The Hiker's Guide
to **HOT SPRINGS**
in the Pacific Northwest

by
Evie Litton

Helena, Montana

Falcon Press is continually expanding its list of recreational guidebooks using the same general format as this book. All books include detailed descriptions, accurate maps, and all information necessary for enjoyable trips. You can order extra copies of this book and get information and prices for other Falcon guidebooks by writing Falcon Press, P.O. Box 1718,
Helena, MT 59624. Also, please ask for a free copy of our current catalog listing all Falcon Press books.

Cover photo by Roger Phillips, Upper Loon Hot Springs,
  Frank Church River of No Return Wilderness, Idaho.
Book photos and maps by Evie Litton.

Litton, Evie.
  The hiker's guide to hot springs in the Pacific Northwest / Evie Litton.
      p.   cm.
  "Completely revised & expanded."
  "A Falcon guide."
  ISBN 1-56044-167-4 :
  1. Hiking—Northwest, Pacific—Guidebooks.   2. Hot springs—
  Northwest, Pacific—Guidebooks.   3. Northwest, Pacific—Guidebooks.
  I. Title.
  GV199.42.N69L58   1993   92-54612
  917.95'0433—dc20   CIP

♻ Text pages printed on recycled paper.

To all the volunteers who struggle patiently and often ingeniously to create and maintain soaking pools for everyone to enjoy; and to those who value hot springs in a natural setting enough to pack out the trash left by others, this book is gratefully dedicated.

ACKNOWLEDGMENTS

My heartfelt thanks to Ellen, the best friend a would-be writer ever had, who not only allowed me (armed with piles of scribbled notes) to attack her own computer after every field trip—but who also spent endless hours trying to teach a strictly "no-tech" novice the fine art of taming it. Without her help, this project would never have gotten off the ground!

All the changes and additions in the second edition would still be in handwriting without my good friends Joanne and Dennis—who gave me full access to their home computer as well as their expertise in handling it (under April's canine supervision). I'm grateful to computer-whiz Gerry for solving jams I got into that were beyond anyone else's nightmares to fix. Thanks are also in order for all the honest feedback I got from Jon—who took the time to "play reader."

For their invaluable input into the first edition and updates for the second, I'm indebted to the many district rangers of Umpqua, Willamette, and Mt. Hood National Forests in Oregon; of Olympic National Park and Mt. Baker-Snoqualmie National Forest in Washington; and of Clearwater, Boise, Payette, Sawtooth, Challis, and Salmon National Forests in Idaho.

For help with the new hot springs and hikes in the second edition, I'm indebted also to the many district rangers of Deschutes National Forest and the Bureau of Land Management in Oregon, of Gifford Pinchot National Forest in Washington, and the Ministry of Parks and Ministry of Forests in British Columbia. All did their best to supply me with accurate and up-to-date information.

And last but not least, I want to express my gratitude to the friendly folks over at Falcon Press for guiding this stray missile to a safe and happy landing. Without their help with both editions, it would still be orbiting somewhere over the Pacific Northwest.

CONTENTS
(* New hot springs in this edition)

WASHINGTON

INTRODUCTION

Halfway through a peanut butter and carrot sandwich, as I sat on a warm rock gazing up at the Chinese Wall, the sky suddenly turned darker than Slate Creek below. I'd just gulped down the last bite when the drops started to fall, and the drizzle turned to a spitting downpour before I was halfway down the trail. I'd no sooner leaped into the car when the sky turned a sickly shade of yellow and let loose a wild volley of hailstones. The ground, covered with dancing snow peas, turned white in an instant. I slithered the last mile up Slate Creek Road with a smile on my face because the perfect antidote to foul weather was close at hand. While sleet and hail pelted the crude shelter, I was soon waiting out the storm in total comfort—immersed in a cocoon of steamy water.

Being devoted to both hiking and hot springing, experiences like the one above taught me early on that the two go together like cream cheese and lox on a bagel. Whether it's a hot dip sandwiched between strolls or a muscle-melting soak at the end of a rugged trek, the contrast creates a dynamite combination!

I began to comb the backwoods and wildlands of the Pacific Northwest, caught in the clutches of a powerful addiction. Between trips, I'd haunt the library to pour over geothermal maps for hot springs hiding in prime hiking country. As the list lengthened, I felt a growing urge to share it with kindred souls.

And so, the pages of this book began to emerge—often under the most adverse conditions. I'd return to camp and just get all the paperwork spread out on a picnic table when the wind would scatter the lot or a sudden

For author Evie Litton, the old bathhouse at Slate Creek Hot Springs offered a fine shelter plus a five-star soak. Dave Bybee photo.

rainstorm turn it to pulp. Often I'd be scribbling away long after dark with the aid of a dim flashlight while trying to dodge the nighttime Kamikaze bugs.

With no space in my tiny car for a laptop computer on top of all the camping gear, an astronomical number of pencils, erasers, and notebooks were consumed in the painstaking process of stringing words together. And I learned that the most grueling hike out there is nothing compared to the effort of capturing it on paper. But at long last the pages are filled (and safely bound), and I leave the final task to you, the reader—to follow the attempts of a first-time writer to share some of her favorite experiences.

I welcome any feedback you aficionados out there might care to toss my way. It's not an easy task keeping track of so many hot springs, and it's an even harder job staying abreast of all the changes they undergo. If your experience was different from mine, I'd enjoy hearing about it. I'm "on the road" much of the year, but if you don't bump into me at one hot pool or another along the way, I can always be reached through Falcon Press. In the meantime, happy soaks!

WHAT IT'S ALL ABOUT

"Hot springs? What kind of hot springs?" you wonder skeptically. "Fancy resorts with wall-to-wall bodies packed into chlorinated pools, or just trickles oozing down some slimy bank into algae-coated mud puddles?" Or else, vaguely offended, you mutter, "What's this, hot springs and hikes in one book? Why on earth mix them together—what's the connection?" In either case, you'd like to know what this is all about.

As to the first question, the gems described in these pages aren't the commercial variety. All but a few are located on prime public land within our national forests and parks—where primitive soaking pools are improvised (strictly by volunteer labor) to collect the flow of any spring equipped with roughly the right temperature, output, and location. A hot trickle is no good to anybody without a proper pool to contain it.

Part of the adventure in seeking them out is that you can never be sure what you'll find. One year there might be a rock-lined pool on the bank of some sylvan stream. The next, it may have vanished and been replaced by a different pool, a hand-crafted soaking box, or possibly even a crude bathhouse patched together to shelter users from the elements. If you're the first arrival this season, you may have the fun of devising your own dip.

Streamside pools are subject to washouts during the spring runoff months and by late summer may be left stranded high on the bank—too hot for comfort without cold water for a mix. For off-season use, the ideal spring would be located well above the river's grasp and have either a temperature within the comfort zone or a side stream flowing by that could be diverted.

In the five-star soaks, in addition to other virtues, both the temperature and the flow rate can be manually controlled if need be. This is often accomplished by merely adjusting a rock or two, but sometimes more ingenious methods are called for to channel both hot and cold water from more distant sources. A strong flow keeps the pools constantly (and naturally) cleaned between soaks.

What you're likely to find also depends on the use a particular hot spring

Streamside pools like this gem at Bonneville in Idaho are submerged at high water and must be remodeled every summer. The temperature can be lowered by shifting rocks on the outer edge to let cold water trickle in.

gets. The soaking pools located closer to the larger population centers tend to receive more volunteer care as well as more stress, while the condition of those in more remote areas will be more primitive but more pristine as well.

As for the second question (assuming you haven't asked what's a hike): What are hot springs and hikes doing together in one book, and what's the connection? Well, there happen to be several good reasons and an excellent connection.

You've probably gathered by now that it's entirely possible to find soaker-friendly hot pools located in precisely the kinds of places you've always enjoyed hiking: deep river canyons, or misty woods, in the mountains of some beautiful national forest or park—and even a few choice wilderness areas!

Now, doesn't such a delightful treat make as worthy a target for a hike as some peak with a view from the top that you might just have time to catch a quick shot of—if the clouds would move over a bit? Or a remote lake with a finicky fish or two flipping around at the bottom? Well, certainly no crazier, anyway. . .

OK, so we've established the legitimacy of hot springs as a hiking goal or destination. But not all of these bubblies require a lengthy trek to locate; many lie near the road in some scenic area that offers a choice of intriguing trails nearby. As a prime example, the Sawtooths in Idaho happen to have strategically spaced hot dips close to almost every trailhead.

"So what", you ask. "I came here to climb Mt. Whatzits'name, or to spend a quiet week up at Such'n'such Lake." Fine! But wouldn't it feel great afterwards, back at the trailhead, to ease away all those aches and pains (not to mention the dirt) immersed in a totally natural Jacuzzi shrouded by evergreens? Or, suppose you got yourself drenched and/or frozen up there and are still faced with either a soggy roadside campsite or a miserable drive back home. Yup, you guessed it (you're learning fast)—time for a nice long soak over at Whozit's Hot Springs!

Well, since you're still reading, this offbeat guidebook must be meant for you: the active outdoor hedonist who enjoys experiencing the wonders of nature the hard way—on foot, but who also turns on to the contrasting image of a blissful dip at the end of the trail in one of nature's own steamy creations.

It just so happens that the Pacific Northwest is a mecca not only for superb scenery and hiking but also for first-class primitive hot springs. A chain of these pearls runs through the Cascades of Oregon and Washington, clusters can be found across southern British Columbia, and in central Idaho you'll discover a profusion of precious gems—including no less than ten buried in the River of No Return Wilderness.

The best of both worlds is presented here in one package: a detailed guide to an even hundred of the finest natural hot soaks in Oregon, Washington, British Columbia and Idaho, and a trail guide to more than eighty scenic hikes that either lead to them or begin nearby. Whether you're already a confirmed wilderness buff and hot springs fanatic or new to either pursuit, this book should be a welcome companion to your travels.

UNDERSTANDING
THE DESCRIPTIONS

Hot Springs for Hikers in the Pacific Northwest is a guidebook to both hot soaks and hikes in Oregon, Washington, British Columbia, and Idaho. The springs marked on the locator maps are listed numerically. Beneath them in the text, you'll usually find a list of one or more hikes. For example, in Oregon we start with 1. Umpqua Hot Springs, followed by Hikes 1a-c. In Washington, 19. Olympic Hot Springs is followed by Hikes 19a-c, etc.

The hikes fall into three basic categories: 1) hikes to reach a hot spring, 2) hikes continuing on from the spring, and 3) hikes located in the same area. One or more of the three types may be found listed under each hot spring (or sometimes following two or more springs located close together).

Headings for Hot Springs

Hot springs located less than a mile from a road are not written up as hikes. They normally have just four headings: a general description, the best map to use, directions for getting there, and the hot spring itself.

General description: This is a nutshell summary that includes what you'll find there, the distance from the road, general location, customary swimwear or lack thereof, and elevation (a useful gauge for estimating seasonal access). For example: A quiet soaking pool cloaked in greenery at the end of a 0.5-mile creekside path, east of Lewiston. Swimwear optional. Elevation 2,900 feet.

Map: This heading lists the best road map for finding your way there—in most cases a Forest Service recreation map. (Note: Travel Maps, printed yearly in many national forests in the U.S., are a good source of updates on the older forest maps.) If a hot spring is administered by an agency other than the Forest Service (such as the Bureau of Land Management or the National Park Service), the appropriate map is listed.

Finding the hot springs: This covers the nuts and bolts of getting there. Start with the Locator Map (found at the start of each state or province) along with a highway map to get your bearings, then follow the directions with the aid of the road map listed. It's noted here whether or not the spring is shown on the recommended map, or if it isn't marked on the state geothermal map (see below).

You'll find the agency address for each hot spring and hike under the heading For More Information at the start of each state or province along with the Locator Map and An Overview. The district offices listed can provide you with the road map recommended as well as up-to-date information on the hot springs and hikes.

The hot springs: Last but not least comes a short paragraph or two describing such things as what the soaking pools are like, the temperature and whatever primitive means there may be of controlling it, the general setting and scenery, an idea of how much company you can expect, and how visible the pools are. As a rule of thumb, the swimwear custom (or degree of "skinnydip-pability") equates with the degree of visibility or distance from the road. A useful formula.

Headings for Hikes

The hikes are provided with the following basic headings: a general description, elevation gain and loss, trailhead elevation, high point, hiking quad(s), road map, finding the trailhead, the hike, and last (for a hot spring hike) the soak itself.

General description: This is a brief statement that includes all the basics: the degree of difficulty (easy, moderate, or strenuous), the distance, and whether it's usually a day hike or an overnighter. For example: An easy five-mile, round-trip day hike to. . . It ends with information about which type of hike it is and where it goes.

For a hike to a hot spring you'll learn what's there, the general location, and the customary swimwear (. . . to a bubbly soaking box in the Glacier Peak Wilderness, northeast of Everett. No need to pack a swimsuit.) For hikes continuing on from a hot spring or any spot other than a roadside trailhead, the starting point is made clear. For a hike located in the same area, the destination is summarized and the hot spring given for reference.

The degree of difficulty is determined by the steepness of the trail with minor adjustments made for length, short steep pitches, or extreme roughness. A hike is rated as easy if the grade is up to five percent, moderate between five-ten percent, and strenuous if the grade is over ten percent. You can use the following formula to calculate the grade of any hike: elevation gain divided by 5,280 (gain in miles) divided by length of trail x 100 = percent grade.

Elevation gain and loss: These figures indicate the rigors of a hike. The elevation gain is given in one direction only. A round-trip hike that gains 1,000 feet and loses 200 feet on the way in would lose 1,000 feet and gain 200 feet on the way out. This would be written: +1,000 feet, -200 feet. Or, suppose a hike gains 1,600 feet, loses 400 feet, gains another 800 feet, then loses another 200 feet. The total gain and loss would be +2,400 feet, -600 feet. Only one figure is listed if the hike is virtually all uphill or all downhill.

A loop hike lists just one figure because no matter how many ups and downs there are, the total gain is always the same as the total loss. Consider Hike 33b: the consecutive figures are +2,800, -280, +40, -40, +480, -240, +120, -120, +440, -3,200. The total gain is 3,880 feet, and the total loss adds up to the same magical number.

Trailhead elevation and high point: These are useful figures to know when trying to determine the access at different times of year. Normally the trailhead is the low point, but sometimes just the opposite is true—as with all the hot springs in the River of No Return Wilderness. In these "upside down" hikes, the headings are changed to make this clear (High point: Trailhead, 8,120 feet. Low point: Kwiskwis Hot Springs, 5,680 feet.) The elevation gain and loss in this case is +340 feet and -2,780 feet since the hike is nearly all downhill.

Hiking quad(s): This heading lists one or more topographic quadrangles for each hike. In the U.S., those most commonly used are the USGS quads. The more detailed 7.5-minute series listed has finally replaced the 15-minute quads. Most have contour intervals of forty feet, cover areas of about seven by nine miles, and are drawn on a scale of 1:24,000.

In British Columbia, the standard quads are the National Topographic Series (NTS). The newer series recommended has a standardized scale of 1:50,000 and contour intervals of 100 feet. Although hot springs and even hiking trails often go unmarked, the more detailed scale is an improvement over the old 1:125,000 series.

Note: Most university libraries have both USGS and NTS maps as well as a helpful staff and copy machines. This makes a great combination when planning trips that wind through three or four quads. The price you pay for such frugality is having to learn a few vital skills: how to line up sections of a large map on a small copier, make a sturdy patchwork quilt out of all the pieces you copy, and draw on your copies all the important streams and lakes (since blue doesn't reproduce well).

In Washington and Northern Oregon, a 15-minute series published by Green Trails is also listed. These popular maps are specifically designed and updated for hikers. The trails are drawn in bold lines with route numbers, and distances are marked between points.

Hiking quads may be ordered directly from the publisher or government agency, but it's often more convenient to stop at a local store. Most mountaineering or sporting goods stores carry regional quads, and bookstores that sell hiker's guides are another likely source. In smaller towns you'll often find local quads in fishing supply or even hardware stores.

The U.S. Forest Service offers contour maps of most wilderness areas. Although drawn with less detail than the USGS quads, they tend to be more up-to-date. They feature clearly marked trails and roads with route numbers and some even mark distances between points. If available, a wilderness map is listed. Many national forests also print updated quads of each district. Although bulky and often hard to read, these are useful for hikes with recent trail changes not marked on other maps.

A trail map may also be found in the text along with each hike. Intended as a general introduction to a given area, these maps should never be substituted for the hiking quads recommended.

The map legend on the next page has a complete list of the symbols used.

MAP LEGEND

U.S. Highway	(00)	River or Creek	~~~
State Route	(000)	Lake	⬭
Forest Road	[0000]	Hot Spring	●
Paved Road	▬▬▬	Meadow or Swamp	☵
Dirt Road	= = = =	Falls or Rapids	⟋⧸⟍
Trailhead and described Trail	⊖---	Campground	▲
Other Trails	- - - - -	Peak and Elevation	x⁰⁰⁰⁰
Cross-country Route	··········	Glacier	⬭
		Pass or Saddle	⫽
Wilderness, Park, or NRA Boundary	⟨···········⟩	Ranger Station	♟
		Bridge	⋊
Wild River Boundary	— · — · —	Building	▪
		Lava	⬭
Map Scale (miles)	0 0.5 1	Power Line	▪-▪-▪

LOCATOR MAPS

Paved Road ——— Dirt Road – — —

Road map: See Maps in Headings for Hot Springs.

A note on state geothermal maps: An official map that marks hot springs along with other geothermal data is published by each state for the U.S. Department of Energy. These maps are gigantic (Oregon's measures four by five feet) but very useful for pinpointing possible soaks. They can usually be found in university libraries. Geothermal Resources of Oregon may be ordered from the State Dept. of Geology and Mineral Industries, 1005 State Office Building, Portland, OR 97201. Geothermal Resources of Washington may be ordered from the Dept. of Natural Resources, Geology and Earth Resources Division,

Olympia, WA 98504. Geothermal Resources of Idaho is unfortunately long out of print.

Finding the trailhead: See Finding the hot springs under headings for hot springs.

The hike: Here you'll find out what the route is like, any nasty stream crossings or other obstacles to expect, possible extensions or side trips, campsites, and whatever outrageous viewpoints or other rewards lie in wait.

The hot springs: On hikes to a hot spring, this final heading covers all the nitty gritty described above in descriptions for hot springs.

TOUCHING THE LAND LIGHTLY

Principles of Low-Impact Camping

"Some call it low-impact use or the minimum-impact method. Others refer to it as wilderness manners or no-trace camping. Whatever you call it, the practice of outdoor ethics is essential in the backcountry. It's a state of mind rather than a list of approved methods. It relies on clear judgment rather than inflexible rules. And not only does common sense protect the backcountry, it can also enhance your outdoor adventures." (FIELDBOOK, Boy Scouts of America).

1. Concentrate use when in popular or high-use places

The key is to concentrate your use on those places that have already been damaged by previous use and to encourage the next group to also concentrate use on the same spots. Choose a well- impacted campsite. Stay within the impacted area and don't enlarge the site. Build campfires only within existing fire rings. Stay on established hiking trails. Cutting across switchbacks or walking outside of established trailbeds can lead to erosion.

2. Disperse use when in pristine areas

The key is to minimize the number of times a place is stepped on and to leave nothing that will encourage others to walk or camp where you did— thus allowing the site time to recover from your stay. Choose a previously-unused site to camp. Disperse foot traffic around camp and between camp and any water source. Minimize the use of campfires and remove all evidence of fire before you leave. Only hike off-trail if prepared to use extra care. Spread out when walking. Try to select routes on hard ground. Avoid fragile surfaces like wet places and steep slopes. If your group must cross a meadow, fan out to avoid trampling a path through vegetation.

3. Other basic rules

Choose your campsite thoughtfully and use it lightly. Pick a spot (at least

100 feet from water or trail) where you won't have to clear any vegetation or level a tentsite. Camp on mineral soil, never in meadows or soft grassy areas that compact easily. Leave the area clean and in its natural condition. Make it look as if no one had been there.

The use of backpack stoves conserves firewood. Campfires have been permanently prohibited in many heavily-used areas and in others are banned in summer and fall due to the danger of wildfire. If a fire is allowed (and really needed), dig out the native vegetation and topsoil and set it aside. Don't build a fire ring with rocks. When breaking camp, drown the fire thoroughly, bury the cold ashes, and replace the native soil.

Keep all wash water at least 200 feet from water sources and don't use soap or detergents in or near water. Even biodegradable soaps are a stress on the environment. Clean your cookware with soapless hot water and a bit of sand or gravel—it's often more effective than soaps. If soap must be used, wash in a basin well away from lakes or streams.

Always answer the call of nature well away from any campsites or open water. Dig a hole six to eight inches deep, bury everything carefully when finished, then cover it with sod or topsoil. If you fish, dispose of entrails by either burying, burning completely, or packing out.

Garbage that can't be burned must be carried out. This includes even the tiny items like gum wrappers and cigarette butts. The plastic-coated foil packages commonly used by packpackers don't really burn and must be packed out as well. Never bury food scraps, because animals will dig them up.

Hot springs are as fragile as any other water source and should be treated with the same respect. Soaking pools are precisely that. They're not bathtubs where you can lather up with soap and shampoo. Whatever drains out flows directly into nearby streams, and what can't drain out is there for the next user to find. Also, the damp ground around the springs is often steep and easily eroded, and delicate plant life can be swiftly crushed.

Many of the popular hot springs in Oregon and Washington are already on the endangered species list simply because too many eager visitors haven't learned the basics of backcountry etiquette. At one of these imperiled gems, I was criticized by volunteer caretakers for wanting to share it with the world at large by writing a guidebook. My defense was the sincere hope and belief that you, the educated reader, will treat the hot springs you visit with responsibility and tender loving care.

This campsite came complete with a kitchen work area and a level slab for the backpack stove (and the cook) to sit on.

MAKING IT A SAFE TRIP

Backcountry safety is largely a matter of being well prepared and using common sense. For starters, this means carrying proper survival and first aid equipment, compass, and topographic map—and knowing how to use them. Secondly, tell somebody where you're going and when you plan to return.

Study an area before leaving home, then gather last-minute information from the ranger station nearest your destination. Rangers can tell you about any potential problems or hazards in their area (approaching storms or forest fires, high water, etc.) as well as the current condition of roads, trails, and streams. See **For More Information** sections for each area.

Take along proper equipment. The basics in every hiker's gear should include sturdy but comfortable footwear and warm clothing that will keep its insulating properties when wet, plenty of water (brought from home), extra food, and a dependable tent. You may enjoy beautiful dry weather, but storms can hit at anytime.

Select a hike within the abilities of all in your group and stay together on the trail. If it's getting dark or a storm looks likely, make camp as soon as possible. Never hike at night. Be aware of the dangers of hypothermia and take the proper steps to avoid it.

If you get lost, don't panic. Sit down and try to locate landmarks that will help orient you. Check out the topo map and take compass readings. Plot a rational course of action before you move on. And remember, many hikers have spent unplanned nights in the woods and survived.

Don't take a chance: boil or treat all open water used for drinking—no matter how clean it may look. For day hikes, carry a canteen from home with an ample supply. It's a sad fact that wilderness water sources are no longer safe to drink, with the exception of remote springs and fresh snowmelt. Increasing cases of backcountry dysentery, caused by a waterborne parasite called Giardia lamblia, show the impact that water pollution has in the wilds.

Giardia is spread by water contaminated by either animal or human waste. Halazone and chlorine don't work against it, and iodine (besides being dangerous in itself) will kill only ninety to ninety-five percent of all the cysts. Experts say the safest bet is to boil all water; recommendations vary from a minute to ten or even twenty minutes. There are also a number of filters on the market that are an effective (but expensive and rather slow) means of purifying water.

Don't attempt to ford major streams during the spring runoff. Fast water can easily sweep hikers off their feet—and sometimes to their deaths. In early summer, creeks and rivers can have ten times their average flow in a year of average snowfall. Consult with the district ranger before attempting hikes that involve a ford; when in doubt, wait until midsummer.

Search for a log crossing or for boulders to hop across. Leave your boots on for better traction on the slippery bottom and avoid the current's full force by staying sideways to the flow. Go slowly and deliberately, planting each foot securely. Some hikers carry a sturdy branch for extra support. During the spring runoff or when crossing a glacial stream, the water will be at its lowest level during the morning hours.

Be cautious around hot springs. Some emerge from the ground at temperatures that can boil eggs and would-be bathers alike. Avoid bare feet until you're sure where any hidden hot spots or other hazards are. If a soaking pool feels too hot, don't use it unless you can find a way to lower the temperature. And never mix a prolonged soak with drinking alcohol; it can cause severe stress on the circulatory system.

To prevent problems in bear country, keep all food well wrapped and hang it at night (along with garbage, lotions and soaps) from a strong tree limb at least twelve feet above the ground and at least five feet from the trunk and other branches. Some hikers use two evenly weighted stuffsacks hung by the counterbalance method.

Driving in the backcountry often involves negotiating narrow one-lane roads—some heavily traveled by huge logging trucks and others deserted for hours just when you get stuck. Drive cautiously and exercise common sense. Carry plenty of gas, water, and spare supplies.

Many hot springs flood the ground with scalding water before reaching a comfortable soaking temperature. The spectacular source of Vulcan Hot Springs is NOT the place for bare feet.

HOT SPRINGS IN OREGON

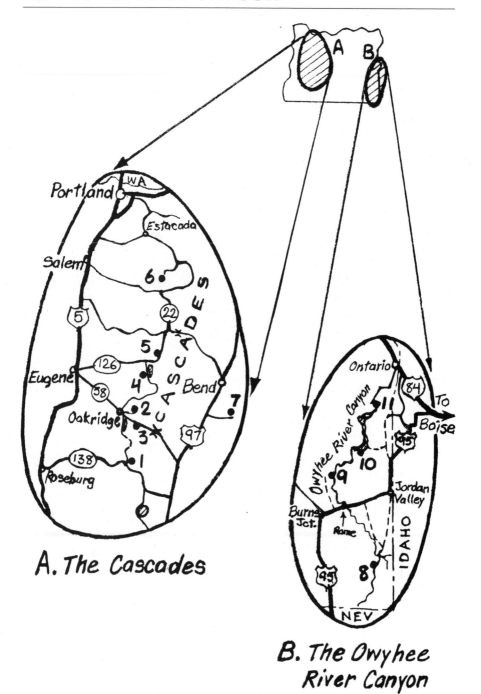

A. The Cascades

B. The Owyhee
River Canyon

OREGON

An Overview

The state of Oregon is amply endowed with primitive hot springs. The ones described are located in two distinct areas. Most can be found in the Cascade Mountains to the west, but we also have a few in the desert country of the Owyhee River Canyon to the east. Other good soaks in eastern Oregon were rejected simply for lack of interesting hikes or scenery. The reader will find a total of eleven wild dips marked on the Oregon Locator Map—seven lined up in the Cascades and four spread out in the Owyhee River Canyon.

A. The Cascades

Hot spring enthusiasts visiting the southern Cascades will enter primeval forests and discover a chain of inviting soaking pools framed by evergreen boughs. The seven listed are all found in national forests, with easy access via paved roads and short paths.

In addition, superb hiking can be found on nearby trails that ramble through lush woods to lakes and waterfalls, ancient lava flows, and overlooks of many volcanic cones. On the east side of the crest, hikers can even explore lava caves. The hikes listed include a sampling of four of the wildlands now linking the high country in an almost unbroken line.

Directions are given from major towns along Interstate 5 and U.S. Highway 97, but it's also entirely feasible to travel directly between all dips but Paulina (see below). In general, the forest roads and hiking trails are well maintained and easy to follow, the campgrounds developed and frequently full, and the bubbly soaking pools often brimming over (at least in summer) with other equally eager beavers.

Direct routes between dips: A combination of highways and forest roads makes it possible to jump from one hot pool to the next without coming up for air, if the reader is so inclined. The one exception is Paulina, in a class by herself farther east. Read the listings for directions and carry the appropriate forest maps. Bear in mind that gas stations and stores are few and far between and that many mountain roads are open only in summer.

Hot springers can get from Umpqua to Wall Creek and McCredie by way of two forest roads that form a twisty fifty-mile link (paved except for one twenty-mile middle stretch) between State Routes 138 and 58. The route starts in Umpqua National Forest as Toketee-Rigdon Road (34), heads north past the turnoff to Umpqua, and crosses a 5,000-foot pass into Willamette National Forest. Forest Road 2134 combines road numbers to connect it with Rigdon Road (21) ending near Oakridge.

To go from Wall Creek and McCredie to Cougar and Bigelow, you can take one paved fifty-five-mile road that links State Routes 58 and 126. Forest Road 19 goes north from Oakridge and passes Cougar on the west side of Cougar Reservoir. From Cougar to Bigelow, drive north to State Route 126 and follow it past Belknap Springs to the bridge at Deer Creek Road (a total hop of twenty-two paved miles).

A series of six paved roads will lead you north from Bigelow to Bagby in a grand total of 100 miles. From Bigelow, drive to the end of State Route 126, jog east on U.S. Highway 20, then north on State Route 22 to Detroit. Follow signs "to Breitenbush" on Forest Road 46, trading Willamette for Mount Hood National Forest, and go about forty miles. Then follow signs "to Bagby Hot Springs" on Forest Roads 63 and 70.

The Owyhee River Canyon

From its origins in the snowcapped mountains of northern Nevada, the Owyhee River carves a rugged canyon through an almost roadless wilderness in the sagebrush hills and plains of southeast Oregon, passes through a long reservoir above the Owyhee Dam, and drains ultimately into the Snake River. Congress has included nearly 200 miles of the Owyhee and its tributaries in the National Wild and Scenic Rivers system, and many parts are under wilderness study.

The state geothermal map lists no less than eight hot springs buried in the Owyhee River Canyon. Of these, four turned out to be virtually unreachable or unusable, but the remainder proved worthy of being added to the book. The four listed are widely spaced—no direct routes between these dips, except maybe by raft. All but one require a hike to reach.

State highway maps don't begin to tell the story here, and forest maps don't apply. Luckily, the Bureau of Land Management prints a 30-minute series detailing roads and land features, available at any district office. The appropriate BLM road map for each write-up is listed along with a hiking quad.

Directions are given from towns along U.S. highways 95 and 20/26. The access roads tend to be long and dusty, hiking routes strictly cross country, campsites primitive, and the hot springs (with one exception) "wild and woolly."

For More Information

Visitors should contact the following Forest Service or Bureau of Land Management (BLM) district offices for updates on hot springs, road and trail conditions, stream crossings, etc. If the receptionist can't answer your questions, ask for someone in recreation. Maps may be purchased here, and most districts offer free trail printouts.

Hot Springs 1 and Hikes 1a-c: Diamond Lake Ranger District, Umpqua National Forest, HC 60, Box 101, Idleyld Park, OR 97447; 503-498-2531 (or contact the Toketee Lake Ranger Station).

Hot Springs 2,3 and Hikes 3a,b: Oakridge Ranger District,Willamette National Forest, 46375 Highway 58, Westfir, OR 97492; 503-782-2291.

Hot Springs 4 and Hike 4a: Blue River Ranger District, Willamette National Forest, Blue River, OR 97413; 503-822-3317.

Hot Spring 5 and Hikes 5a,b: McKenzie Ranger District, Willamette National Forest, McKenzie Bridge, OR 97413; 503-822-3381.

Hot Springs 6 and Hikes 6a-c: Estacada Ranger District, Mount Hood National Forest, 595 NW Industrial Way, Estacada, OR 97023; 503-630-6861.

Hot Springs 7 and Hikes 7a-c: Fort Rock Ranger District, Deschutes National

Forest, 1645 Highway 20 East, Bend, OR 97701; 503-388-5664. Or contact Paulina Lake Resort about the springs: Box 7, La Pine, OR 97739; 503-536-2240.

Hot Springs 9-11 and Hikes 8a through 11a: Vale Ranger District, Bureau of Land Management, 100 Oregon St., Vale, OR 97918; 503-473-3144.

Hot Spring 10: Bureau of Reclamation, Central Snake Project Office, 214 Broadway Ave., Boise, ID 83702.

A. THE CASCADES

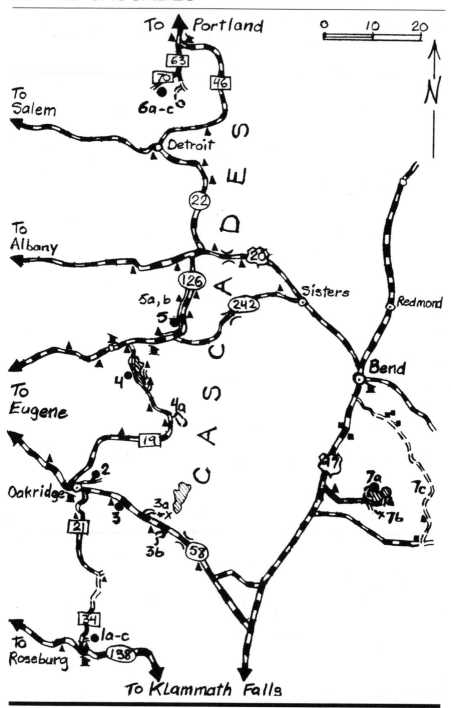

A. THE CASCADES

Hot springs and hikes

Umpqua Hot Springs (1) and nearby strolls are found east of Roseburg. Southeast of Eugene near Oakridge, soaks at quiet Wall Creek and popular McCredie mix well with hikes in the Waldo Lake and Diamond Peak wildlands. East of Eugene is the ever-popular Cougar, (4) with a loop hike in the Three Sisters Wilderness, and nearby Bigelow, (5) hidden between hikes along the McKenzie River. Southeast of Portland, a walk to the unique Bagby (6a) combines with nearby treks in the Bull of the Woods Wilderness. And south of Bend, on the volcanic east side of the range, comes a hike-in soak on the shores of Paulina Lake (7a) and an assortment of hikes in and around Newberry Crater.

Season

All the hot springs can be reached and enjoyed throughout the year except for Paulina, snow-bound through the winter months at 6,300 feet, and Bigelow, submerged during spring runoff. Regardless of weather, Cougar and Bagby see long lines of winter visitors. The hiking season ranges from all year for the low-elevation hikes near Umpqua and Bigelow to summer months only for the higher routes in the vicinity of McCredie, Cougar, Bagby, and Paulina. Summer weather west of the crest can vary from bright sunshine to damp rain clouds (sometimes in a matter of minutes) while the east side around Paulina stays "high and dry."

1 Umpqua Hot Springs

General description: A grand old soaking pool on a short new path, overlooking a wooded canyon east of Roseburg. Keep swimwear handy. Elevation 2,640 feet.
Map: Umpqua National Forest.

Background: Umpqua has a history of challenging approach routes. Some years ago, the hopeful hot springer had a difficult choice. A jeep track followed by a primitive path snaked down the far bank from "the Meadows". The alternative was a muddy slide to do a tightrope act on a slippery log. Then, just a few years back, the Forest Service built the hazard-free North Umpqua Trail along the far bank. This route provided not only a cool walk through a quiet forest but also a comfortably uneventful access.

Nowadays, a sturdy bridge spans the North Umpqua and offers the ultimate approach. It leads to a 0.25-mile path joining the last segment of the North Umpqua Trail (Hike 1a). No more jeep roads, muddy banks, or slippery logs to bar your way but help ensure your privacy at this once secluded spot. Be prepared to wait your turn for a soak—especially on summer weekends.

Finding the hot springs: From Roseburg, drive east on State Route 138 about sixty miles to Toketee Junction and turn left on paved Toketee Rigdon Road

(34). At the bottom of the hill, bear left at the "Y" and drive past Toketee Lake and Campground. Turn right at 2.3 miles onto graded Thorn Prairie Road (3401) and drive two miles to the parking area. The path crosses the bridge and joins the North Umpqua Trail to climb the steep riverbank. A few more dips and rises east and you'll emerge from the woods to spot a three-sided shelter on the edge of a bluff. Umpqua is named on the map.

The hot springs: Sculpted from colorful travertine deposits, a pool measuring about four by five feet perches on a bare cliff 150 feet above the North Umpqua River; the free-flowing curves make a uniquely attractive container for the 106-degree water trickling through it. Shaded from the elements within a three-sided, shingle roofed shelter, a sun deck on the open side provides a pleasing view over the canyon below.

HIKE 1a *Umpqua Hot Springs via North Umpqua Trail*

General description: An easy 3.6-mile, round-trip walk to the hot springs on a wooded path near the route described above.
Elevation gain and loss: 140 feet.
Trailhead elevation: 2,500 feet.
High point: Umpqua, 2,640 feet.
Maps: Trail 1414 printout, Umpqua National Forest.

Finding the trailhead: Follow the directions above to Thorn Prairie Road and follow it 0.6 mile to a grassy pullout on your left just before a bridge. This trail is so new that it isn't shown on the 1986 Toketee Falls and Potter Mountain USGS quads, but both the path and the springs are marked on the latest forest map.

The hike: The alternate route to Umpqua is included for those readers interested in sampling a slice of the recently built river trail which now stretches from Idleyld Park on up to the Pacific Crest Trail near Maidu Lake— the headwaters of the North Umpqua River. It offers a pleasantly lonesome walk as well as a bit of exercise to make the hot soak even more welcome.

The trail climbs well above the canyon floor and undulates through a forest of western red cedar and Douglas-fir. The roar of the river follows you, but the screen of trees hides it from view most of the way. The route detours at the halfway point to cross Deer Creek upstream on a log bridge.

In 1.5 miles, the new short cut cuts in just beyond a bare slope easily mistaken for the one below the springs. The combined route climbs steeply above the river and contours through woods for the last 0.25 mile. Watch your footing on the slick rock around the shelter, or you'll end up with a cold plunge in the river instead of a hot bath in the "tub!"

The shelter at Umpqua Hot Springs faces a broad view over the North Umpqua Canyon.

HIKE 1b *Clearwater River Trail*

General description: A 3.4-mile round-trip (or 1.7-mile one way) riverside walk through an age-old forest, near Umpqua Hot Springs.
Elevation gain and loss: 200 feet.
Trailhead elevations: West end, 2,440 feet; east end, 2,640 feet.
High point: 2,640 feet.
Maps: Trail 1490 printout, Umpqua National Forest.

Finding either trailhead: At Toketee Junction on State Route 138, take Forest Road 34 to the bottom of the hill. Bear right at the "Y" onto graded Forest Road 4776, the west entrance to Toketee Ranger Station. Drive 0.25 mile to a pullout on the right and the west marker. The east trail sign is found two miles farther up the road just before it rejoins the highway.

The hike: Clearwater River Trail meanders through a twilight forest along the riverbank. Shaded by a dense canopy of cedar and Douglas-fir mixed with rhododendrons, alder, and dogwood, it passes lively rapids interspersed with deep pools. The gentle path parallels Toketee Ranger Station Road and can be walked from either end.

HIKE 1c *Toketee and Watson Falls*

General description: Two last short strolls through lush woods, near Umpqua Hot Springs.
Elevation gain and loss: Toketee Falls, sixty feet; Watson Falls, 230 feet.
High points: Toketee Falls, 2,380 feet; Watson Falls, 2,950 feet.
Maps: Trail 1496 and 1495 printouts, Umpqua National Forest.

Finding the trailheads: To see Toketee Falls, drive to Toketee Junction on State Route 138 and take Forest Road 34 to the bottom of the hill. Bear left at the "Y" and follow signs to the parking area. To visit Watson Falls, drive 2.2 miles east of Toketee Junction on State Route 138 (or 0.3 mile east of the east entrance to Toketee Ranger Station) and follow signs to the picnic area parking lot.

The hikes: Toketee Falls, a double waterfall plunging a total of 120 feet, lies at the end of an easy 0.4-mile path along the North Umpqua River near Toketee Lake. At one spot, the river tumbles through a tight gorge filled with water sculpted pools. Mottled sunlight filters through a colorful grove of Douglas fir, cedar, maple, and Pacific yew en route to a viewing platform.

Watson Falls, with its 272-foot drop, is the third highest waterfall in Oregon. A steep 0.6-mile trail follows the plunging creek through an age-old forest of Douglas fir and western hemlock. The understory of ferns, Oregon grape, and salal blends tints of green with the velvet coat of moss draped over the creekside boulders. A footbridge along the way offers an excellent viewpoint, and the path comes to rest in the misty spray at the base of the falls.

HOT SPRING 1   *Umpqua Hot Springs*
HIKE 1a   *Umpqua Hot Springs via North Umpqua Trail*
HIKE 1b   *Clearwater River Trail*
HIKE 1c   *Toketee and Watson Falls*

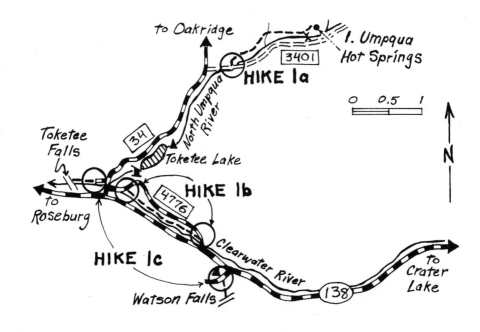

2 Wall Creek Hot Springs

General description: A warm soak in a sylvan setting at the end of a short path, southeast of Eugene. Swimwear optional. Elevation 2,200 feet.
Map: Willamette National Forest.

Finding the hot springs: From Eugene, take State Route 58 forty miles southeast to Oakridge. Turn left to city center, then right on East 1st Street which soon becomes Salmon Creek Road (24). Continue northeast, past Salmon Creek Campground, on pavement. *Campers:* You'll also pass a number of primitive sites sandwiched between the creek and the main road.

At nine miles, turn left on a gravel road (1934) signed to Blair Lake. Watch for a pullout on your left in 0.4 mile, now marked with a hiker's symbol and a "No Camping Here" sign. A 0.3-mile path follows Wall Creek to the pool. The springs are marked without a name on the forest map.

The hot springs: A clearing in a virgin forest reveals a pool, (aptly) called Meditation Pool by some users, built directly over the source springs. Bubbles rise gently to the surface in long streamers, currently heating the water to around 96 degrees. (*Note:* The temperature appears to be rising lately, a degree or so a year.) The rectangular pool is roughly ten-by-fifteen feet. It sits on the bank of a small but lively creek surrounded by countless acres of green solitude.

Bubbles perk up through the sandy bottom of a pool bordered by age-old trees at Wall Creek Hot Springs

3 McCredie Hot Springs

General description: A highway pit stop that puts McDonalds and Burger King in the minor leagues, southeast of Eugene. A strong skinnydipping tradition despite visibility. Elevation 2,100 feet.
Map: Willamette National Forest.

Finding the hot springs: From Eugene, take State Route 58 forty miles southeast to Oakridge. Follow the highway ten miles farther (0.5 mile past Blue Pool Campground) to a large turnout on the right. A forty-yard path heads upstream to the pools. McCredie is named on the forest map.

The hot springs: This soaker-saturated site, sandwiched between Salt Creek and a major highway, offers a variety of soaking pools with temperatures ranging from 95-105 degrees. The "party pool" measures about fifteen-by-twenty feet and has a knee-deep bottom varying from sandy muck to sharp rocks and bits of broken glass.

Anytime is party time at McCredie. The action varies from mild (on weekdays) to industrial strength over the weekends. Easily accessible throughout the year, you're likely to find Winnebago City assembled in the large pullout. A nearby vantage point frequently houses a lineup of truck drivers-cum-birdwatchers.

A few quieter pools may be found directly across the broad creek. To reach these with dry feet, drive another 0.5 mile up the highway and take Shady Gap Road across a bridge. Bear right for 0.1 mile to a pullout, then hunt for an overgrown path that follows the creek 0.3 mile back downstream.

Nighttime closure: The Forest Service, long plagued with problems of overuse similar to those found at Cougar (see 4 below), has since followed suit and posted "Day Use Only" signs both at the hot springs and all nearby parking areas.

Truck drivers have traditionally used the large pullout as an overnight rest stop, but that's now a thing of the past. For those of you with smaller "rigs," there are still a few primitive campsites in the nearby woods or full facilities at Blue Pool Campground 0.5 mile down the road.

The popular pools at McCredie see few moments as tranquil as this.

HIKE 3a *Fuji Mountain*

General description: A brisk three-mile, round-trip day climb to a mountaintop overlooking a long line of volcanic peaks, near McCredie Hot Springs.
Elevation gain and loss: 964 feet.
Trailhead elevation: 6,180 feet.
High point: Fuji Mountain, 7,144 feet.
Hiking quad: Waldo Lake area or Diamond Peak Wilderness (Forest Service) or Waldo Lake USGS.
Road map: Williamette National Forest.

Finding the trailhead: Drive about fifteen miles southeast of Oakridge (or 5.5 miles past McCredie) on State Route 58. Watch for a train trestle over the highway and turn left just beyond it onto Eagle Creek Road (5883). With the help of the forest or wilderness map, follow this gravel road for 10.3 miles uphill to a small trail sign on the left and an equally small pullout on the right.

The hike: With a peak named Fuji, how can you miss? The short climb is a piece of cake, and the summit offers an overview of no less than three of the wilderness areas that now link the Oregon Cascades in an almost unbroken line. The route described here is a short cut to the summit overlooked by most hikers.
The lightly used path (3674) climbs moderately to a signed junction in 0.25 mile, then traverses along the west side of a steep ridge in a gentle climb through tall stands of mountain hemlock and true fir coated with tufts of moss. The last 0.5 mile is a steeper grade eased by switchbacks. Snow patches often obscure the route until mid-July.
Looking south from the summit, snow-capped Diamond Peak presides over the Diamond Peak Wilderness (see Hike 3b). Waldo Lake, framed by a landscape of wooded knolls and ridges, spreads out directly below. Fuji Mountain itself forms the southern boundary of the 39,200-acre Waldo Lake Wilderness. The massive Three Sisters Wilderness lies just beyond it to the northeast; the glacier-capped peaks of the North and South Sisters, along with several other volcanic cones, can be spotted in a straight line fading into the distance.

HIKE 3b *Diamond Creek Loop and Vivian Lake*

General description: A moderate 6.5-mile, round-trip day hike (including a 2.5-mile loop) featuring waterfalls, wildflowers, and a wooded lake in the Diamond Peak Wilderness, near McCredie Hot Springs.
Elevation gain and loss: 1,486 feet (loop, 280 feet; 1,206 feet to Vivian Lake).
Trailhead elevation: 4,000 feet.
High point: Vivian Lake, 5,406 feet.
Hiking quads: Diamond Peak Wilderness (Forest Service) or Diamond Peak USGS.
Road map: Same as Hike 3a.

Finding the trailhead: From Oakridge, take State Route 58 about twenty-two

HIKE 3a *Fuji Mountain*

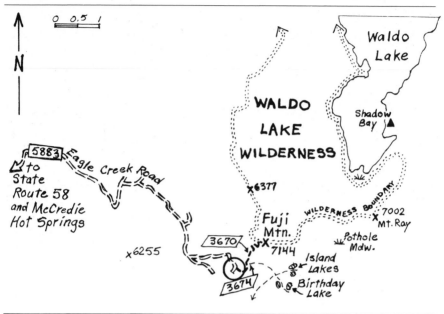

HIKE 3b *Diamond Creek Loop and Vivian Lake*

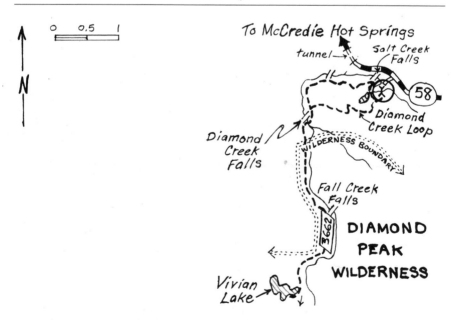

The band of trees around Vivian Lake hides all but the tip of one of Mt. Yoran's angular lava crags.

miles southeast (twelve miles past McCredie) and through the highway tunnel to Salt Creek Falls Viewpoint and trailhead parking.

The hike: A pleasant half-day outing through a shaded forest bursting with rhododendrons leads to waterfalls and a wooded lake. The first mile is part of a newly constructed loop trail not yet marked on the maps to Diamond Creek Falls. The route described combines the new loop with a two-mile extension from the far end south to Vivian Lake.

Diamond Creek Trail (3598) passes the spur to Salt Creek Falls and bridges Salt Creek to a second junction. Bear left and begin a gentle climb in a forest of hemlock and Douglas fir. Thickets of bright pink rhododendrons and the solitary white blooms of beargrass highlight the way. The new route crosses a dirt road in 0.5 mile and once again just before reaching the far end of the loop.

Take the left fork at the junction to reach Vivian Lake. After crossing the same road once more, followed by the Southern Pacific Railroad tracks and then yet another road, you'll welcome the final crossing—the wilderness boundary line! Next, the trail climbs a steep grade beside Fall Creek Falls, then tapers off a bit in the last 0.5 mile along the rushing creek. Thick woods hide the lake until the last minute.

The Diamond Peak Wilderness has expanded to presently cover 52,337 acres centered on the snow-crowned roots of an old volcano (8,744-foot Diamond Peak) and the 7,100-foot and 7,138-foot lava crags of Mount Yoran. The peaks are flanked by forested ridges, tree-rimmed lakes, and a multitude of lakelets gouged out by glaciers.

Vivian Lake, a relatively small lake marked by an irregular shoreline, sits in a shallow basin walled in by trees. A few tiny clearings offer possible campsites or picnic areas. Looking across the green water, Mount Yoran peeks an angular head above the treetops a couple of miles south.

Retrace your steps to the junction and bear left on Diamond Creek Trail to complete the loop. The path soon reaches a close range overlook of Upper Diamond Creek Falls. The second viewpoint is found via a spur that drops to bridge the creek and return to the base of the falls. The homeward route offers a few more vistas across the rugged canyon and a short spur to the rhododendron-rimmed shore of Too Much Bear Lake. Be sure to see 286-foot Salt Creek Falls, Oregon's second highest plunge, before leaving the area.

A visitor at Cougar, if so inclined, can take a cold shower between hot soaks.

4 Cougar Hot Springs

General description: An idyllic chain of (too) well-known soaking pools reached by a short path, east of Eugene near Cougar Reservoir. Skinnydippable with discretion. Elevation 2,000 feet.
Map: Willamette National Forest.

Finding the hot springs: From Eugene, drive about forty-two miles east on State Route 126 to Blue River. Continue four miles to paved Forest Road 19 and follow it along the west side of Cougar Reservoir. At 7.5 miles, you'll pass a lagoon with a waterfall on your right followed by a parking area on the left. Park and walk back past the lagoon to the trail sign. The well-worn .3-mile path hugs the shore, then climbs through a darkening forest to the pools. Cougar (also known as Terwilliger) isn't marked on the forest map.

The hot springs: Enveloped in the dark hues of a primeval woodland, Cougar is brushed by mottled light filtering down from treetops high above. Five soaking pools spaced apart by giant logs are laid out in steps down a steep ravine. Spring water tumbles directly into the uppermost and hottest pool, and cold water flowing down a log flume provides an eye-opening shower.

Each rock and gravel pool is slightly cooler than the one above; they range in temperature from 108 down to 95 degrees. The moss-coated trunk of one ancient log spanning the cleft plays host to a budding growth of ferns.

Some years back, a volunteer group working with the Forest Service built log steps and railings down the slippery bank, replanted the eroded ground cover around the pools and added walkways, built an outhouse up the hill, and had a resident caretaker there to help protect the fragile grounds—a difficult job due to steadily increasing use/abuse problems.

Reminder: If you value a pristine environment, please observe the basics: no soap or shampoo, no glass containers, pack out what you pack in, leave your pets at home, and be kind to the soil by staying on established paths. Cougar needs all the help it can get!

Nighttime closure: As the crowds kept increasing, so did the difficulty of dealing with the drinkers, dopers, and a few just plain "crazies." The Forest Service was eventually forced to take over the headache of managing Cougar and came up with a strictly enforced nighttime closure. Signs posted at both the parking area and trailhead now read "Day Use Area. Closed Sundown to Sunrise." Camping along the reservoir is limited to very few primitive sites and a developed campground near either end.

HIKE 4a *Rebel Creek/Rebel Rock Loop*

General description: A fairly strenuous 12.5-mile, loop day hike climbing through a lonesome slice of the Three Sisters Wilderness, near Cougar Hot Springs.
Elevation gain and loss: 3,271 feet.
Trailhead elevation: 2,040 feet.
High point: 5,311 feet.
Hiking quad: Three Sisters Wilderness (Geo-Graphics or Forest Service) or Cougar Reservoir, Chucksney Mountain, and Grasshopper Mountain USGS.
Road Maps: Willamette National Forest.

Finding the trailhead: Follow the directions above to Cougar and continue south 6.5 miles (fourteen miles total from State Route 126). The parking loop is on the left, and the newly combined trailhead splits a short way above.

The hike: There has been more volcanic activity in the area of the Three Sisters Wilderness during the past few thousand years than in any other part of the entire Cascade range. The Three Sisters are the star attractions in this 285,202-acre wildland: The striking peaks with their fourteen separate glaciers draw a multitude of climbers, hikers, and sightseers along boot-beaten paths to the east and north, while the western side remains relatively free of crowds.

The Rebel Creek/Rebel Rock Loop offers a quiet route stretching through virgin backcountry. Rebel Creek Trail climbs from creekside greenery and old-

HIKE 4a *Rebel Creek/Rebel Rock Loop*

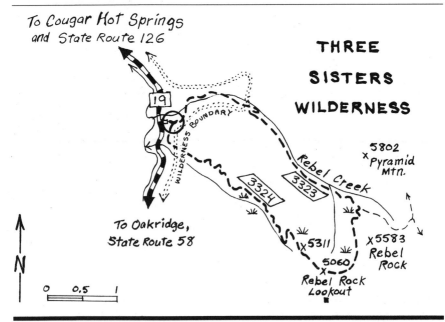

growth trees up through meadows dotted with pine and fir. It connects with Rebel Rock Trail, a ridgetop route offering rear balcony views of the Three Sisters and Mount Jefferson before circling back down through more meadows and woods to end at the original trailhead.

It's best to follow Rebel Creek Trail up and Rebel Rock Trail back, as the gain is more gradual this way. Turn left just above the parking loop onto Rebel Creek Trail (3323). Ferns and thimbleberries overgrow the path, and ancient stands of Douglas-fir, cedar, and western hemlock wrap it in many shades of green. It's a gentle climb along the creek, and the only two crossings are on split-log bridges. The trail leaves the creek and begins a moderate 5.7-mile climb to a junction at 4,480 feet.

Take the right fork, Rebel Rock Trail (3324), and climb one more ridge. You'll pass the base of 5,583-foot Rebel Rock while slicing through fields of knee-high flowers. The high meadows are peppered with mountain hemlock and true fir. As the ridgeline route slowly curves, it offers a variety of views en route to a large meadow on a 5,311-foot plateau. From here you can gaze out across the wilderness to several of the highest distant peaks.

It's all downhill from this point. The path plunges through more meadows so overgrown that the route is barely visible until you reach the lower woods. Here, hundreds of invisible spiderwebs span the trail between anchoring trees, ignoring the hiker's right of way. Ferns and thimbleberries again choke the path, and the forest closes in overhead.

5 Bigelow Hot Spring

General description: A secret soaking pool in a fern grotto on the Mckenzie River near a paved road, northeast of Eugene. Skinnydippable with discretion. Elevation 2,000 feet.
Map: Willamette National Forest.

Finding the hot spring: From Eugene, take State Route 126 about fifty-seven miles east to Belknap Springs. Continue four miles north (.4 mile past Milepost 15) and turn left onto Deer Creek Road (2654). (*Campers:* There are primitive sites in the nearby woods and a developed campground a mile or so up the highway.) Cross the river and park just past the bridge. Follow the lower path a short way downstream to the pool. Bigelow Hot Spring (also known as Deer Creek) isn't marked on the forest map.

The hot spring: This little jewel, well camouflaged among the many look-alikes along the riverbank, is a closely guarded secret. Rafting downstream, it would never catch your eye. Walking right above it on McKenzie River Trail (Hike 5a), you wouldn't see the pool through the trees. Even driving across the nearby bridge and looking right at it, there are no telltale signs to give it away unless it's occupied.

With the inlet at the bottom of the bubbly pool, hot water seeps in quietly to provide an optimum soaking temperature of 102 to 104 degrees. Riverside rocks line the outer edge, while the inner side forms a small grotto carved out of the steep riverbank. Luxuriant ferns overhang the pool, and moisture

Bigelow bubbles up from below into a fern grotto pool well hidden along the riverbank.

condenses overhead to drip back down on the steaming surface in cool droplets.

Nighttime closure: Following in the footsteps of first Cougar and then McCredie, Bigelow has recently joined the list of hot springs in Willamette National Forest with a night closure. The area around the pool is now officially off limits from sundown to sunrise.

"Waking nightmare:" I parked by the bridge (the only vehicle on a rainy Friday night) on my first visit to Bigelow in several years. The next morning I awoke to discover the lot rapidly filling to capacity. People were gathering in small clusters and talking with animation. Huge motorhomes pulled in, and more folks piled out.

I finally squeezed my door open and jokingly asked a lady where the line began. She gave me a blank look and a polite laugh, then hurried off. I finally learned to my great relief that it wasn't Bigelow Hot Spring at all but a running marathon on the McKenzie River Trail that had drawn the crowd!

HIKE 5a *McKenzie River National Recreation Trail*

General description: A variable-length riverside stroll featuring virgin forests, lava flows and waterfalls, near Bigelow Hot Spring.
Elevation gain and loss: up to 1,750 feet.
Trailhead elevation: 1,450 feet.

High point: Clear Lake, 3,200 feet.
Maps: Forest Service brochure, Willamette National Forest.

Finding the trailheads: Drive about fifty-two miles east from Eugene on State Route 126 to McKenzie Ranger Station, where you can pick up a free brochure/map listing the many trailheads and exact mileages between points.

The hike: The riverside path above Bigelow Hot Spring is part of the twenty-seven-mile McKenzie River National Recreation Trail. Designated a National Wild and Scenic River in 1988 and also listed as a State Scenic Waterway around the same time, the McKenzie is a whitewater river that originates in the high Cascades. Beginning just west of McKenzie Ranger Station and ending near Clear Lake and the river's headwaters, the route is a gentle climb upvalley parallel to State Route 126. There are eleven parking areas along the way that provide a variety of easy access points at signed trailheads.

The lower eight to ten miles are usually free of snow year around. The hiker treads through dim forests of 600-year old Douglas-fir mixed with hemlock, cedar, and dogwood. Thick mats of Oregon grape, wildflowers, and salal crowd beneath vine maple and other hardwoods. The upper part passes areas where lava flows once spewed from nearby craters, filling the McKenzie Canyon and forcing the once mighty river through underground channels (see Hike 5b). Tamolitch, a broad valley of lava, remains a dry watercourse except in times of heavy runoff.

Graceful log bridges are a common sight along the McKenzie River Trail.

Above Tamolitch Valley, the trail passes two impressive waterfalls created by lava. Koosah Falls, a seventy-foot drop into a deep pool, is outclassed by magnificent Sahalie Falls, a broad 100-foot plunge over a lava dam followed by a series of cascades that tumble another forty feet. Clouds of spray billow outward over green banks.

Clear Lake, the next to last stop, was created some 3,000 years ago when a giant lava flow dammed the river and caused the wide valley upstream to fill in. Submerged trees can be seen through the clear surface near the north end—well preserved in the icy, mineral-free water. Springs that average 43 degrees act as outlets for the buried river and well up from below to feed the lake. Great Springs, one of the largest, can be seen from the trail on the northeast side.

The McKenzie River Trail finally comes to rest near the Old Santiam Wagon Road just north of Clear Lake. This was the historic route over the Santiam Pass which became an early link between the mid-Willamette Valley and the lands in central and eastern Oregon.

HIKE 5b *"The Blue Hole" and Tamolitch Falls*

General description: A four-mile, round-trip stroll to uncover one of the stranger sights along the McKenzie River Trail, near Bigelow Hot Spring.
Elevation gain and loss: 240 feet.
Trailhead elevation: 2,160 feet.
High point: "The Blue Hole," 2,440 feet.
Maps: Same as Hike 5a.

Finding the trailhead: One could walk upstream to "the Blue Hole" from Bigelow, a pleasant round trip of fourteen miles, but there's a much closer access point. Take State Route 126 five miles farther north to Trail Bridge Reservoir. Cross the river bridge to a junction and bear right (the left fork goes to Trail Bridge Campground). Continue straight where the main road forks right again. As the road makes a sharp left, watch for a small turnout and trail marker 0.5 mile from the highway.

The hike: One of the highlights on the McKenzie River Trail (Hike 5a) is a spot known locally as "the Blue Hole"—a brilliant blue pool of icy water that marks the place where the river rises from its underground channel, near the south end of Tamolitch Valley, to continue its course in a more normal fashion. It's quite a sight to see this strange pool, with no visible inlet, channeling out into a whitewater river.

Follow the McKenzie River Trail north for an easy two miles through deep woods. At one point, you'll cross a fern-laden marsh on a curving bridge hewn from logs. The route gradually emerges into the open at Tamolitch, the Valley of Lava. A drier landscape prevails across a riverbed of moss-coated volcanic rock that culminates in a sixty-foot dropoff into "the Blue Hole." Called Tamolitch Falls on the Forest Service brochure, the bone-dry cliff would confound any camera-clicking sightseer out to capture one more waterfall on film. But so would a river flowing downstream from nowhere!

HOT SPRING 5 *Bigelow Hot Spring*
HIKE 5a *McKenzie River National Recreation Trail*
HIKE 5b *"The Blue Hole" and Tamolitch Falls*

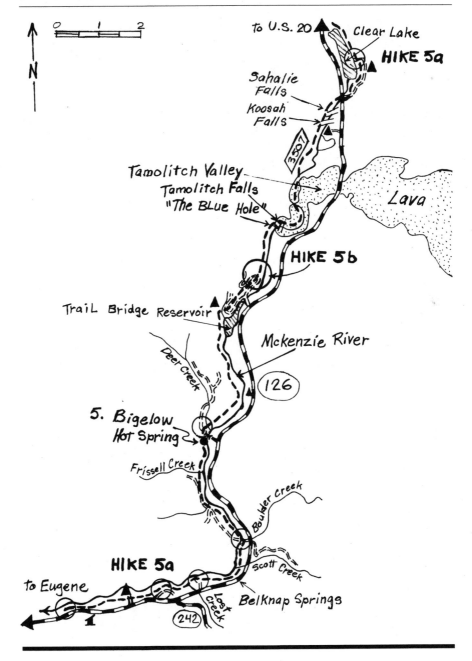

to U.S. 20

Clear Lake

HIKE 5a

Sahalie Falls

Koosah Falls

3507

Tamolitch Valley

Tamolitch Falls

"The Blue Hole"

Lava

HIKE 5b

Trail Bridge Reservoir

McKenzie River

Deer Creek

126

5. Bigelow Hot Spring

Frissell Creek

Boulder Creek

HIKE 5a

to Eugene

Scott Creek

Belknap Springs

Lost Creek

242

1

The McKenzie River surfaces abruptly from its underground water course through "the Blue Hole."

6 Bagby Hot Springs

HIKE 6a *To Bagby Hot Springs*

General description: A delightful three-mile, round-trip day hike through lush woods to the Shangri-la of hot soaks, a treasure buried southeast of Portland. No need to pack a swimsuit.

Elevation gain and loss: 190 feet.

Trailhead elevation: 2,080 feet.

High point: Bagby, 2,270 feet.

Hiking quads: Battle Ax Green Trails or Bagby Hot Springs USGS.

Road map: Mount Hood National Forest.

Finding the trailhead: Bagby Hot Springs, located seventy miles southeast of Portland, is reached by following State Route 224 to Estacada and on into Mount Hood Forest. Take a right on Forest Road 46 at 0.5 mile past Ripplebrook Ranger Station, and bear right in 3.5 miles onto Forest Road 63. Turn right again in 3.5 miles onto Forest Road 70 and drive six miles to the trailhead parking lot.

You'll pass several developed campgrounds on the way in, and there's also a primitive camp adjacent to the parking lot. "Car clouting" has become an increasing problem here, so park close to other vehicles, get your goodies out of sight, and lock up tight. The roads are paved and well signed, and Bagby is named on the maps.

The hike: For the ultimate experience in natural hot springs, come to Bagby. A talented group of volunteers working with the Forest Service has built three rustic bathhouses, fed by two nearby springs, in a sylvan forest setting. The tubs are drained and cleaned daily by the hardworking Friends of Bagby who have also added decks with log benches, outhouses, pathways, and landscaping. This unique group welcomes anyone interested in helping them preserve the area. You can send donations or apply for membership to Friends of Bagby, Inc., P.O. Box 15116, Portland, OR 97215.

The 1.5-mile Bagby Trail (544) is a delight in itself as it undulates through a grand old forest of Douglas-fir and cedar with an understory of vine maple. Moss-coated logs litter the way, and the path slices between cross sections with five-foot diameters. The gentle creekside route passes emerald green pools spaced between rapids. Cross three bridges, then leave the creek behind just beyond the last bridge and climb a short hillside to the springs.

The hot springs: The bathhouse at the upper spring, built in 1983, has a single six-foot round cedar tub enclosed by minimum walls and maximum trees. The ceiling is pure sky. This is the spot for a family or cozy group to enjoy total privacy. A log flume 150 feet long diverts the 135-degree spring water into the tub, and a crude faucet admits cold water.

The communal bathhouse, finished in 1984, is another minimum wall/maximum tree and sky affair but on a larger scale. Three huge cedar logs, hollowed out to form long and narrow soaking tubs, are spaced a few feet apart; these

In the communal bathhouse at Bagby are three hand-hewn soaking tubs hollowed out from giant logs.

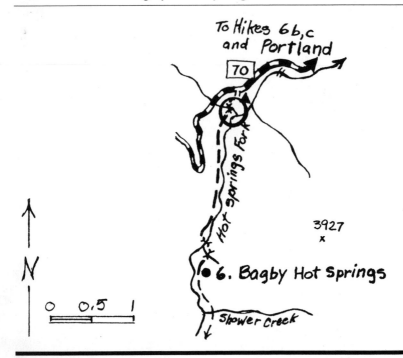

rustic log tubs are all that remain from the original bathhouse that burned down in 1979. At one end of the airy room is another six-foot round tub. An adjoining bathhouse, completed in 1986, is a fully roofed replica of the one that burned; it offers five hand-hewn log tubs in private rooms.

A cleverly designed system of log flumes channels 135-degree water from the lower spring into each tub, and individual gates may be opened or closed to control the flow. Tub water drains out through another set of gates into long troughs that run beneath each house. One last flume feeds cold water into a centrally located well, and buckets are provided to carry it to the tubs.

Overnight camping isn't permitted at Bagby but is allowed at Shower Creek 0.25 mile farther on. At Spray Creek, 2.5 miles from the Bagby trailhead, the path enters the Bull of the Woods Wilderness. It continues through more verdant scenery, climbing 1,330 feet in the next eight miles to Silver King Mountain. From a high point at 4,600 feet along a ridge, you could drop east on Trail 573 to reach Twin Lakes in another two miles.

HIKE 6b *Bull of the Woods*

General description: An easy 7.5-mile, round-trip day hike the Bull of the Woods Wilderness with a view of Mount Jeffers... Hood, not far from Bagby Hot Springs.
Elevation gain and loss: 883 feet.
Trailhead elevation: 4,640 feet.
High point: Bull of the Woods, 5,523 feet.
Hiking quads: Battle Ax Green Trails or Bull of the Woods USGS.
Road map: Same as Hike 6a.

Finding the trailhead: Follow the directions above to the junction of Forest Roads 63 and 70 (the turnoff to Bagby) and continue two miles south on 63. Turn right on gravel Forest Road 6340 and climb to a three-way junction in ten miles. A sign on the right marks the location of the new trailhead. Park here and put your boots to work.

The hike: The lookout that caps 5,523-foot Bull of the Woods is the logical spot to survey one of Oregon's newer wildlands. The 34,900-acre Bull of the Woods Wilderness is a spoonful of wooded lakes spread out around the central peak. The small area, which includes the headwaters of the Collawash, Breitenbush, and North Santiam rivers, adds yet another link in the chain of wilderness gems running through the Cascades. The broad view from the summit includes many prominent peaks.

Follow Bull of the Woods Trail (550) on a gentle climb through a forest of Douglas-fir and western hemlock. Rhododendron, bear grass, and lupine brush the path in alternating bursts of pink, white, and blue/purple. The route hugs the west side of a ridge topped by North and South Dickey Peaks; it's basically one short and sweet traverse with a couple of hairpins at the end that offer previews of coming attractions.

The lookout tower on top of Bull of the Woods offers an expanse of undulating mountain ranges dotted with volcanic cones.

41

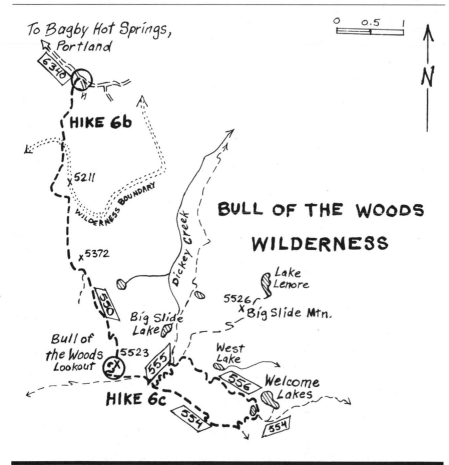

To Bagby Hot Springs,
Portland

6340

HIKE 6b

x 5211

WILDERNESS BOUNDARY

x 5372

BULL OF THE WOODS

WILDERNESS

Dickey Creek

Lake
Lenore

5526
x Big Slide Mtn.

550

Big Slide
Lake

Bull of
the Woods   5523
Lookout

West
Lake

555

556   Welcome
Lakes

HIKE 6c

554

554

0   0.5   1

N

The lookout has expansive open views of glacier-draped peaks from the Three Sisters north to Mount Rainier. Most prominent is the angular white face of Mount Jefferson standing out at 10,495 feet to the southeast. The massive shape of 11,239-foot Mount Hood rises dramatically to the northeast. A pleasant loop may be made from the lookout east to the Welcome Lakes (Hike 6c).

HIKE 6c *Bull of the Woods to the Welcome Lakes Loop*

General description: A moderate five-mile, round-trip day hike or overnighter (including a 3.3-mile loop) from the lookout to lakes and more views of Bull of the Woods Wilderness, not far from Bagby Hot Springs.
Elevation gain and loss: 1,243 feet (283 feet to start of loop; loop, 960 feet).
High point: Trailhead, 5,523 feet.
Low point: Upper Welcome Lake, 4,440 feet.
Maps: Same as Hike 6b.

Finding the trailhead: Follow Hike 6b to Bull of the Woods.

The hike: The Welcome Lakes Loop makes a pleasant side trip from Bull of the Woods Lookout down through a bit more backcountry east of the summit. The five-mile circuit passes through old-growth timber and open ridges, and it intersects a network of trails en route that could keep a backpacker busy for days.

The route begins by dropping steeply from the lookout through deep woods, then veering east over a rockslide area. A junction is reached in 0.9 mile, 280 feet below the summit, with Schreiner Peak Trail (555) plunging downhill on the left. To follow the loop in a clockwise direction, turn north here and descend tight switchbacks past Dickey Creek Trail branching left down to Big Slide Lake. Continue beyond a pond to a junction with the lower trail to the Welcome Lakes.

Turn right onto West Lake Way (556) and drop gradually through low forest, traversing 250 feet above West Lake, treading an open rocky area with good views around the scenic basin. The path contours gently downhill along the face of a slope and rounds a corner to arrive at Upper Welcome Lake. Orbit the small lake to intersect the Welcome Lakes Trail at 2.7 miles.

Upper Welcome Lake sits on a ledge a few hundred feet from the trail with a large dry campsite nearby. The surface is brushed in late summer with the yellow blooms of pond lilies. From the viewpoint east of the lake, you can look 240 feet down onto Lower Welcome Lake. An unsigned spur heads down from the Welcome Lakes Trail to the larger lake, adding a mile round trip to the hike.

Turn onto Welcome Lakes Trail (554) for the second half of the loop. The path zigzags up a ridge through meadows and more rockslide areas, passing the Geronimo Trail veering off to Elk Lake. The route makes a dip, then rises to follow the crest with views into West Lake Basin and across to Big Slide Mountain to the northeast. Pass the junction with Schreiner Peak Trail, bear right at one last junction 0.2 mile to the west, and retrace your steps back up the mountain.

7 Paulina Lake Hot Springs

HIKE 7a *To Paulina Lake Hot Springs*

General description: An easy four-mile round-trip (or 7.5-mile loop) day hike to a batch of "now you see 'em, now you don't" hot springs on a lake inside a volcanic crater, south of Bend in Newberry National Volcanic Monument. Carry a swimsuit and shovel.
Elevation gain and loss: 180 feet.
Trailhead elevation: 6,340 feet.
High point: 6,520 feet at "red slide."
Hiking quads: Paulina Peak and East Lake USGS quads or Forest Service trail printout.
Road map: Deschutes National Forest.

Finding the trailhead: Drive twenty miles south of Bend on U.S. Highway 97, then follow signs thirteen miles east to Newberry Crater and Paulina Lake. The springs are on the far shore and can be reached on the Paulina Lake-Shore Loop Trail 2.75 miles from Paulina Lake Campground or two miles from Little Crater Campground. Everything here is well signed and easy to find—except the hot springs, which aren't marked at all. Snow blocks the roads in winter, and the prime time for digging a hot pool is said to be June-August.

The volcano: The recently created (late 1990) Newberry National Volcanic Monument is a slice of Deschutes National Forest housing much of the "lava lands" on the east side of the Cascades plus the largest ice-age volcano in Oregon. Several violent eruptions over the past half million years formed the five-mile wide caldera called Newberry Crater. Within are two scenic lakes. At one time a single body of water, Paulina and East Lakes were eventually split apart by further eruptions.

East Lake has no visible inlet or outlet and is fed, aside from snowmelt, by submerged hot springs bubbling up near the southeast shore. The springs clock in at a staggering 175 degrees, but the heat is instantly lost to the cold lake. Paulina Lake, however, offers an array of usable hot springs on the northeast side in addition to submerged ones along the rocky east coast. Except for snowmelt, their combined flow constitutes the lake's only inlet. Paulina Creek, the outlet, forms the only breach in the rim of the crater.

The hike: Although the round trip to the hot springs from Little Crater Campground is short and sweet, the full loop hike around the lake is well worth the added mileage. The path hugs the photogenic shoreline, leaving it only briefly to climb "red slide." Thick forest shades the way without blocking views of Paulina Peak (Hike 7b) and the Big Obsidian Flow. The springs can be found between "red slide" and the Inter-Lake Lava Flow, along a meadow-lined beach near a hike-in/boat-in campground.

The hot springs: The springs at Paulina are a tad out of the ordinary. Elusive even once found, they lurk not underwater but under gravel. You can walk

The perennial foot warmer at Paulina Lake needs a few buckets of cold water to cool it into the comfort zone.

down the beach, turn and literally watch your footsteps fill with hot water! The challenge is twofold—trying to coax the good stuff out of hiding (that's where the shovel comes in), and then once you've got it, trying to hang onto it long enough for a soak. The springs range from 96-113 degrees, so if you stumble onto a live one, a bucket might be in order. (Actually, a sturdy bucket can double for both digging a pool and tossing in lake water.)

I consulted a hydrologist and a geologist, both familiar with Newberry Crater, and was told that the hot springs here bubble up from the depths and simply ride the top layer of the lake's water table. Hot water filters up through the shoreline gravel at the same level as the lake itself. When the lake recedes, the hot water can be tapped, but the trick is to dig deeper than the level of the lake. Then you can sit back and watch it fill—and stay filled!

There's a shallow, log-lined soaking pool (113 degrees) over by "red slide" that appears to be a perennial. It sits on bedrock and can't be deepened, but it should fill up when the lake level's just right. It has a nice platform spanning one end to sit and dangle feet from. All it needs is some cold water thrown in.

Paulina Lake Resort offers boat rentals and rustic accommodations under a special use permit from the Forest Service, and "Paulina Joe" keeps a sharp eye on the lake, roads, and weather. The summer visitor center at Paulina Lake or the ranger station in Bend can help with other questions.

HIKE 7a *To Paulina Lake Hot Springs*
HIKE 7b *Paulina Peak*

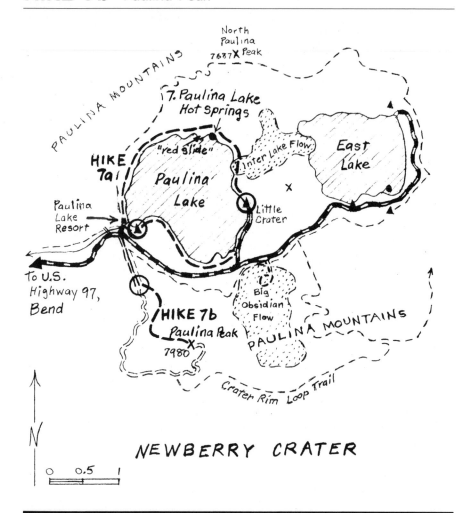

North Paulina 7637X Peak

PAULINA MOUNTAINS

7. Paulina Lake Hot Springs

HIKE 7a

"red slide"

Paulina Lake

Inter Lake Flow

East Lake

Paulina Lake Resort

Little Crater

To U.S. Highway 97, Bend

Big Obsidian Flow

HIKE 7b
Paulina Peak
X
7980

PAULINA MOUNTAINS

Crater Rim Loop Trail

N

0   0.5   1

NEWBERRY CRATER

HIKE 7b *Paulina Peak*

General description: A strenuous five-mile, round-trip climb to the high point on the rim of Newberry Crater, near Paulina Lake Hot Springs.
Elevation gain and loss: 1,480 feet.
Trailhead elevation: 6,500 feet.
High point: 7,980 feet.
Hiking quad: Paulina Peak USGS.
Road map: Deschutes National Forest.

Finding the trailhead: Follow the directions above to Paulina Lake. Take a right just before the visitor center on a washboard forest road (500) signed to Paulina Peak. Drive 0.8 mile to a small pullout and trail sign on your left. (The actual trailhead, back at the junction, adds an extra mile and 160-foot gain to the hike.)

The hike: Although you can drive to the top of Paulina Peak, the present road is in rough shape. Also, it climbs the back side of the mountain. The hiking route contours up the front side and offers views of the lake en route. There's been some talk of relocating the road and the trail, so it wouldn't hurt to check with the Forest Service before setting out. (Newberry Crater, long dormant, is currently experiencing activity of a human variety resulting from its "upgrading" to a national monument.)

Crater Rim Loop Trail presents a steady eleven percent grade, but the north-facing slope and thick woods combine forces to shade the way. The lodgepole forest includes a sprinkling of hemlock and ponderosa interspersed with rock and lava slopes. Near the end, a spur trail accesses the craggy summit.

Paulina Lake unfolds below. On the far shore, you can spot "red slide," the landmark for the hot springs (Hike 7a). The Inter-Lake Lava Flow and Big Obsidian Flow can also be seen. Beyond the crater rim, the panorama takes in much of the Cascades. The massive cones of Mount Bachelor and South Sister top the northwest horizon, and to the southeast is Fort Rock.

HIKE 7c *Other Trips in the Newberry Area*

Newberry Crater

The crater contains a network of hiking routes to suit every taste. Crater Rim Loop Trail climbs Paulina Peak (Hike 7b) and then continues around the rim for some twenty miles. It can also be entered via the 4.25-mile Lost Lake Trail to provide a ten-mile loop, or via Newberry Crater Trail, bisecting the crater floor from east to west.

Not to be missed are the 0.5-mile Paulina Falls Trail, which offers an exceptional view from the base of the 100-foot plunge, and the one-mile Obsidian Flow Loop, snaking across frozen cataracts of black volcanic glass. The 1,300-year-old flow is the most recent volcanic eruption in Oregon. The Paulina Peak and East Lake USGS quads cover Newberry Crater, and the Deschutes Forest map handles the roads.

Newberry lava tubes

A lava tube (or lava cave) is a natural underground cavity formerly occupied by lava—in other words, a roofed-over section of a lava river. Fluid lava streaming underground has created a variety of tubes and complex systems that are fascinating to explore, and most of those in central Oregon are found on the flanks of Newberry Crater. The Newberry lava tubes are known to be at least 6,800 years old, as they contain ash from the eruption of Mount Mazama (better known as Crater Lake).

Exploring lava caves needn't be a risky endeavor if you simply practice common sense and basic rules of safety, and take appropriate gear. In total

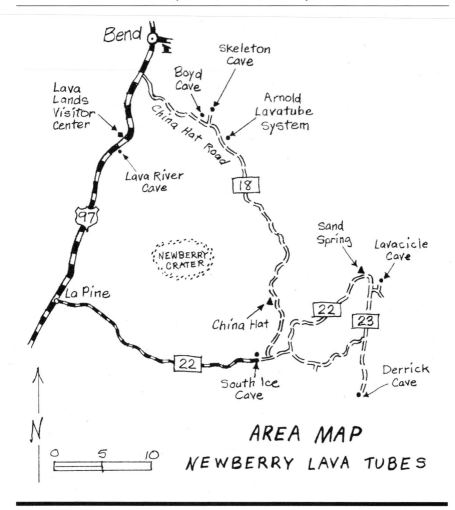

Bend

Skeleton Cave

Boyd Cave

Lava Lands Visitor Center

Arnold Lavatube System

China Hat Road

Lava River Cave

18

97

NEWBERRY CRATER

Sand Spring

Lavacicle Cave

La Pine

China Hat

22

23

Derrick Cave

22

South Ice Cave

N

0   5   10

AREA MAP

NEWBERRY LAVA TUBES

darkness, every 100 feet feels like a mile. Experienced cavers carry three sources of light. A good combination is a Coleman lantern, a powerful flashlight, and a candle for the time when all else fails. Head protection is advisable, as are boots with lug soles. Wear plenty of warm clothes—cave temperatures in central Oregon fall generally in the thirty-five to fifty-degree range.

The Newberry lava tubes lie widely scattered within a crescent shaped area centered to the east of the crater. The easiest access is via a loop drive on forest roads leaving U.S. Highway 97 south of Bend and returning at La Pine. (See Area Map.) All of the caves are marked on the Deschutes Forest map.

The well known *Lava River Cave*, located near the Lava Lands Visitor Center twelve miles south of Bend, is the longest continuous lava tube in the state. The interpretive trail is 1.5 miles long, of which a full 1.1 miles is underground.

One 1,500-foot section has become unstable and is now closed. This is one of Oregon's three commercial caves, and gas lanterns are rented for the trip. With marked paths, stairways over collapsed rubble, and smooth floors, it makes a good introduction to caving.

Boyd Cave is a single lava tube 1,800 feet long. It has a single entrance with a sturdy stairway, and the walking is fairly easy over sand and scattered rubble.

Nearby is popular *Skeleton Cave*—a must for the more adventurous. This lava tube is 3,000 feet long and has a fork just beyond the halfway point that can easily turn you around. The name came from the abundance of Pleistocene-age bones found within. The floor is smooth sand until well past the "junction room."

The collapsing remains of the *Arnold lava tube system* also are found nearby—including the once famous Arnold Ice Cave and such colorful names as Bat Cave No. 1, Hidden Forest Cave, Wind Cave, and Charlie-the-Cave. The complex system once extended about 4.5 miles, but most of what's left today is considered either hazardous or difficult scrambling. It's worth a visit just to view the gaping entrance holes.

Lavacicle Cave Geological Area is a narrow, lengthy lava tube with stalagmites of frozen lava. Its two opposing sections total 4,231 feet. Discovered in 1959, it was badly vandalized before the Forest Service gated the entrance. Contact the Lava Lands Visitor Center for information on summer group tours.

Derrick Cave is a complex lava tube 1,200 feet long. The first section is an easy walk to an area where skylights overhead cast eerie rays down the walls. Beyond, it narrows into intriguing and challenging passageways. This cave is on Bureau of Land Management land. The access roads aren't well signed but are well used and fairly obvious.

South Ice Cave is a high ceiling cave with permanent ice. It has two sections, one on either side of the ramped entrance, with a total of 1,000 feet. The cave is managed by the Forest Service as an improved recreation site.

B. THE OWYHEE RIVER CANYON

Hot springs and hikes

Upstream and south of Jordan Valley, a canyon hike leads to a great soak at Three Forks (8a). The next two far-flung dips (in the lower canyon) remain nameless on the maps and even the state geothermal. The adventurous route to No. 1 (9a) can be found north of Rome; No. 2 (10a) is accessed along with a companion hike from spectacular Leslie Gulch. Farthest north comes a dip at the popular Snively (11) and a nearby desert walk. *Note to campers:* Malheur County prohibits open fires and requires fire pans for those camping within 0.25 mile of the banks of the Owyhee River.

Season

The best time to track down the first three on the list is June/July through October/November when the river level is low, the access roads dry, and competition from river rats gone for the season. Snively alone is accessible and usable all year. Daytime temperatures in the desert often climb to 90 degrees or higher through the summer months but drop markedly overnight. The weather tends to be dry and clear, and sunscreen replaces raingear as the number one item in the pack.

B. THE OWYHEE RIVER CANYON

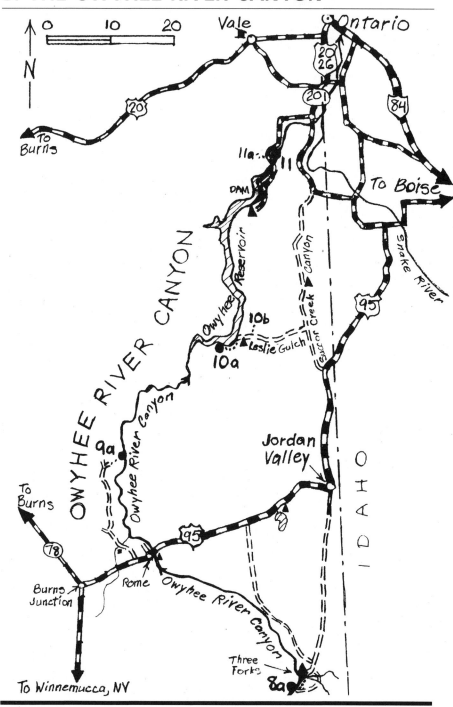

8 Three Forks Hot Springs

HIKE 8a *To Three Forks Hot Springs*

General description: An easy 5.5-mile scenic loop day hike or overnighter to secluded springs and a Jacuzzi/waterfall pool in the upper Owyhee River Canyon, south of Jordan Valley. Swimwear optional.
Elevation gain and loss: 260 feet.
Trailhead elevation: 3,980 feet.
High Point: 4,200 feet.
Hiking quad: Three Forks USGS.
Road map: Jordan Valley 30-minute BLM.

Finding the trailhead: Two gravel roads fifteen miles apart travel south from U.S. Highway 95 to Three Forks. If coming from Burns Junction, go about thirty miles east to a road signed "Three Forks—35" at Milepost 36. This route has the bonus of passing the Owyhee Canyon Overlook. Or, if coming from Jordan Valley, head due south, bearing right at a fork in three miles. The latter route is a bit longer, but the first eight miles are paved. Either way, it's a long haul and shouldn't be traveled in wet conditions.

The two roads eventually join up around three miles from the canyon rim. The final 1.5-mile stretch to the bottom is quite steep and should never be attempted when the road is muddy. Find a niche to park at the primitive BLM camping area in a grassy flat by the river. The springs are marked on both maps.

The hike: This remote spot, reached by fishermen and a few hardy river runners, marks the confluence of three tributaries of the Owyhee River—hence the name Three Forks. The Middle and North forks of the Owyhee come together 0.5 mile to the east and flow into the main fork of the river at the BLM camp and launch site.

A three-mile jeep road takes a roundabout route from Three Forks to the hot springs. This is the principal access, but when the river level is low (usually June-September) a nice loop hike can be made by walking up the river canyon to the springs and then following the road back to camp.

The route starts by fording the combined Middle and North forks at the launch site. You won't have to wade the main fork; the route stays on the east side all the way. Jagged walls shadow the deep canyon, and an intermittent path reaches the springs about 2.5 miles upstream.

To complete the loop, follow the jeep road up the steep bank and swing east to breathtaking views of the gorge. The track curves around a hill (the high point on the hike at 4,200 feet), then dips across a sagebrush valley and drops down to ford the Middle Fork.

The North Fork is bridged, and the rocky gorge upstream makes an inviting side trip. The road improves in the short distance back to camp, tempting the unwary driver to try it, but it offers some surprises and almost no place wide enough to turn around when you change your mind.

Three Forks Hot Springs features a warm Jacuzzi pool beneath a waterfall.

The hot springs: Clusters of 95-degree springs are located on both sides of the river, and the rugged Owyhee Canyon forms a magnificent backdrop. There's an unofficial camping area along the east bank where several warm streams snake through tall grass to the river. Above are two tiny pools, each with a sit-down shower provided by a length of pipe. But the best is yet to come.

On the opposite bank, several thermal waterfalls pour into the river at 3,750 liters per minute, all emanating from Warm Springs Canyon. You may spot a rope descending from a boulder above the largest falls. That's your target. (But don't aim for it during the spring runoff or you're likely end up downstream at Rome!)

Ford the cold river and climb to a large soaking pool enclosed between boulders. This gem is a good three feet deep and has a gravel bottom. It's kept clean as a whistle by the scouring action of three cascades pouring into it, and the resulting warm Jacuzzi is delightful. There's another pool or two upstream, but beyond the source the side canyon is dry.

Note: The springs are located on unposted private land. Please pack out what you pack in, observe fire restrictions, and respect the landowner's rights.

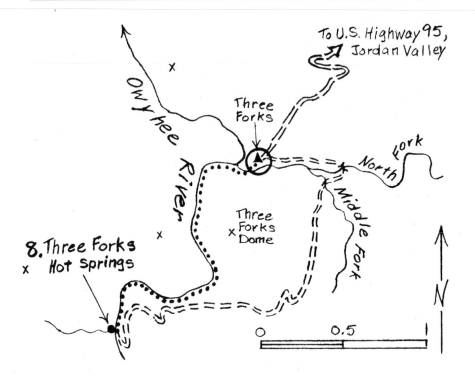

9 Unnamed Hot Spring No. 1

HIKE 9a *To Unnamed Hot Springs No. 1*

General description: A fairly easy, eight-mile round-trip bushwhack to a hot spring known only to a few river runners, north of Rome in the lower Owyhee River Canyon. Swimwear: a hat and bug juice.
Elevation gain and loss: 440 feet.
High point: Trailhead, 3,560 feet.
Low point: Hot spring, 3,120 feet.
Hiking quad: Lambert Rocks USGS.
Road maps: Crooked Creek and Skull Spring 30-minute BLM.

Finding the trailhead: Take U.S. Highway 95 to Rome, the launch site for raft trips down the lower canyon. Go four miles west 0.2 mile east of Milepost 58) and watch for a stop sign on the north side of the highway at the crest of a low hill. Nothing else marks the spot. Whatever you do, don't even consider taking this seasonal road if the ground is at all damp. You'll never make it.

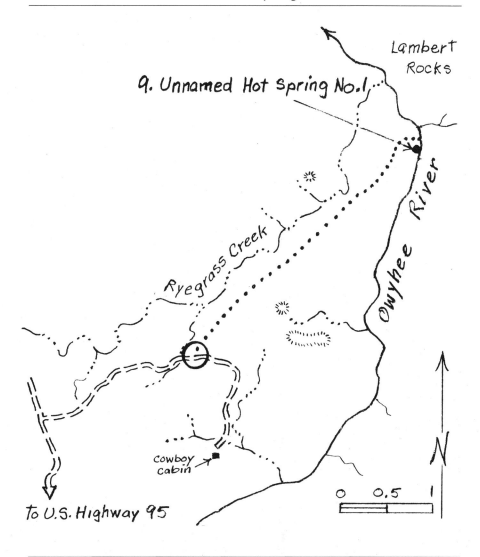

Drive 3.5 miles north to a ranch on Crooked Creek. The gravel ends at the doorstep. Back up and take the obscure right fork past the ranch (please be sure to leave the gate as you found it or as signs request). *Note:* There's a classic swimming hole in the creek at the bottom of the hill. See story at end.

The route, a boundary road for Wilderness Study areas on either side, continues north and roughly parallels the Owyhee Canyon just visible to the east. It's slow going over rocks, potholes, and sandy washes. You'll eventually cross a plateau strewn with lava rocks and drop into the broad valley of Ryegrass Creek.

Watch for a "Y" in the road about fifteen miles from the fork at the ranch. Bear right and park in a mile or so. The hot spring isn't marked on either map and misplaced to the north on the state geothermal.

The challenge: The fun with this hot spring isn't the soak so much as the adventure of locating it. Neither map sheds a clue, but both are essential for navigation. Reports from river rats place it on the riverbank close to Ryegrass Creek. But each map pinpoints a different spot (nearly a mile apart) where the creek joins the river!

The USGS quad correctly marks the confluence to the north, and the coordinates on the geothermal map (once you manage to subdivide a section that isn't square) place the hot spring nearby. That confirms it, right? Not so. The actual location of the spring is a mile south, near the spot where the BLM map erroneously shows the confluence. Most confusing!

The hike: The route itself is a gentle downhill grade, but the trick is to keep track of key landmarks emphasized on the enclosed trail map. The banks of Ryegrass Creek are visible across the valley, and the route parallels the canyon. Notice a rounded hill close to a long low one. Make sure you keep those hills on your right, or you'll end up in another drainage.

Strike out in a northeast direction between the creek canyon and the rounded hill and work your way over a grassy desert floor scattered with sagebrush and lava rocks. Soon you'll see a pyramid-shaped hill over by the creek. When you're midway between the two hills, the canyon veers north.

Continue straight, aiming for a peninsula across the river. A faint drainage system (the Ryegrass Creek marked on the BLM map) will lead you eastward to the easiest route down the rocky bank. The unnamed spring, sometimes referred to as Ryegrass, can be found a short way upstream.

The hot spring: Water emerges from the ground at 110 degrees, and several steamy channels lined with orange algae flow down the bank into small pools hidden in the tall grass at the river's edge. The shallow, algae-coated pools reportedly get some TLC during the float season, but at low water you'll have them all to yourself. If you decide on a soak, you'll need a bucket to cool them down with river water. But the river may look a lot more inviting on a hot summer day.

The river runners' camp is a grassy beach near the big bend downstream. A colorfully banded rock formation known as Pruitt's Castle stands out to the north at the true outlet of Ryegrass Creek. Across the river, a jeep track winds down the steep peninsula by Lambert Rocks.

The spring lies within the Wild and Scenic River corridor. The BLM office says it may be in the Wilderness Study Area or possibly on privately owned land. In any case, please treat it with respect, pack out your trash, and observe fire restrictions.

"Midsummer madness": *I stopped on the return drive at the large pond in Crooked Creek just outside the ranch gate. This desert oasis, hidden on a dead-end road with no tire tracks on it but my own, turned out to be the ideal retreat for the upcoming Fourth of July.*

At Unnamed Hot Spring No. 1, hikers can enjoy a plunge in the river as well as a hot-water soak.

I managed to escape the mad holiday weekend parked smack dab in the middle of the road, stark naked for three blissful days, enjoying both the backwaters of the surging currents of humanity and the eddies of the creek swirling out of a culvert through a swimming hole guaranteed to match any you can conjure up from childhood memories!

10 Unnamed Hot Spring No. 2

HIKE 10a *To Unnamed Hot Spring No. 2*

General description: A difficult, ten-mile round-trip, trailless hike to a hot showerbath enjoyed by a few river rats, northwest of Jordan Valley on the Owyhee Reservoir in the lower Owyhee River Canyon. Wear what you normally shower in.
Elevation gain and loss: +400 feet, -320 feet.
Trailhead elevation: 2,680 feet at Leslie Gulch boat ramp.
High point: Roughly 3,000 feet, along cliff above reservoir.
Hiking quads: Rooster Comb and Diamond Butte USGS.
Road map: Sheaville 30-minute BLM.

Finding the trailhead: From Jordan Valley, take U.S. Highway 95 about eighteen miles north. Turn left onto an all-weather gravel road signed to Succor Creek State Park. Follow signs to Succor Creek for ten miles, then turn left onto another gravel road that reads "Leslie Gulch—15." This BLM National Back Country Byway twists down a canyon marked by vertical towers and pinnacles jutting from steep slopes (Hike 10b). Even without the hot spring, it's worth the long drive just to experience Leslie Gulch!

The road ends at a boat ramp on the Owyhee Reservoir, where rafts running the lower canyon take out, and you can park at the nearby BLM campground. It's a total of twenty-five miles from the highway or forty-three miles from Jordan Valley. The hot spring is marked on both maps.

The choices: This remote spring can be reached on foot by following the reservoir's shoreline upstream from Leslie Gulch, but only when the water level is low (usually July-November). At other times, it might be reached overland in dry weather via thirty miles of rough roads followed by a precipitous bushwhack off a landmark called "the Tongue" (see recommended maps).

A dubious plan of attack might be to find a route up the ravine near the boat ramp and cross a high saddle, with a staggering gain of nearly 1,300 feet in 1.5 miles, then bushwhack down to Spring Creek and into the Owyhee Canyon.

Even the shoreline holds one major obstacle: a cliff attached to a huge hill blocks the start upstream. The route described here is a short-cut best suited to bighorn sheep and steeplejacks that traverses the face of the cliff—with a relatively modest gain of maybe 400 feet in a mile.

The hike: Walking upstream from the boat ramp, you'll notice a faint path angling up a meadow, then climbing steeper slopes to disappear just above a rock outcrop. This lofty route is but one of many engineered by the bighorn sheep of Leslie Gulch (current population over 200). All in all, they do a decent job of maintenance—their lives depend on it. The dropoff is awesome, but the path is wider than it appears from below (ten inches on the average) and well packed. The gain is strenuous but short.

After crossing above the first pinnacle and rounding a bend, the track does

Unnamed Hot Spring No. 2 rewards those who find it with an improvised hot shower.

indeed continue. It undulates across the face and passes above several more outcrops before finally dropping steeply to the river at Spring Creek. From here, it's a piece of cake.

Just follow the long reservoir about three miles upstream, tracking the bends with those on the map. When you think you're closing in, watch for a few rivulets of warm water crossing your path and follow them uphill to their source.

The hot spring: Well hidden on the bank above, you'll discover a niche in the rocks with an ingeniously rigged overhead shower pipe. Lo and behold, out gushes a lovely stream of 103-degree water! Follow the steamy flow farther uphill, past a tentsite on a sagebrush flat, and you'll find a pool or two sporting a healthy growth of algae. If you find these a tad too hot for comfort, head back to the showerbath for a soothing neck massage while enjoying the broad view up the canyon.

Note: This spring, due to its location on the shoreline of the Owyhee Reservoir, is administered by the Bureau of Reclamation (BOR). The agency is currently developing a resource management plan for the reservoir and is concerned about protecting sensitive resource values associated with the spring. Indian Hot Spring (as it's called by the BOR) is definitely a resource worth preserving, so please treat it with care.

HIKE 10a *To Unnamed Hot Spring No. 2*
HIKE 10b *Juniper Gulch*

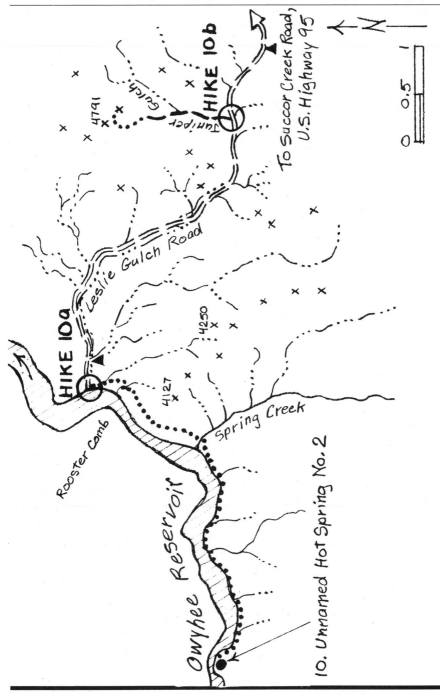

HIKE 10b *Juniper Gulch*

General description: An easy to strenuous three-mile round-trip day hike up a side canyon in Leslie Gulch featuring unique and colorful rock formations, not far from Unnamed Hot Spring No. 2.
Elevation gain and loss: 1,200 feet.
Trailhead elevation: 3,400 feet.
High point: 4,600 feet at the crest.
Map: Rooster Comb USGS.
Road map: Same as Hike 10a.

Finding the trailhead: Follow the directions above to Leslie Gulch and drive about midway between the Overlook point and the boat ramp at the end. Watch for a prominent pullout on the north side of the road 0.5 mile west of a cabin. You'll find restrooms, garbage cans, and a Wilderness Study Area sign near the trail.

The hike: Leslie Gulch is a moonscape of bizarre rock formations capping steep hills. Of igneous origin, the talus slopes are said to be an ash flow tuff from volcanic eruptions fifteen million years ago, with a harder core of more erosion-resistant rhyolite forming the spires. Side canyons offer access but with few exceptions are too vertical to be feasible routes. Juniper Gulch, however,

The spires at Leslie Gulch have a honeycomb effect caused by trapped gases in the cooling lava.

provides easy access up slot canyons into a land of Swiss cheese rocks and eerie shapes. The hike culminates at an eagle-shaped spire perched on the crest, with an 800-foot gain in the final 0.5 mile.

A well-defined path follows Juniper Gulch north between high walls which gradually constrict. Early on, you'll pass a huge Cheshire cat grinning down at you. Bear left into a second slot canyon 0.5-mile up and you'll soon see the eagle rock standing tall on a skyline of convoluted shapes up ahead.

With care, it's possible to scramble all the way up to stand beside it. From the crest, you can enjoy a face-on confrontation with the towering bird as well as a panoramic view of Leslie Gulch.

11 Snively Hot Spring

General description: A roadside/riverside attraction at the lower end of the Owyhee Canyon below the dam, south of Ontario. Swimwear essential when standing up. Elevation 2,280 feet.
Map: Mitchell Butte 30-minute BLM.

Finding the hot spring: From Ontario, head twenty miles south on U.S. Highway 20/26, followed by State Route 201, to Owyhee Junction. Follow signs

Snively Hot Spring has a scenic backdrop that's hard to beat.

south toward Lake Owyhee State Park. From a prominent pipeline spanning the mouth of the canyon, continue 1.5 miles.

Watch for a concrete source pool on your left where spring water boils up from the bottom at 135 degrees. A "Please pack it out" sign, too often unheeded, marks the turnoff to a BLM camping area by the riverside pool. (If you cross a cattleguard, you've gone too far.) The spring is shown on the USGS quad for the following hike.

The hot spring: Scalding water flows from the source pool through a ditch into one large shallow pool dammed by rocks. The result is an eye-opening swirl of hot and cold currents as the source and the river mix. The hot floats on top of the cold, so you'll have to keep stirring it up to stay comfortable. The overall temperature is adjustable by shifting the riverside rocks.

Unfortunately, Snively exhibits some symptoms of overuse/abuse disease. This is due mainly to the easy access via paved roads. As a result, evenings (at least in summertime) have a tendency toward boisterous partying, while mornings are usually a peaceful scene marred only by the beer cans and other litter from the night before.

The setting is nothing short of spectacular. Redrock cliffs and graceful cottonwoods line the deep canyon on both sides. Snively can be reached and enjoyed year-round, as the upstream dam controls the flow of the river and partially protects the pool during spring runoff.

HIKE 11a *"Henry Moore" Rock*

General description: A moderate 5.5-mile round-trip bushwhack up a desert wash beside Deer Butte, near Snively Hot Spring.
Elevation gain and loss: 1,040 feet.
Trailhead elevation: 2,280 feet at Snively.
High point: 3,320 feet.
Hiking quad: Owyhee Dam USGS.
Road map: Mitchell Butte 30-minute BLM.

Finding the trailhead: Follow the directions above to the parking area at Snively Hot Spring. The unmarked route starts by the fence across the road.

The hike: The Owyhee River Canyon between Snively and the Owyhee Reservoir offers cross-country routes up any number of side canyons or ridges. Here's one that follows an intermittent stream around the west side of a prominent butte to a hidden amphitheater in the rock walls.

Climb the gate near the cattleguard and follow the wash due west through a desert valley alongside Deer Butte, aiming for a low wall of rocks a mile away. As you draw near, the wall becomes a jumble of gigantic boulders that seem to block the tiny canyon, but there's a route over them on the right.

Around the next few bends are two short pouroffs that must be climbed, but after that the way again opens up. Sagebrush dots the rolling hills, while tamarisk and tall grasses hug the streambed. The wash curves north around the end of the butte to reach one more fence about two miles up.

HOT SPRING 11 *Snively Hot Spring*
HIKE 11a *"Henry Moore" Rock*

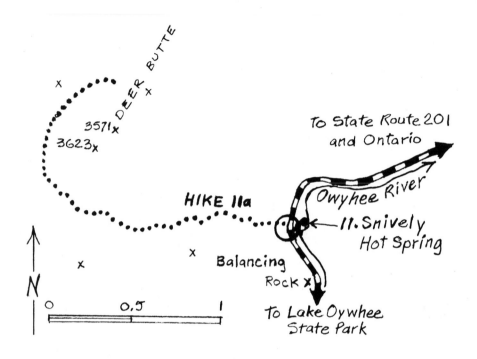

Step across the gate and continue the northeastward curve that leads into a three-sided amphitheater with colorful walls of banded layers of rock. In the center of this gallery, standing on a tall pedestal, is a rock statue with a tiny head that looks for all the world like a sculpture by the 20th century American artist Henry Moore.

HIKING NOTES

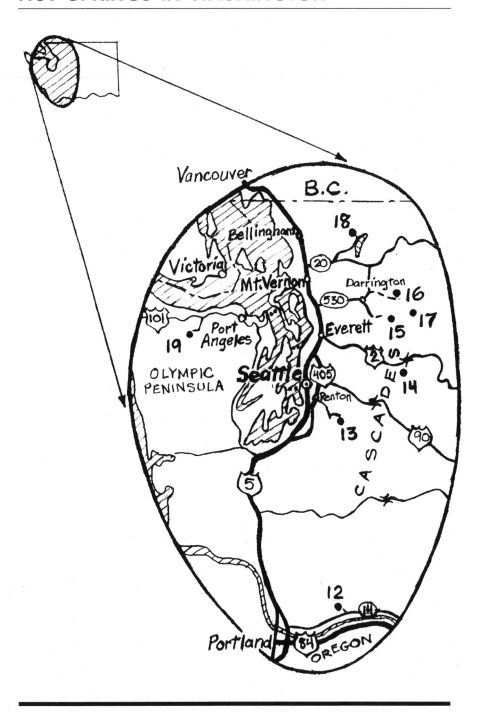

WASHINGTON

An Overview

The Evergreen State has surprisingly few hot springs on public land that are both reachable and usable. (See Other hot springs, below.) However, the eight shown on the Washington Locator Map are all located in magnificent hiking country, and all but Green River Gorge, Sulphur, and Gamma have fairly easy access with great soaks guaranteed. Although they don't form a chain like those in Oregon or convenient clusters like the ones in Idaho, Washington's scattered bubblies are worth visiting.

The eight hot springs listed are found in two highly scenic areas—one gem in the Olympic Mountains, which form the jagged core of the Olympic Peninsula—and the remaining seven in the northern Cascade Range, with its many sharply sculpted glacial peaks. Both areas abound in craggy summits to rival the Swiss Alps, alpine meadows bursting with wildflowers, shrouded rain forests, and seething rivers with waterfalls that thunder into vast canyons. The potential here is limited only by the hiker's imagination.

Directions are given from major towns along State Route 14, Interstates 5 and 405, and U.S. Highway 101. As a general rule, the access roads are paved and well signed, the campgrounds developed and heavily used, and the hiking trails maintained and teeming with other avid hot springers during the short summer months.

Other hot springs: The following is a list of the ones marked on the state geothermal that have been tracked down but, due to a variety of technical glitches, sadly failed to qualify.

Packwood—Alive (contrary to official report) but not well. A 70-degree trickle, on bedrock with no usable pool, often submerged by the Cowlitz River, no access path, and reached via private road. In Gifford Pinchot National Forest.

Deception Creek—Newly discovered but a mere 70 degrees, no usable pool, and no access path. In Gifford Pinchot National Forest.

Orr Creek—Again, only 70 degrees, no usable pool, and a nasty bushwhack. In Gifford Pinchot National Forest.

Ohanapecosh—Boggy seeps of historical interest only, on Hot Springs Nature Trail at Ohanapecosh Visitor Center, in Mount Rainier National Park.

Lester—Reportedly great soaks but no public access. Owned by Tacoma Watershed. On the Green River and almost in Mount Baker-Snoqualmie National Forest.

Goldmeyer—Fantastic pools in a sylvan setting, but privately owned and at last report charging $10/day. Surrounded by Mount Baker-Snoqualmie National Forest and the Alpine Lakes Wilderness.

Swift Creek—Buried under a huge landslide in the late 1970s. Unreachable anyway due to trail bridge washouts. In Mount Baker-Snoqualmie National Forest.

For More Information

Visitors should contact the following Forest or Park Service district offices for updates on hot springs, road and trail conditions, stream crossings, etc.

If the receptionist can't answer your questions, ask for the recreation officer. Maps may be purchased here, and most districts offer free trail printouts.

Hot Springs 12 and Hikes 12a,b: Wind River Ranger District, Gifford Pinchot National Forest, Carson, WA 98610; 509/427-5645.
Hike 12c: Columbia Gorge Ranger District, Mount Hood National Forest, 31520 SE Woodard Road, Troutdale, OR 97060; 503/695-2276.
Warm Spring 13: District Ranger, Kanaskat-Palmer State Park, 3201 Kanaskat Cumberland Road, Palmer, WA 98051; 206/886-0148. Or contact Green River Gorge Resort, 29500 Green River Gorge Rd., Enumclaw, WA 98022; 206/886-2302.
Hot Springs 14 and Hikes 14a,b: Skykomish Ranger District, Mount Baker-Snoqualmie National Forest, P.O. Box 305, Skykomish, WA 98288; 206/677-2414.
Hot Springs 15-17 and Hikes 15a-c, 16a and 17a: Darrington Ranger District, Mount Baker-Snoqualmie National Forest, Darrington, WA 98241; 206/436-1155.
Hot Springs 18 and Hike 18a: Mount Baker Ranger District, Mount Baker-Snoqualmie National Forest, 2105 Highway 20, Sedro Woolley, WA 98284; 206/856-5700.
Hot Springs 19 and Hikes 19a-c: Olympic National Park, 600 East Park Ave., Port Angeles, WA 98362; 206/452-4501. Or check at the Elwha Ranger Station on Olympic Hot Springs Road.

Hot springs and hikes

We start at the Columbia Gorge with a great soak at Wind River (12) and hikes to waterfalls and panoramic views, then move north to a potluck dip at Green River Gorge (13) near Seattle. Southeast of Everett comes a hike-in soak at Scenic (14a) and a climb in nearby Alpine Lakes Wilderness. Forest roads out of Darrington access the Glacier Peak Wilderness and the hiker's soaking box at Kennedy (15a) (an ideal base for high-country treks) and hunts for hidden pools at Sulphur and remote Gamma (16a, 17a). Baker (18), north-east of Mount Vernon, has an easy-access dip and a companion climb to glacier views. And on the Olympic Peninsula, soaks at Olympic (19a) mix well with alpine rambling in Olympic National Park, with over 600 miles of hiking trails.

Season

Although summer and fall is the prime time for hot springing, some pools can be reached and used off season. Winter road closures and deep snow impede access to Baker, Kennedy, and especially to Sulphur and Gamma. Spring runoff won't bury the tub at Scenic or the uppermost pools at Olympic, and both can be accessed through the winter by cross-country skiers. The low-elevation springs at Green River Gorge and Wind River can be reached on foot all year, but the pools are submerged during high water.

Hiking trails in the Columbia Gorge are enjoyable all year, but the high-country hiking season doesn't get comfortably underway until late July, and even then blue skies can't be guaranteed. In an average year, the mountains west of the Cascade crest are cloud-free one day out of every six. The months of November through April bring torrents of rain to the lowlands and snow to higher elevations. Intermittent storms are common through June and likely to return by early September.

12 Wind River Hot Springs

General description: Riverside pools at the end of a slippery .75-mile path, east of Stevenson near the Columbia Gorge. A swimsuit/birthday suit mix— please use common courtesy. Elevation 160 feet.

Map: Gifford Pinchot National Forest.

Finding the hot springs: Follow State Route 14 along the Columbia River Gorge five miles east of Stevenson (or fifteen miles west of Hood River) to Home Valley. Take Berge Road a mile north, then go left on Indian Cabin Road. The road twists between the legs of a power pole tower, then turns to gravel and follows the powerline down to the river.

The road-end parking area, 2.5 miles from the highway, is privately owned. Please respect all posted signs. You'll find a notice to visitors and a registration box where the owner collects a small fee. Overnight camping is discouraged, but there's a county campground in Home Valley.

The walk starts on a wooded path (thick with poison oak) along an eroded and slippery bank, then drops down to a riverside scramble over slick boulders. When a small waterfall upstream comes into view, you've reached the first pool. The hot springs aren't marked on the forest map.

The hot springs: Wind River (also called Shipherd) Hot Springs consists of two soaking pools nestled between riverside boulders. Hot water bubbles up

Downstream travelers often drop in for a warm-up at Wind River Hot Springs.

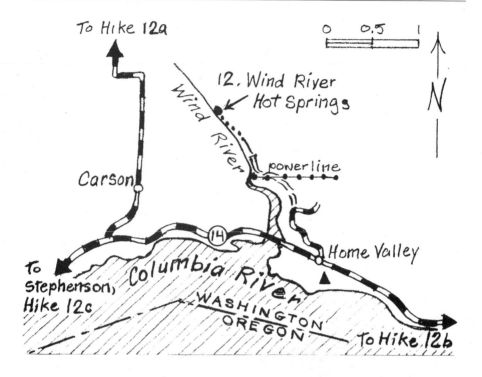

To Hike 12a

0   0.5   1

N

12. Wind River
Hot Springs

Wind River

powerline

Carson

Home Valley

14

Columbia River

To
Stephenson,
Hike 12c

WASHINGTON
OREGON

To Hike 12b

from bedrock through a sandy bottom, and an ample flow keeps the pools clean. The temperature can be lowered by adjusting rocks at the river's edge.

The downstream dip is smaller, right at water level, and registers around 102 degrees. The upper pool, about 105 degrees, is a tad higher on the bank and enjoys a longer season of use. Users often dig a gravel pool at one end to mix the outflow with river water for a cooler soak. A third spring nearby has dried up beneath a pool of stagnant water.

Thick forest borders the river, and the upstream view includes Shipherd Falls. A proposed study would include the Wind River within the National Wild and Scenic Rivers System. If this plan comes to pass, it may safeguard a very special place.

HIKE 12a *Falls Creek Falls*

General description: An easy three-mile round-trip day hike to a triple waterfall, near the Columbia Gorge and Wind River Hot Springs.
Elevation gain and loss: 600 feet.
Trailhead elevation: 1,400 feet.
High point: 2,000 feet at the falls.
Hiking quads: Wind River Green Trails or Wind River USGS.
Road map: Gifford Pinchot National Forest.

Finding the trailhead: Follow State Route 14 along the Columbia Gorge three miles east of Stevenson (or two miles west of Home Valley, if coming from Wind River Hot Springs). Turn north on Wind River Road and go through Carson. Pass the road to the ranger station in 8.5 miles and the turnoff to Mineral Springs in about fourteen miles.

Take a right in a mile on gravel Forest Road 3062. Bear right in another two miles on a road signed Lower Falls Creek Falls-Trail 152A. You'll soon reach the road-end trailhead, a total of seventeen miles from State Route 14.

The hike: For connoisseurs of waterfalls, this one's a must! A broad cascade pours over cliffs high above, churns over a shelf partway down, then yet another shelf, to reach the bottom in a total of 250 feet in three graceful tiers.

Successive tiers at Falls Creek Falls form a liquid staircase down the narrow canyon.

HIKE 12a *Falls Creek Falls*

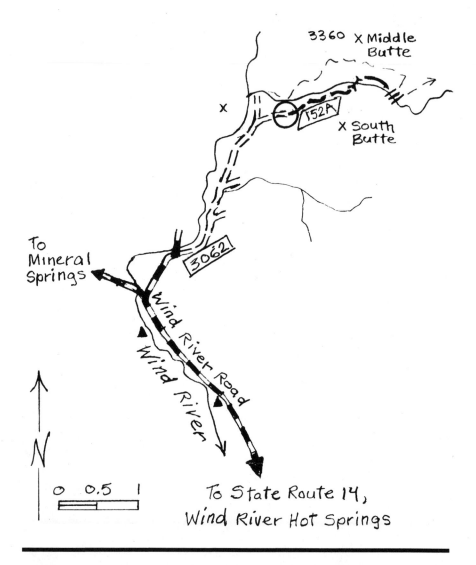

Clouds of spray billow out across the narrow canyon. If you're taking pictures, afternoon's the best time to catch sunlight on the falls.

Trail 152A wanders through a forest of Douglas-fir, hemlock, and larch along the south bank of Falls Creek. It bridges the creek at the halfway point, then climbs above the north bank in a moderate grade. Shortly after crossing a boulder-strewn ravine comes a view of the upper and middle tiers soon followed by the final viewpoint across from the middle and lower descents.

HIKE 12b *Dog Mountain*

General description: A strenuous five-mile round-trip climb to wildflowers and views of the Columbia Gorge, near Wind River Hot Springs.

Elevation gain and loss: 2,340 feet.

Trailhead elevation: 160 feet.

High point: Former lookout, 2,500 feet.

Hiking quads: Trails of the Columbia Gorge (Forest Service contour map showing the new trail) and Forest Service trail printout.

Road map: Same as Hike 12a.

Finding the trailhead: Follow State Route 14 along the Columbia Gorge about nine miles east of Stevenson (four miles past Home Valley, if coming from Wind River Hot Springs) or about eleven miles west of Hood River. The parking area and trail sign are on the north side of the highway just west of Milepost 54.

The hike: Open slopes bursting with over 200 species of spring wildflowers coupled with a bird's-eye view of the Columbia Gorge are the hiker's reward for a short but stiff climb to the site of a former lookout cabin perched on the south-facing flanks of Dog Mountain. A newly rerouted trail both eases the ascent and offers intermediate viewpoints.

Prime time for the flower display is Mid-March through May. The route is usually passable all year because of the low elevation, but it's a hot climb

The view from Dog Mountain stretches across the Columbia Gorge into Oregon.

HIKE 12b *Dog Mountain*

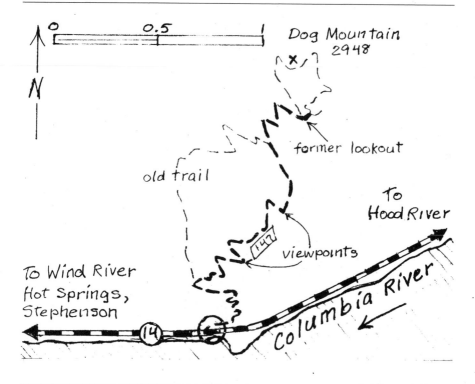

in the summer unless you get an early start. Watch out for poison oak on the lower slopes.

Dog Mountain Trail 147 switchbacks up a hillside where ponderosa pine mixes with Douglas-fir and alder. Here along the gorge, vegetation typical of both the dry eastern climate and the wet northwest can be seen. This unusual coexistence is made possible by the unique sea level corridor carved through the Cascades by the Columbia River.

Bear right at a junction 0.5 mile up the trail where the old route shoots up an abandoned logging road. The new path contours up the front side to pass the first viewpoint in another 0.5 mile and reach a second in 1.5 miles.

Enjoy a taste of what's to come as you gaze across flowered slopes to the gorge below, then continue past a fork where the old route rejoins the way. At 2.5 miles, you'll reach a shelf dug from the hillside where the lookout cabin once stood.

Here the ground comes alive with color. Purple daisies and asters blend with blue penstamon and lupine, while golden buttercups and sunflowers vie with flaming red paintbrush. And here the broad blue-green band of the Columbia River bisects the surrounding uplands in its journey to the sea. Look down at Wind Mountain to the west and across the channel to the white tip of Mount Hood jutting above cliffs green from waterfall spray.

If this isn't enough, you can take the new loop trail on up to the 2,948-foot summit. The three miles round trip and 450-foot gain are offset by a panoramic view. The uppermost slopes of Dog Mountain are blanketed with balsamroot and tiny pink spreading phlox, and massive Mount Hood dominates the southern skyline at 11,225 feet.

HIKE 12c *Eagle Creek Trail*

General description: An easy twelve-mile round-trip day hike or overnighter to popular waterfalls on the Oregon side of the Columbia Gorge, near Wind River Hot Springs.
Elevation gain and loss: +1,080 feet, -320 feet.
Trailhead elevation: 120 feet.
High point: 1,200 feet at Tunnel Falls.
Hiking quad: Same as Hike 12b.
Road map: Mount Hood National Forest.

Finding the trailhead: From the Portland area, take Interstate 84 east to Eagle Creek Park (Exit 41). Westbound travelers must make a U-turn at Bonneville Dam (Exit 40) to reach Exit 41. Those coming from the Wind River area cross into Oregon over a toll bridge at Cascade Locks and continue west as outlined above (about twelve miles total). Follow signs past the campground to parking for Eagle Creek Trail 440.

The hike: The Oregon side of the Columbia Gorge is famous for its profusion of waterfall hikes, and the well traveled Eagle Creek Trail into the Columbia Wilderness ranks as one of the finest. It gets the heaviest use in summer, but low elevation makes it quite enjoyable during the off-season as well.

Highlights include a verdant forest backed by cliffs, views from high bridges, and a succession of waterfalls along narrowing canyon walls. A variety of loops can be made with a longer trip, but the sheer drop of Tunnel Falls at the six-mile mark makes a good destination for a day hike.

Eagle Creek Trail 440 meanders through old-growth woods above the glacially carved canyon of Eagle Creek and soon traverses a railed section carved from rock. A spur at 1.5 miles leads to a distant view of Metlako Falls, and another drops to Lower Punch Bowl Falls. The main trail comes to the upper falls in 2.1 miles.

Punch Bowl Falls may be a bit modest as waterfalls go, but it's exquisitely graceful. It forms a perfect punchbowl shape in its delicate descent, spilling over the rimrock into a circular pool below. Nearby benches offer a pleasant overlook.

Next, the route spans two lush side canyons on high steel bridges. At 3.3 miles, it crosses the now narrow gorge of Eagle Creek itself, a full eighty feet below, on High Bridge. The route soon passes Tenas Camp, then bridges the gorge once again to pass more tentsites at Wy'east Camp.

HIKE 12c *Eagle Creek Trail*

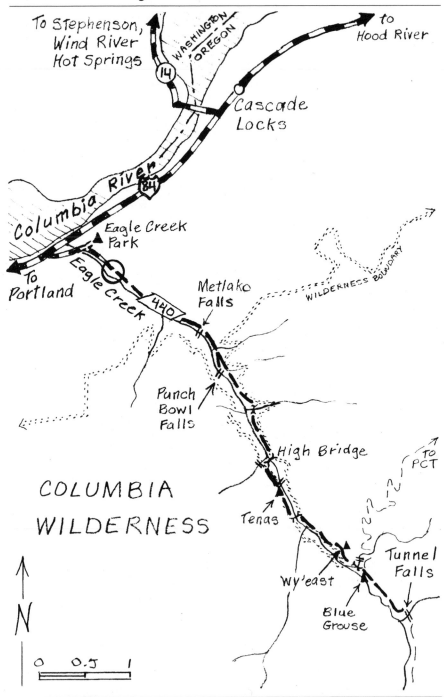

To Stephenson,
Wind River
Hot Springs

to
Hood River

14

WASHINGTON
OREGON

Cascade
Locks

Columbia River

84

To
Portland

Eagle Creek
Park

Eagle Creek

440

Metlako
Falls

WILDERNESS BOUNDARY

Punch
Bowl
Falls

High Bridge

TO
PCT

COLUMBIA
WILDERNESS

Tenas

Wy'east

Tunnel
Falls

Blue
Grouse

N

0   0.5   1

Just beyond the wilderness boundary comes a junction in five miles with the Eagle-Benson Trail, which climbs 2,900 feet in three miles to the Pacific Crest Trail (PCT) and Benson Plateau. Pass another waterfall nearby, then Blue Grouse Camp at 5.3 miles—the last stop before Tunnel Falls.

The route past Tunnel Falls actually slices a twenty-five-foot tunnel through sheer rock behind the falls. Spray drifts across the side canyon to shower anyone nearby, and the roar reverberates from nearby walls. Seen from across the ravine, hikers approaching the plunge resemble a trail of ants.

Beyond are more waterfalls, views, and remote camps. Side trails offer tempting choices. A backpacker could loop back via Eagle-Tanner and Tanner Butte trails or continue on to join the PCT at Wahtum Lake, returning across beautiful Benson Plateau or perhaps down quiet Herman Creek to Government Cove.

13 Green River Gorge Warm Spring

General description: A transitory warm spring found .5 mile from a highway bridge in a highly scenic canyon, southeast of Seattle. Swimwear recommended during rafting season. Elevation 400 feet.

Map: Mount Baker-Snoqualmie National Forest or Cumberland USGS.

Finding the warm spring: From Interstate 405 at Renton, take State Route 169 south to Black Diamond. Turn left on Green River Gorge Road and drive four miles (just past the bridge) to a small resort by that name where Jim Easton, the owner, will point you in the right direction. The route begins on his land. The spring, located on undeveloped state land beside a parcel which once housed a coal mine, isn't marked on any map.

The choices: When the river level is right, it's possible to float a small craft downstream from Green River Gorge Resort. People also run the gorge by raft—putting in at Kanaskat-Palmer State Park several miles upstream. If interested, call the park ranger for information and the Army Corps of Engineers (206/767-6702) for an update on water level. River runners rate this stretch as class IV to V, meaning hazardous whitewater with expert skill required.

Access by land involves a 0.5-mile bushwhack that feels more like a mile on a badly overgrown trail. You'll stoop under branches until you're sure you've gone too far (bypassing a side path that ends at the rim) to reach a sign on a tree that reads *Hot Spring*, with an arrow pointing right.

Whack a few more bushes aside until you see another arrow pointing down an eroded bank. Tree roots help brake the slide, and at the bottom you'll find a warm trickle emerging from a collapsed mine shaft. A few cables mark the spot.

The warm spring: Green River Gorge, with a temperature range of 80-100 degrees, certainly qualifies as a thermal spring. But it isn't marked on any map simply because it didn't come about by natural processes. Originally a cold spring that filtered through a steep riverbank, it was fired up a few decades

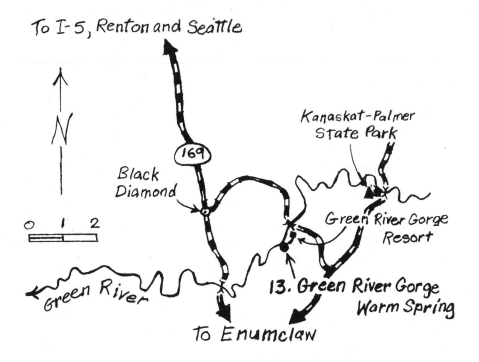

To I-5, Renton and Seattle

N

Black Diamond

169

Kanaskat-Palmer State Park

Green River Gorge Resort

Green River

0 1 2

13. Green River Gorge Warm Spring

To Enumclaw

ago by a coal mine burning underground in its path!

When I was there, I found only a fragmented pool in the rocks that barely registered 80 degrees. The park ranger, however, told me that he had rafted by a few months earlier and found "a nice little 90-degree pool" that some enterprising volunteer had built.

Avid hot springers will go to great lengths to add a new dip (official or otherwise) to the list. Thus, despite difficult access, uncertain temperature, and no guarantee of a soak, a few hardy souls do check it out. The only thing guaranteed is first-class scenery in the rocky gorge.

Keep an eye peeled for hidden clues on the overgrown path to Green River Gorge Warm Spring.

14 Scenic Hot Springs

HIKE 14a *To Scenic Hot Springs*

General description: A rugged four-mile, round-trip day hike featuring an aptly named gem hidden southeast of Everett near the Cascade crest. Naked bodies welcome.

Elevation gain and loss: 1,140 feet.

Trailhead elevation: 2,360 feet.

High point: Hot springs, 3,500 feet.

Hiking quads: Stevens Pass Green Trails or Scenic USGS.

Road map: Mount Baker-Snoqualmie National Forest.

Finding the trailhead: From Everett, take U.S. Highway 2 about fifty miles southeast to Skykomish. Continue ten miles to Scenic, the service depot for the Burlington-Northern Railroad's Cascade tunnel (see Hike 14b). Cross the highway bridge that spans the tracks and watch for a primitive road on your right 0.2 mile east of Milepost 59. Unless you've got a high clearance vehicle, it's best to park near the bottom and walk up. The springs aren't marked on any map.

At Scenic Hot Springs, hot water is fed through a pipe into a user-built soaking box perched on the steep hillside.

The hike: Tucked away high on a hillside overlooking Windy Mountain and the broad canyon just west of Stevens Pass, Scenic Hot Springs lives up to its name. A user-built soaking box collects the flow, and evergreen branches frame the view. Used mainly by locals and a few wintertime ski buffs, it's bordered by Mount Baker-Snoqualmie Forest and the northern tip of the Alpine Lakes Wilderness. The springs and access route are on a tiny plot of private land within the forest, but the owners don't object to visitors as long as they continue to show respect for the property.

The rocky road climbs a steep 0.5-mile slope to a string of powerlines, then gets steeper and rockier yet as it turns to follow them eastward. The towers have number plates. After you pass No. 5, look for a faint path to the right which contours uphill in a 0.5-mile arc leading to the springs.

The hot springs: The waist deep, five-foot square soaking box commands an outstanding view. The spring water gushing into it at 108 degrees can be cooled by diverting the incoming pipe, and a copious flow keeps the water clean. This isn't the place for wearing treadless sneakers or pitching a tent, as the ground around the springs is steep and slippery. Scenic Hot Springs, also known as "Great Northern," feeds a few smaller soaking boxes and pools nearby in addition to the main tub.

HIKE 14a *To Scenic Hot Springs*
HIKE 14b *Surprise Lake*

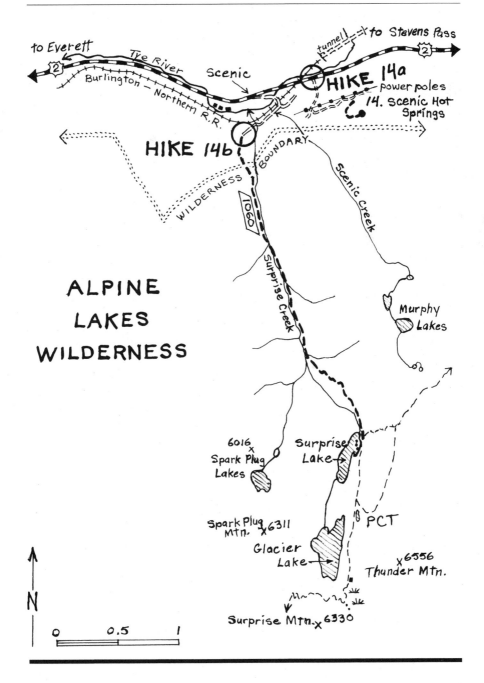

to Everett

Tye River

Scenic

Burlington – Northern R.R.

tunnel

to Stavens Pass

HIKE 14a

power poles

14. Scenic Hot Springs

HIKE 14b

WILDERNESS BOUNDARY

1060

Scenic Creek

Surprise Creek

ALPINE
LAKES
WILDERNESS

Murphy Lakes

6016 ×
Spark Plug Lakes

Surprise Lake

Spark Plug Mtn. × 6311

Glacier Lake

PCT

× 6556
Thunder Mtn.

Surprise Mtn. × 6330

N

0   0.5   1

HIKE 14b *Surprise Lake*

General description: A moderate eight-mile, round-trip day hike or overnighter climbing past waterfalls to the first in a group of secluded lakes in the Alpine Lakes Wilderness, near Scenic Hot Springs.
Elevation gain and loss: 2,300 feet.
Trailhead elevation: 2,200 feet.
High point: Surprise Lake, 4,500 feet.
Maps: Same as Hike 14a.

Finding the trailhead: Follow the road access to Scenic given in Hike 14a. Turn right, 0.7 mile east of Milepost 58, on an unmarked road that bridges the Tye River and drops down to cross the train tracks and intersect a side road. Turn right and drive about 0.25 mile to the parking area and trail sign.

The hike: An image of evergreenery walled in by white granite is mirrored in the glassy surface of Surprise Lake. Three tiny islands near the outlet stipple the reflection. The oblong lake lies at the end of a brisk four-mile climb which soon joins the Pacific Crest Trail (PCT) and leads on to other alpine delights.

Surprise Creek Trail (1060) starts by swinging away from the creek in a moderate climb up an open hillside but swings back in 0.5 mile to enter cool woods along Surprise Creek. Soon shrouded under a canopy of age-old trees, it hugs the creek banks in a gentle 2.5-mile stretch upvalley past waterfalls and blue pools. Rocky walls slowly converge as the canyon narrows.

The final mile is a steep climb up the headwall in a series of tight hairpins that parallels the cataract of the rushing stream below. The old route of the PCT branches off to twist straight up the east canyon wall just before the path reaches the north tip of the lake at four miles.

Surprise Lake, nestled in a hanging valley flanked by cliffs, makes a delightful spot to enjoy a picnic lunch. For a longer trip, follow the trail 0.7 mile south to the PCT and on up to Glacier Lake, lying in a bowl of granite at the base of Surprise Mountain. Grassy campsites tempt the visitor to stay and explore the alpine basin or to climb the 6,330-foot peak for an overview of other lakes and mountains in the magnificent 305,407-acre Alpine Lakes Wilderness, Washington's third largest wildland.

DARRINGTON AREA

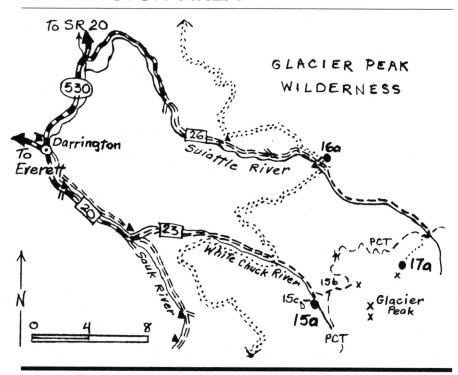

15 Kennedy Hot Spring

HIKE 15a *To Kennedy Hot Spring*

General description: An easy eleven-mile, round-trip day hike or over-nighter featuring a bubbly soaking box in the Glacier Peak Wilderness, east of Everett. No need to pack a swimsuit.

Elevation gain and loss: +1,100 feet, -100 feet.

Trailhead elevation: 2,300 feet.

High point: Kennedy, 3,300 feet.

Hiking quads: Glacier Peak Green Trails or Pugh Mountain, Lime Mountain, and Glacier Peak West USGS.

Road map: Mount Baker-Snoqualmie National Forest.

Finding the trailhead: To reach this alpine hideaway from Interstate 5, take State Route 530 about thirty-two miles east to Darrington. Turn right onto the Mountain Loop Highway (20) and drive ten miles south along the Sauk River. Turn left onto White Chuck Road (23) and drive eleven dusty miles east to the road-end parking area and trail sign. Kennedy is named on all the maps.

The hike: Remember Badfinger singing "You'd better hurry 'cause it's going fast"? Well, Kennedy Hot Spring, currently down to 92 degrees, has been dropping about a degree every year according to one oldtimer who can remember when it was once 102. Despite the lukewarm temperature and a yellowish cast (iron oxide) to the water, Kennedy remains a favored goal for day trippers as well as a popular stopoff for longer distance trekkers on the nearby Pacific Crest Trail (PCT).

The Glacier Peak Wilderness surrounding Kennedy fills 576,865 prime acres of the North Cascades and forms the largest wildland in the state of Washington. Measuring thirty-five miles long by twenty miles wide, it offers 450 miles of hiking trails. Most of the passes aren't snow-free before mid-

The "standing room only" cedar box at Kennedy can accommodate a crowd of vertical soakers—including many who find their toes dangling in space.

August, but this varies from year to year. The PCT snakes through the heart of the wildland as it swings around Glacier Peak, Washington's fourth highest and most remote volcanic cone.

The White Chuck Trail (643), probably the most popular walk in the Glacier Peak area, winds gently up the canyon of the White Chuck River. An understory of ferns and vine maple flourishes under a ceiling of ancient cedar and Douglas-fir. The river can be constantly heard but only glimpsed through the trees. Side streams cross the path in a headlong rush to join the cascade below. At one point, the route drops to river level along a gravel beach; at another, it passes beneath pumice rockslides and cliffs of volcanic tuff.

Kennedy Ridge Trail branches left at five miles to climb up beside alpine meadows and glaciers (Hike 15b). The main trail soon bridges Kennedy Creek, intersects the spur branching right to the hot spring, then ends in 1.5 miles at a junction with the PCT. One could ramble south from this point through Glacier Peak Meadows and on over White Pass in another ten miles, or travel north to Kennedy Ridge past glaciers and tumbling streams to cross Fire Creek Pass and drop down to Gamma Hot Springs (see Hike 17a).

The short spur to the hot spring passes many campsites along and above the river; a cold spring at the guard station provides good drinking water. The path bridges the river to a junction: the right fork leads to more campsites, then shoots up to Lake Byrne (Hike 15c) and beyond; the left fork follows the river a short way upstream to reach Kennedy Hot Spring in a total of 5.5 miles.

The hot spring: The extraordinary soaker here consists of a four-by-five-foot, cedar box recessed into the ground. As the depth is over five feet, the strategy is to do your soaking in a vertical position. A surprising number of bodies can squeeze into the small box in this unusual fashion—either standing up, if they're tall enough, or by just gripping the sides with toes suspended!

Spring water filters in through the rocky bottom and rises in warm bubbles to the surface. A small platform borders the box, with a handy rack nearby for clothes and towels. Nestled into the bank between the milky river and a wall of trees, Kennedy's magic bubble box offers highly scenic therapy for aching muscles.

HIKE 15b *Kennedy Hot Spring to Glacier Creek Meadow*

General description: A moderate nine-mile, round-trip day hike or overnighter from the hot spring to high meadows and glacial icefalls, in the Glacier Peak Wilderness.
Elevation gain and loss: +2,450 feet, -100 feet.
Trailhead elevation: 3,300 feet at Kennedy.
High point: Glacier Creek Meadow, 5,650 feet.
Hiking quads: Glacier Peak Green Trails or Lime Mountain and Glacier Peak West USGS.
Road map: Same as Hike 15a.

Finding the trailhead: Follow Hike 15a to Kennedy Hot Spring.

The rocky moraine above Glacier Creek Meadow offers hikers a close-up look at Scimitar and Kennedy glaciers just beneath 10,541-foot Glacier Peak.

The hike: An exhilarating side trip from the hot spring climbs to an alpine meadow bisected by a gurgling glacier-fed stream. The grassy banks along the creek make an idyllic spot to sit and dangle hot toes in icy water, enjoy a picnic lunch, and contemplate the world around you. Head farther upvalley, if you can tear yourself away, for a face-to-face confrontation with nearby glaciers.

From Kennedy, retrace your steps 0.5 mile to the point where White Chuck Trail meets Kennedy Ridge Trail (639). Tree roots across the path form randomly spaced steps as the route climbs 875 feet in two miles to join the PCT at 4,150 feet. Continue on up the ridge with increasing glimpses through the trees of silvered glaciers and peaks. The PCT emerges into the lush meadow bordering Glacier Creek (at 5,650 feet) in another two miles.

The heather meadow bursts with lupine and glacier lilies. Marmots stare down from rocky castles, and tiny birds sing out from invisible perches. Glacier Creek ripples down the slope in rocky steps to form small pools between cascades. A campsite bedded in a plush-green carpet lies just downstream from the path. The dark moraine above Kennedy Glacier juts into view at the head of the long meadow.

For a view of distant peaks and a close-up of two glaciers, leave the trail behind and follow the creek up beyond the valley. A faint climber's route leads up the side of a moraine and follows the rocky crest ever closer to the glistening 10,541-foot cone of Glacier Peak. Scimitar Glacier can be seen to the southeast, and the double tongue of Kennedy Glacier looms before you. Ribbons of water emerge from the base of the icefall to twist and braid their way downhill over glacial debris.

HIKE 15c *Kennedy Hot Spring to Lake Byrne*

General description: A grueling five-mile, round-trip day hike or overnighter climbing from the hot spring to an alpine lake and panoramic vistas in the Glacier Peak Wilderness.
Elevation gain and loss: 2,250 feet.
Trailhead elevation: 3,300 feet at Kennedy.
High point: Lake Byrne, 5,550 feet.
Hiking quads: Glacier Peak Green Trails or Glacier Peak West USGS.
Road map: Same as Hike 15a.

Finding the trailhead: Follow Hike 15a to Kennedy Hot Spring.

The hike: The bubble box at Kennedy makes the ultimate base for yet another outing, more demanding but every bit as rewarding as the climb to Glacier Creek Meadow (Hike 15b). Lake Byrne, nestled in a rock basin directly across the deep canyon of the White Chuck from Glacier Peak, offers a face-on view of the massive pyramid—that is, if the curtain of clouds parts far enough to let you look across! The short climb is a real backbreaker, but the spectacular scene is worth the price.

Looking east from Lake Byrne, the massive cone of Glacier Peak can be seen across the canyon of the White Chuck River.

HIKE 15a *To Kennedy Hot Spring*
HIKE 15b *Kennedy Hot Spring to Glacier Creek Meadow*
HIKE 15c *Kennedy Hot Spring to Lake Byrne*

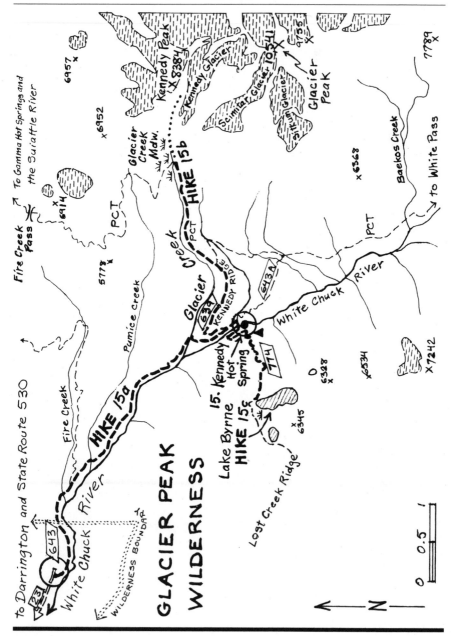

The Lake Byrne Trail begins at the bridge by Kennedy. A relentless series of tight switchbacks drags the path straight up the canyon wall; luckily, the route is shaded by an obliging forest. In about 1.5 miles, the path levels off long enough to pivot southwest and then north around a sharp knoll, passing a heather dappled meadow with the first open views across the canyon. The final stretch of hairpins is open to both the sun's rays and increasingly broad panoramas. The path fords the gushing outlet to reach the northern tip of Lake Byrne in 2.5 miles.

Fragile meadows fringe one side of the oblong lake while scattered clusters of subalpine fir cling to outcrops of rock on the far side. Ice can often coat the deep blue lake (and snow obscure the trail) until mid-August. Camping is banned within 0.25 mile of Lake Byrne, but there are two good campsites north of the outlet and an unconventional, open-air privy near the trail.

Experienced scramblers can roam the steep ridges that wall the lake. The high knob at the south end offers one of the finest views in the North Cascades. Looking due east, 10,541-foot Glacier Peak fills the foreground. On a clear day, you can see the distant white cones of Mount Baker (see Hike 18a) and Mount Shuksan to the northwest. A combination of boot tread, tree blazes, and cross-country travel lures the more adventurous traveler westward from Lake Byrne to a chain of lakes and meadows along Lost Creek Ridge.

16 Sulphur Warm Springs

HIKE 16a *To Sulphur Warm Springs*

General description: A relatively easy 3.6-mile round-trip hike, plus a very tricky hunt for warm seeps hiding in a primeval forest in the Glacier Peak Wilderness, northeast of Everett. Swimwear superfluous.
Elevation gain and loss: +480 feet, -120 feet.
Trailhead elevation: 1,560 feet.
High point: 2,040 feet.
Hiking quads: Lime Mountain and Downey Mountain USGS or Glacier Peak and Cascade Pass Green Trails.
Road map: Mount Baker-Snoqualmie National Forest.

Note: Save this one for late summer when the water level is down, the creek safer to cross, and any pool more likely to have surfaced. Also, check with the Forest Service on the current condition of the Suiattle River Road. It's been closed for the past few years due to a washout.

Finding the trailhead: From Interstate 5 north of Everett, take State Route 530 about forty miles east and north, past Darrington, to the Suiattle River Road (26). Drive 21.5 dusty miles east to Sulphur Creek Campground, near the road-end trailhead for the following hike to Gamma. The springs are named on the USGS and forest maps but misleadingly called hot.

HIKE 16a *To Sulphur Warm Springs*

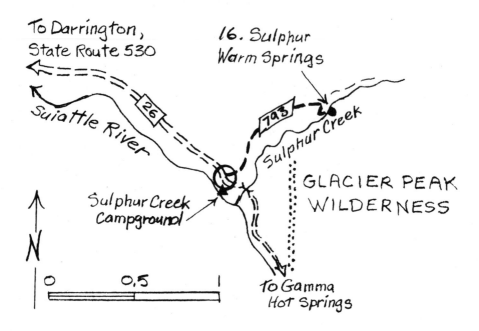

The hike: In this neck of the woods, Sulphur Warm (or Hot) Springs ranks second only to Gamma for sheer elusiveness. It's pinpointed on the maps on the edge of Sulphur Creek at the 1,920-foot contour line and listed by the Forest Service as being across the creek from a point precisely 1.8 miles up Trail 793, but stumbling across it on the ground is another matter.

Sulphur Creek Trail 793 begins across the road from the campground, climbs the bank and contours past gullies, through a dimly lit forest. As it finally drops, you'll enter a wildland of fallen logs and rushing water.

The trick is to gauge the 1.8 miles, beyond which the trail fades into a fishermen's route, and then watch for a faint track angling downhill to a haphazard line of footlogs crossing the torrent. If you've picked the right track and managed to balance your way over the right logs, the springs should be lurking close by.

The warm springs: One guidebook stated: "Several hot springs seep and flow down a heavily vegetated slope from the south into Sulphur Creek. The main spring issues from a crack in the bedrock immediately adjacent to the creek bank. There is a pool that will accommodate two people comfortably dug into the bank." The flow was listed at ten gpm and the temperature as 98 degrees.

In contrast, the Forest Service printout had this to say: "The springs consist of small colored pools, smelling of hydrogen sulphide gas, and are not large enough to take a dip in." The temperature listed was a mere 80 degrees. The district ranger states: "The springs (about the size of a quarter) seep out of the ground, and the landmarks are not established because the creek washes all signs away."

Then, to further confuse the issue, I met a ranger from Gifford Pinchot National Forest who claims that he's not only found a pool at the described location but has actually soaked his bones in it. When pressed as to what it was like, a secretive smile crossed his lips as he simply replied "not bad at all."

And what did your fearless reporter discover firsthand after zigzagging back and forth across every log in sight at least twice, and bushwhacking for hours through primeval ooze armed with machete, magnifying glass, divining rod, and infrared scanner? You guessed it. Nothing. Not even a two-bit seep.

Conclusion? If some industrious elf has gotten there ahead of you and dug a cozy little soaker (and perhaps heated it up a few notches), then, if you're persistent and lucky enough to find it, you might possibly end up with something to write home about. But, come to think of it, maybe "the one that got away" makes a better story.

17 Gamma Hot Springs

HIKE 17a *To Gamma Hot Springs*

General description: A challenging thirty-mile round-trip backpack for hard-core fanatics only, following the call of the wild to hot springs buried deep in the Glacier Peak Wilderness, northeast of Everett. Swimwear? You gotta be kiddin'!

Elevation gain and loss: +4,300 feet, -960 feet.

Trailhead elevation: 1,600 feet.

High point: 5,000 feet at Gamma Hot Springs.

Hiking quads: Lime Mountain and Gamma Peak USGS or Glacier Peak Green Trails.

Road map: Mount Baker-Snoqualmie National Forest.

Finding the trailhead: Refer to the note and directions above to Sulphur Creek Campground. Continue another mile southeast to the Suiattle River trailhead at the road end, a distance of 22.5 miles from State Route 530. Gamma is named on the USGS and forest maps.

The call: First, conjure up a pristine spring emerging from bedrock at 140 degrees and swirling into icy pools at the head of a canyon framed by jagged peaks, "light years" from the nearest outpost. Then, fit your humble body into the scene—boldly going where (virtually) no one has gone before, seeking out new soaks and devising a dip with a temperature mix close to heaven!

Bitten by the bug? It's known as the call of the wild hot spring, and the only cure is to follow it. But treatment can be risky unless proper precautions are taken. Check with the Forest Service on current conditions. Get a weather forecast and travel prepared. Go late in the season when the streams are low.

I've been suffering from the Gamma bug for years, but all attempts at a cure have been foiled to date by the washout on the Suiattle River Road. This write-up is therefore based solely on logical deduction (or wishful thinking, as the case may be) combined with a detailed report from the district ranger.

The hike: This far-flung expedition, in addition to requiring twelve long miles by trail with a gain of 2,160 feet to reach Gamma Creek, involves a rough three-mile bushwhack up the narrow canyon, wading sections of the icy creek, and multiple fords from side to side to reach your goal. The final climb up the canyon has a grueling 2,140-foot gain, nearly doubling in the final three miles the elevation gained in the first twelve.

The route up the Suiattle River follows an abandoned road past the wilderness boundary. In a mile, Milk Creek Trail branches right to climb to Fire Creek Pass. The Suiattle River Trail (784) dips and rises along the bank, skirting side streams through an age-old forest. Finally climbing the bank, it reaches several campsites and a footbridge at Canyon Creek in 5.8 miles.

The route offers glimpses through the trees of mountains on the far side of the broadening valley. In another three miles it passes the Miners Ridge Trail. The path then dips and rises past Miners Creek and comes to an end when it intersects the Pacific Crest Trail (PCT) in 11.2 miles.

Take the right fork downhill on the PCT and cross Skyline Bridge. Here you'll leave the Suiattle River and work your way south up a gradual slope across the valley. A primitive path soon forks left to Gamma Ridge as the PCT veers west and drops downhill. It crosses two streams before hitting Gamma Creek at 2,860 feet in another mile.

Note: From this point, one could conceivably do a "double dip" by following the PCT on up over Vista Ridge and Fire Creek Pass and then down to Kennedy Hot Spring (see Hike 15a), some twenty-six highly scenic miles away.

At Gamma Creek you'll leave the PCT and the last vestiges of civilization behind and forge your way into true wilderness. The route upstream changes seasonally depending on water level and whatever obstacles have rolled into place along the canyon floor after the spring runoff. The banks are very brushy, but the district ranger says it's reasonably safe to wade the creek at low water. The final 0.5 mile is a precipitous scramble.

The hot springs: Scalding water seeps up from rock fractures at the headwaters of Gamma Creek and quickly mixes into the glacier-fed stream.
Nearby, small vents bubble to the surface like vintage champagne.
Hot and cold currents swirl side by side within the creek like patterns of marble fudge, and the result should be equally delectable.

You can try poking around downstream for some spot where the cooling temperature suits your fancy and with enough luck enjoy a ready-made soaking pool. But just in case the right temperature comes at the wrong place in the creek, you'd better come prepared to dig your own. If your efforts meet with success, I'd like to hear all about it.

The deep canyon is sandwiched between serrated ridges, the hot springs nestle in the shadow of 7,000-foot Gamma Peak. A bit beyond, Gamma Ridge slices a jagged line between two massive glaciers on the north flanks of 10,541-foot Glacier Peak.

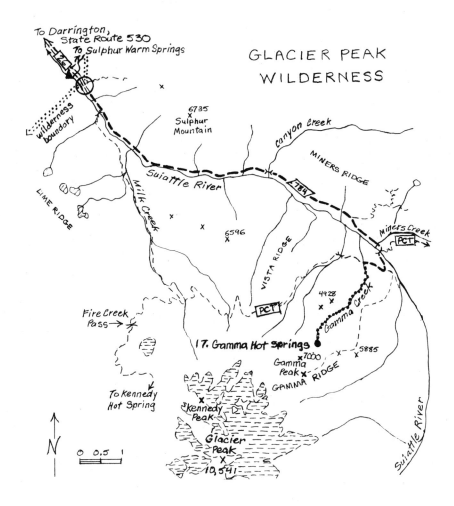

18 Baker Hot Springs

General description: A bather-full bubbly framed by evergreens at the end of a short path, northeast of Mount Vernon. Swimwear recommended due to frequent user complaints about nudity. Elevation: 2,000 feet.
Map: Mount Baker-Snoqualmie National Forest.

Finding the hot springs: From Interstate 5 near Mount Vernon, take State Route 20 about twenty miles east. Bear left at Milepost 22 onto paved Baker Lake Road and follow it up the west side of the lake. Turn left opposite Baker Lake Resort onto gravel Forest Road 1144 and climb 3.2 miles to a large turnout. A primitive 0.3-mile path leads you uphill through a cool forest and emerges into a small clearing at the pool.

Overnight parking is currently not prohibited at the turnout, but you'll pass a variety of nice campgrounds (both developed and primitive) along Baker Lake on the way in. Baker Hot Springs isn't named on the forest map.

The hot springs: Users have dug a shallow pool at Baker out of a sandy bank. The pool varies from four to a maximum of ten feet across and is seldom more than a foot and a half deep. Natural mineral water bubbles up from the bottom at about 104 degrees and cools as it disperses. The water's often a bit murky, but that doesn't seem to faze the aficionados who come for a soak. Unless you feel like sharing your cozy cocoon, try the early mornings or the off-season months.

HOT SPRINGS 18 *Baker Hot Springs*

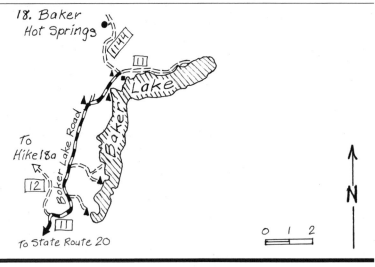

Background: At one time, the Forest Service developed the area as a designated recreation site. They built a boardwalk path to span muddy stretches and even installed a wooden tub over the springs. The tub was later taken out due to bacteria brewing in the cedar walls, and the boardwalk has since been removed as well.

Management problems associated with the increasing public use of the springs have brought about a change in policy, and as the current user-built pools become excessive in size, they will periodically be filled in.

HIKE 18a *Park Butte*

General description: A strenuous seven-mile, round-trip day hike or over-nighter featuring alpine meadows and close views of Mount Baker, both from the lookout and from nearby railroad grade, not far from Baker Hot Springs.
Elevation gain and loss: +2180 feet, -80 feet.
Trailhead elevation: 3,350 feet.
High point: Park Butte Lookout, 5,450 feet.
Hiking quads: Hamilton Green Trails or Baker Pass USGS.
Road map: Mount Baker-Snoqualmie National Forest.

Finding the trailhead: Follow the directions in 18 above and drive around twelve miles up Baker Lake Road. Turn left just beyond a bridge onto Forest Road 12 and follow signs to Mount Baker National Recreation Area and Schriebers Meadow. You'll reach a camping area and the trail sign in another nine miles. *Note:* The trailhead is a twenty-mile drive from Baker Hot Springs.

The hike: This short climb in the Mount Baker National Recreation Area is a hard one to beat for wall-to-wall alpine views. Snow-draped peaks rim the horizon, and the awesome sight of Mount Baker's Easton Glacier steals the foreground. Lush meadows and tiny lakes are cupped between rocky knolls, and tumbling streams carve clefts between ridges and glacial moraines. Fat marmots announce your arrival with piercing cries.

Park Butte Trail (603) begins by bridging Sulphur Creek and undulating through Schriebers Meadow, where heather and huckleberries choke the open spaces and Mount Baker glistens between scattered stands of cedar and fir. Beyond lies a moonscape of rock and rushing streams. Volcanic mudflows and meltwater from the massive Easton Glacier have sliced freeways through the forest here; you'll probably have to boulder-hop a bit to cross the channels, especially on warm summer afternoons.

Next comes the hard part. The path, now wrapped in cool woods, gains 800 feet in a long and very steep mile to Lower Morovitz Meadow. Western hemlock gives way to mountain hemlock en route. Western red cedar yields to a strange looking cousin, the Alaska cedar, whose needles hang in long chains from drooping limbs. The off-white, shaggy bark peels off in long strips as if some bear had been using the poor tree as a sharpening post for giant claws!

This party-size pool at Baker plays host every year to many congenial groups of soakers.

The railroad grade, a knife-edged moraine created by Mount Baker's Easton Glacier, attracts seasoned scramblers along its knobby spine.

The grade tapers on the way to Upper Morovitz Meadow where you'll find superb campsites amid alpine scenery. The main trail goes across the meadow past a junction, with increasing panoramas as it climbs the last mile above Pocket Lake to the summit. The lookout cabin, leased by Skagit Alpine Club of Mount Vernon, is available to the public when not being used by its members.

Park Butte, ringed by peaks far and near, will take your breath away just when you stop to catch it. The 10,778-foot white cone of Mount Baker dominates the view. Its satellite peaks, the Black Buttes, jut above the Deming Glacier in sharp contrast. Looking westward, you'll see the serrated crests of the Twin Sisters range. To the south are Loomis Mountain and Dock Butte, backed in the far distance by Mount Rainier. To the east and southeast rise other distant cones including snow-clad Glacier Peak (see Hikes 15a-c).

Returning to the junction in the upper meadow, there's another direction to go that's well worth exploring. Take the side trail north toward Baker Pass

HIKE 18a *Park Butte*

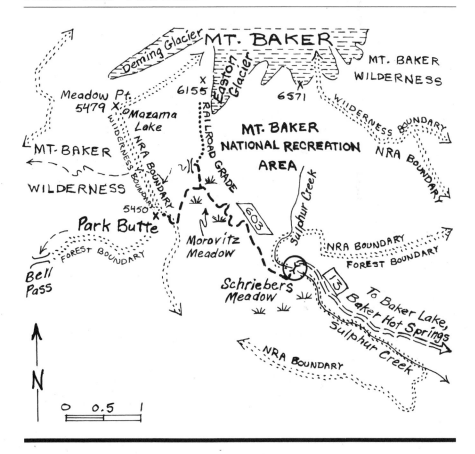

and ramble northeast to intersect the long rocky spine of the railroad grade. Pick your way along the tip of this knife-edged ridge, a moraine built up by the nearby Easton Glacier.

You can gaze eastward across the giant cleft to the massive glacier and barren landscape below the ice or look up, as you're drawn ever closer, to the gleaming-white volcanic cone of Mount Baker. Remote campsites hidden in clusters of subalpine fir speckle the high meadows west of the railroad grade, and further cross-country routes beckon.

---

19 Olympic Hot Springs

HIKE 19a *To Olympic Hot Springs*

General description: An easy five-mile round-trip day hike or overnighter featuring popular soaking pools in a rain forest setting, southwest of Port Angeles in Olympic National Park. Skinnydippable with discretion.
Elevation gain and loss: 260 feet.
Trailhead elevation: 1,800 feet.
High point: Olympic Hot Springs, 2,060 feet.
Hiking quads: Seven Lakes Basin Custom Correct, Mount Olympus Green Trails, or Mount Carrie USGS.
Road map: Olympic National Park brochure.

Finding the trailhead: Drive eight miles west of Port Angeles on U.S. Highway 101. Take Olympic Hot Springs Road ten miles south and west on pavement, past Elwha Ranger Station, to a roadblock and parking area at the signed trailhead. The springs are named on the USGS quad.

Background: Geologists believe that surface water here percolates downward until it reaches the earth's interior. Then, through cracks in the rock, steam and heated water rise back to the surface.

A more poetic explanation is the Native American legend that tells of two lightning fish (dragon-like creatures) who fought a mighty battle long ago here in the Olympics. Neither was able to win, so they crawled into separate caves where both continue to shed hot bitter tears. These tears still provide hot water at both Olympic and nearby Sol Duc Hot Springs (a modernized historic resort). The tears at Olympic range from lukewarm to 118 degrees.

In more recent times, a famous resort at Olympic Hot Springs met a spectacular demise when an electrical short simultaneously ignited a fire and turned on the organ. The resort burned to the ground to the strains of Beethoven's Funeral March!

The hike: Nowadays, the Park Service has barred the final stretch of the access road to motor vehicles in an attempt to curb overuse of the fragile soaking pools and also due to instability of the road surface. The end of the original road was constructed on fault surfaces and continues to slump.

Walk the last 2.2 miles of crumbling pavement, a gentle grade through deep woods, and set your pack down at Boulder Creek Campground. At one time

The largest pool at Olympic mirrors a canopy of evergreens on a quiet summer day.

fully developed with flush toilets and piped water, the site has been transformed into a primitive camp for backpackers. The short path to the springs drops down to bridge Boulder Creek, then meanders downstream passing one soaking pool after another.

A variety of side paths wriggle down the grassy bank and up into the forest; some hit the jackpot while others just circle around in a maze reinforced by the steady tread of hopeful feet. Perseverance mixed with a dash of logic and luck will lead you to the more secluded pools.

The hot springs: Without a doubt the hot spot of the Olympics, this cluster of steaming springs and pools lies sandwiched between a lush forest of fir and hemlock and the whitewater rapids of Boulder Creek. There are a total of seven bubbly soakers with a variety of sizes and temperatures to choose from—including one by a small waterfall. A popular destination for day trippers, it's also the stepping-off point for longer trips into the high Olympics (see the following hikes).

HIKE 19b *Olympic Hot Springs to Appleton Pass*

General description: A strenuous 10.5-mile, round-trip day hike or overnighter from the hot springs to alpine meadows and breathtaking views, in the northern mountains of Olympic National Park.

Elevation gain and loss: +2,920 feet, -120 feet.

Trailhead elevation: 2,200 feet at Boulder Creek Campground.

High point: Appleton Pass, 5,000 feet.

Maps: Same as Hike 19a.

Finding the trailhead: Follow Hike 19a to Olympic Hot Springs.

The hike: Olympic Hot Springs makes a great base for a side trip to Appleton Pass. This deservedly popular route climbs up, up, up through moss-coated primeval forest to an awesome view across High Divide. Wave after wave of snow-capped peaks recedes southward to the horizon like whitecaps on a stormy sea. Mount Olympus, at 7,965 feet, rides the highest crest. Airy campsites dot the pass, and a tempting extension of the route could be made from here across to Seven Lakes Basin and High Divide.

Appleton Pass Trail begins at the upper end of Boulder Creek Campground and winds through twilight woods to a junction in 0.7 mile with Boulder Lake Trail (Hike 19c). The gentle grade continues until the path bridges the North Fork of Boulder Creek. Now the work begins as the route shoots up the canyon of the South Fork of Boulder Creek. Two short spurs a short distance apart lead to cascading falls and a small campsite apiece while the main trail bridges the creek and climbs on.

Avalanche lilies carpet the viewpoint just east of Appleton Pass, and the jagged peaks along High Divide are seen to the south.

Crunch your way along a path littered with the small cones of western hemlock and Douglas-fir mixed with a dash of cedar. Log walkways aid the traverse over fragile marshy areas to a large campsite at 2.5 miles. The route crosses several rockslides spaced between stands of subalpine fir and a wavy tangle of slide alder.

Beyond, you'll cross the South Fork twice and finally emerge into a steep meadow in a high basin just below the pass. A thick mat of summer wildflowers competes with huckleberry, willow and other bushy plants in the waist-deep grass; the humid fragrance is intoxicating. Watch for fat marmots sunbathing on rocky outcrops as you work your way up.

Catch your breath and prepare for the last nine switchbacks up a precipitous slope that's often deep in snow until midsummer. An ice axe is well advised for early season hikers; a far easier snow climb from here crosses past tiny Oyster Lake up a long valley to a viewpoint 0.5 mile east of Appleton Pass.

Views from the pass itself are limited to tantalizing glimpses through the trees, so it's well worth the extra 0.5 mile and 300-foot gain to follow the ridgeline path east to the unnamed viewpoint. Tiny dwarfs of subalpine fir dot the plush green carpet spread out here, and the view unfolds in all directions. The glaciers of Mount Olympus can be seen directly behind the foreground ridge of High Divide.

"Snow Joke": *Fingers and toes half frozen from kicking one precarious step after another into crusty snow on the final steep pitch to Appleton Pass, my knees shook every time I made the mistake of glancing back down the slick wall. Concentrating instead on looking up, I began to see a sight that made me doubt my senses. A volley of snow-white balls was arcing through the blue sky above me, coming from some source just out of sight.*

And there, as I hauled my stiff body onto the crest, wearing only faded cutoffs and sturdy boots, stood a talented snowball juggler practicing his art! He paused long enough to share a precious quart of milk, then gathered up a handful of white avalanche lilies which he promptly consumed for dessert. Then, with a cheerful wave, he leaped over the edge. I blinked twice and peered down just in time to see him disappear far below in a graceful glissade, using only his boots for skis.

HIKE 19c   *Olympic Hot Springs to Boulder Lake*

General description: A moderate seven-mile, round-trip day hike or overnighter from the hot springs to a tree-rimmed lake and high views, in the northern mountains of Olympic National Park.
Elevation gain and loss: 2,150 feet.
Trailhead elevation: 2,200 feet at Boulder Creek Campground.
High point: Boulder Lake, 4,350 feet.
Maps: Same as Hike 19a.

Finding the trailhead: Follow Hike 19a to Olympic Hot Springs.

The hike: Another pleasant outing from the hot springs, not as spectacular as that to Appleton Pass (Hike 19b) but less demanding, climbs to a small lake

HIKE 19a   *To Olympic Hot Springs*
HIKE 19b   *Olympic Hot Springs to Appleton Pass*
HIKE 19c   *Olympic Hot Springs to Boulder Lake*

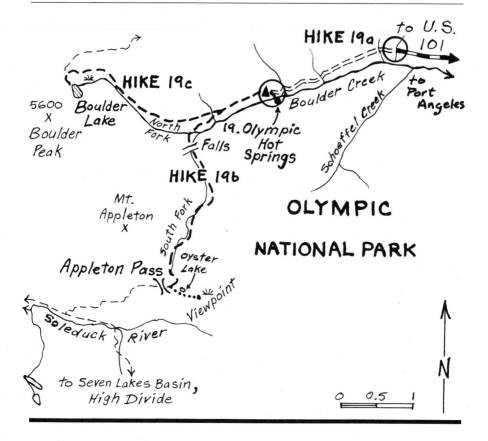

nestled in a wooded basin. The snowfields and cliffs of Boulder Peak rise 1,250 feet above the southwest shore, offering a challenge rewarded by excellent views.

Start toward Appleton Pass from Boulder Creek Campground and branch right in 0.7 mile onto Boulder Lake Trail. The route is a traverse climbing steadily above the North Fork of Boulder Creek, with a forest of Douglas-fir giving way to graceful western hemlock. Beyond Halfway Creek, the trail passes rockslide areas followed by stands of cedar and fir, crosses two rushing creeks, and finally levels into a meadow at the head of the valley. Subalpine firs line the last short rise.

Boulder Lake has a level campsite near the small peninsula on the north shore. The short climb from the lake to the 5,600-foot summit of Boulder Peak is steep but not difficult. The panoramic view includes Mount Appleton (nearby to the southeast) almost eclipsing massive Mount Olympus in the distance, and 7,000-foot Mount Carrie crowning the eastern end of High Divide.

BRITISH COLUMBIA

An Overview

Beautiful British Columbia has her fair share of wild hot springs. The ones described here are concentrated in the southwest and the southeast corners of the province. The former area covers Vancouver Island and the Lillooet Valley on the adjacent mainland. The latter, commonly known as the Kootenay region, includes dips on both the west and east sides. There are also many other springs farther north, which were eliminated merely for lack of convenient access. The reader will find a total of thirteen hot springs, all temptingly close to the U.S. border, marked on the B.C. Locator Map.

The hot springs in the southwest corner see the highest use. This isn't too surprising when you consider that roughly seventy-five percent of B.C.'s population can be found here—concentrated mainly in metropolitan Vancouver, the largest city, and in Victoria, the capital. The soaks in the Kootenays, on the other hand, remain nearly as lonesome as those in Idaho.

A. Vancouver Island and the Lillooet Valley

The west side of Vancouver Island is a maze of inlets, channels, and islands. The rugged coastline boasts not one but two hot springs, eight miles apart, accessible only by boat or plane. Several companies at the road-end town of Tofino offer scheduled service in addition to charters, and the two stops can be combined for a "double dip."

On the nearby mainland, hot spring fans will find no less than four soaks scattered within weekend range of the greater Vancouver area, in a line stretching the length of the Lillooet Valley northwest from Harrison Lake to the upper Lillooet River, bordered on the west by ranges of high peaks in spectacular Garibaldi Provincial Park and to the east by the remote and sparsely developed Coast Mountains.

Hikers in these parts will discover driftwood strewn beaches interspersed with tidal pools on the big island. In contrast, the high country bordering both sides of the Lillooet Valley offers day trippers and backpackers alike such enticements as twilight forests and glacial streams, jagged peaks, a broad range of alpine delights at popular Garibaldi Park, and head-on glacier views at a more remote park in the Coast Mountains.

Directions are given from towns on highways 4, 99, 7, and a variety of back roads. As a general rule, the forest roads are long and dusty from far too many logging trucks, campsites undeveloped, hiking trails primitive outside of the parks, and the soaking pools well used on weekends despite somewhat cumbersome access.

B. The Kootenay Region

The Kootenays encompass an area of fertile river valleys and narrow, glacially carved lakes sandwiched between mountain ranges, with Kootenay Lake running north-south down the center. To the west, three hot springs are clustered above a long lake in the rugged Selkirk Range; to the east, four more are spread out across the southern Rocky Mountain Trench. All are tucked away in sylvan settings, yet most are short walks to reach.

HOT SPRINGS IN BRITISH COLUMBIA
A. VANCOUVER ISLAND AND THE LILLOOET VALLEY

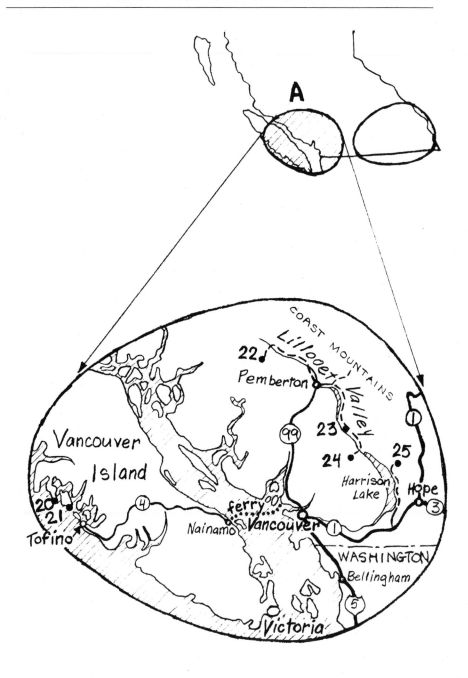

HOT SPRINGS IN BRITISH COLUMBIA
B. THE KOOTENAYS

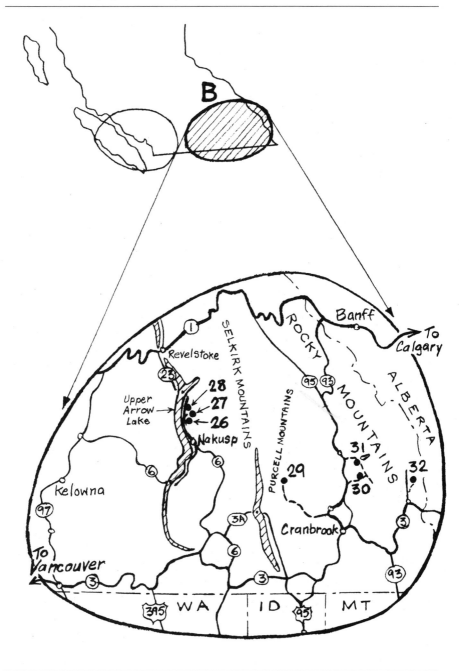

Hikers hereabouts enjoy trails that meander through age-old forests to the many scenic lakes in the area or climb to high overlooks. In addition to the routes described, national parks such as Glacier and Banff (in addition to a variety of provincial parks) offer a wide range of alpine destinations.

Directions are given out of Nakusp on Highways 6 and 23 and Cranbrook on Highways 95A, 93/95 and 3. Back roads and hiking routes run the gamut from short and well maintained to long and poorly defined, campsites vary from developed to primitive, and the bubbly soaking pools generally have room to spare.

For more information

Visitors should contact the following Forest or Park Service district offices for updates on hot springs, road and trail conditions, stream crossings, etc. If the receptionist can't answer your questions, ask for someone in recreation. Both agencies give out recreational road maps and trail printouts of the more popular hikes in each district. The Forest Service maps aren't up to the standards of those in the U.S., but most current roads are sketched in. Travel Infocentres across B.C. are also a good source of regional road maps as well as general information.

Hot Springs 20, 21 and Hikes 20a, 21a: Ministry of Parks, Strathcona District, (Rathtrevor Beach Provincial Park), P.O. Box 1479, Parksville, B.C. V9P 2H4; 604-248-3931.

Hot Springs 22-24 and Hike 24a: Ministry of Forests, Squamish Forest District, 42000 Loggers Lane, Squamish, B.C. V0N 3G0; 604/898-2100.

Hikes 22a, 23a: Ministry of Parks, Garibaldi/Sunshine Coast District, (Alice Lake Provincial Park), P.O. Box 220, Brackendale, B.C. V0N 1H0; 604-898-3678.

Hot Springs 25 and Hike 25a: Ministry of Forests, Chilliwack Forest District, P.O. Box 159, Rosedale, B.C. V0X 1X0; 604-794-3361.

Hot Springs 26-28 and Hike 26a: Ministry of Forests, Arrow Forest District, 845 Columbia Ave., Castlegar, B.C. V1N 1H3; 604/365-8600. Or check at the Infocentre or the ranger station in Nakusp.

Hikes 28a: Revelstoke Forest District, 604/837-7611; Revelstoke National Park and Glacier National Park, 604-837-5155; Arrow Forest District, see above.

Hot Springs 29 and Hike 29a: Ministry of Parks, East Kootenay District, (Wasa Provincial Park), P.O. Box 118, Wasa, B.C. V0B 2K0; 604-422-3212.

Hot Springs 30: Ministry of Forests, Invermere Forest District, 604-342-4200.

Hot Springs 31 and Hikes 30a,31a: Ministry of Parks (see 29 above).

Warm Springs 32 and Hike 32a: Ministry of Forests, Cranbrook Forest District, 1902 Theatre Rd., Cranbrook, B.C. V1C 4H4; 604-426-3391.

VANCOUVER ISLAND AREA MAP

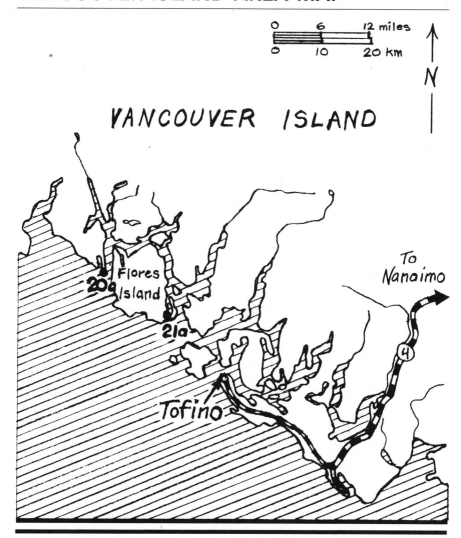

0 6 12 miles

0 10 20 km

N

VANCOUVER ISLAND

To Nanaimo

20a *Flores Island*

21a

4

Tofino

A. VANCOUVER ISLAND AND THE THE LILLOOET VALLEY

Hot springs and hikes

On the west coast of Vancouver Island, short hops by sea or air will drop you at popular Hot Springs Cove (20a) and little-known Ahousat (21a). Back on the mainland, a remote road up the Lillooet River northwest of Pemberton reaches five-star soaks at Meager Creek (22) followed by a trek over the "musical bumps" in magnificent Garibaldi Park. A drive southeast of town accesses a glacier hike in Joffre Lakes R.A. en route down the Lillooet River

UPPER LILLOOET VALLEY AREA MAP

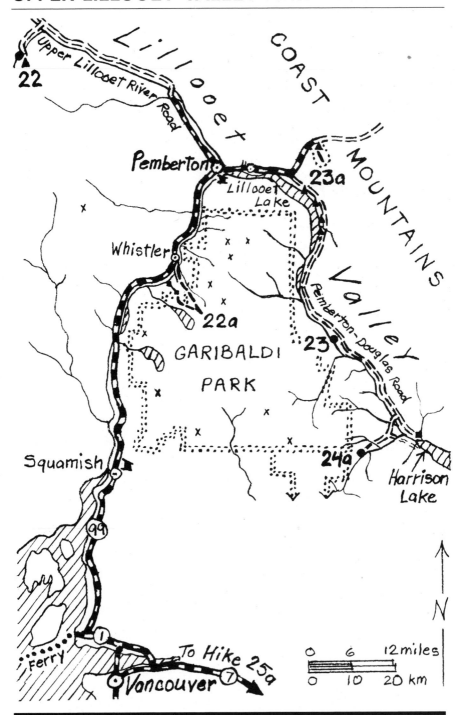

Lillooet

COAST MOUNTAINS

22

Upper Lillooet River Road

Pemberton

23a

Lillooet Lake

Whistler

22a

Pemberton-Douglas Road

GARIBALDI PARK

23

Valley

Squamish

24a

Harrison Lake

99

N

1

Ferry

To Hike 25a

Voncouver

| 0 | 6 | 12 miles |
| 0 | 10 | 20 km |

to a roadside dip in St. Agnes Well (23). Farther downstream is a far-flung hike to Sloquet Creek Hot Springs (24a). And last, a dusty drive up the east side of Harrison Lake north of Kent leads to a hike-in soak at popular Clear Creek (25a).

Season

The springs on Vancouver Island can be reached and enjoyed virtually all year thanks to scheduled transportation and a mild maritime climate. The Lillooet Valley soaks are best in early summer through fall, as winter road closures make access difficult. Spring runoff buries the pools at Sloquet and possibly Clear Creek, but most pools at Meager stay high and dry.

Hikers in the coastal area can expect cool but sunny summers, and mild winters with heavy rains. The hiking season on the mainland is limited to summer months only for the higher routes, with cold winters and heavy snows on west-facing slopes.

20 Hot Springs Cove

HIKE 20a *To Hot Springs Cove*

General description: A pleasant 2.5-mi/four-km round-trip boardwalk stroll to tidal hot pools in a provincial park at Sharp Point, northwest of Tofino on the west coast of Vancouver Island. Swimwear advised.
Elevation: Sea level.
Hiking quad: Hesquiat 92E/8 NTS (optional).
Road map: Provincial Parks of Vancouver Island.

Finding the Trailhead: On Vancouver Island, take Highway 4 west to the road-end town of Tofino. The springs at Sharp Point are on the tiny Openit Peninsula, twenty mi/thirty-two km to the northwest, and can only be accessed by sea or air. One can make arrangements to stop over at Ahousat Warm Spring (see 21), half way up the coast to Sharp Point. The hot springs are marked on both maps.

Transportation: Until recent years, only one charter company (Tofino Air) made the run and in 1989 accounted for twelve percent of the visitors. The remaining eighty-seven percent in that year consisted of: U.S. pleasure boats—forty-six percent, B.C. pleasure craft—twenty percent, and commercial fishing boats and local natives—twenty-one percent. In 1990, seven charter companies carried a total of 5,700 visitors to Hot Springs Cove, with Tofino Air accounting for sixty percent of the season's volume.

Today, you can take a scheduled "sea bus" from Tofino, a scenic one-hour ride leaving twice a day all summer, or fly Pacific Rim Airlines (1-800-663-6679), offering year-round scheduled flights twice a day from Port Alberni, with special summer rates in July and August.

The charter companies include Tofino Air (725-4454), Air Nootka (725-2255), Seaforth Charters (725-4252), Inter-Island Excursions (725-3163), Chinook

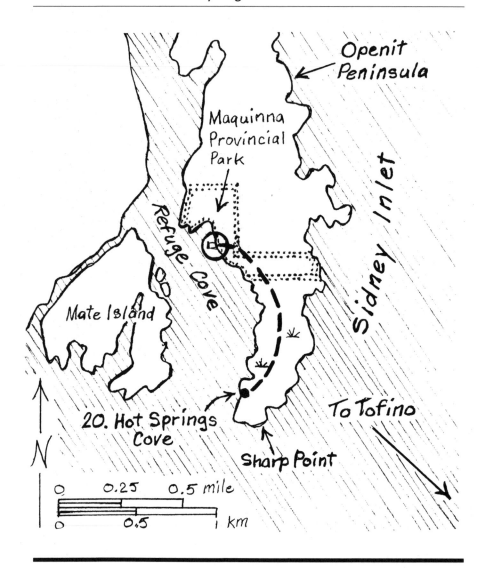

Openit Peninsula

Maquinna Provincial Park

Refuge Cove

Sidney Inlet

Mate Island

20. Hot Springs Cove

To Tofino

Sharp Point

N

0.25   0.5 mile

0   0.5   1 km

Charters (725-3431), and the Whale Centre (725-3163), first season 1991. Contact the Tofino Infocentre for an update on transportation choices and general information about the hot springs. The Area Code for B.C. is 604.

The hike: Visitors are deposited at Government Wharf, the site of an abandoned fish cannery where, until the summer of 1991, a floating house at the dock offered homemade food, hot coffee, and other goodies for sale. The Park Service doesn't expect it to return, but who's to say if another party may take up this role. Sun starfish can be seen at low tide, and sea anenomes grow profusely from the logs of the wharf.

Maquinna Park was named after a famous Nootka Indian chief in an area where habitation can be traced back more than 5,000 years. The tiny park offers no facilities, but tents can be pitched nearby, or you can camp for a fee in the adjacent Indian reserve.

The boardwalk trail spans a marshy area and heads south from the wharf to the rocky tip of the Openit Peninsula. The hot springs are located near the

At Hot Springs Cove, hot and cold currents battle for supremacy in the tidal pools in the rocky shore. Photo courtesy of BC Parks.

end. Beyond, you can explore the shoreline and observe an abundance of fascinating marine life at low tide.

Flores Island, the home of Ahousat Warm Spring (see below), is visible across Sidney Inlet to the east. Tiny Mate Island can be seen across Refuge Cove to the west. *Note:* A second thermal spring (barely warmer than sea water) and a gas vent off the southeast shore of the island, detected by infrared scanning, are reported to be related to the hot springs.

The hot springs: Water issues from bedrock at 129 degrees F/54 degrees C, cascades over a twelve-ft/3.6-m waterfall, and soon drains into three tidal pools the size of bathtubs. Icy ocean waves swirl through the pools with the incoming tide, which dilutes the scalding water to a more comfortable temperature. The uppermost offers the most relaxing soak and a great view of the sea.

Magnificent Hot Springs Cove has become quite a tourist attraction in recent years. Access is no longer a major obstacle, and in the prime summer months (July- September) as many as 100 people or more may flock to the springs in a single day. The best odds for a quiet soak would be weekdays or during the off season.

"A nautical boardwalk:" Ship's name graffiti is known the world over as sailors record their ports of call. At Hot Springs Cove, this graffiti has taken a different twist. Rather than paint their names and deface local landmarks, sailors regularly engrave, burn or chisel their ship's name into a plank and then nail it into the boardwalk. Some even bring their plank already prepared. Others add the date of each successive visit. As of July 1991, more than 150 planks were in place. Nowadays, the boardwalk is becoming a lesson in Who's Who of coastal yachting—not to mention a testimonial to the artistry of visiting seamen.

21 To Ahousat Warm Spring

HIKE 21a *To Ahousat Warm Spring*

General description: An easy two-mi/3.2-km round-trip walk to a warm pool in a marine park on an island off the west coast of Vancouver Island, northwest of Tofino. Swimwear recommended.
Elevation: Sea level.
Maps: Same as Hike 20a.

Finding the trailhead: On Vancouver Island, take Highway 4 west to the road-end town of Tofino. The warm spring is located at the south end of Flores Island, about twelve mi/nineteen km northwest, and can be accessed only by sea or air. Hot spring fans can get in a "double dip" by arranging to stop here en route to Hot Springs Cove (see above). The spring isn't marked on either map.

Transportation: Refer to the list of charter companies in 20a.

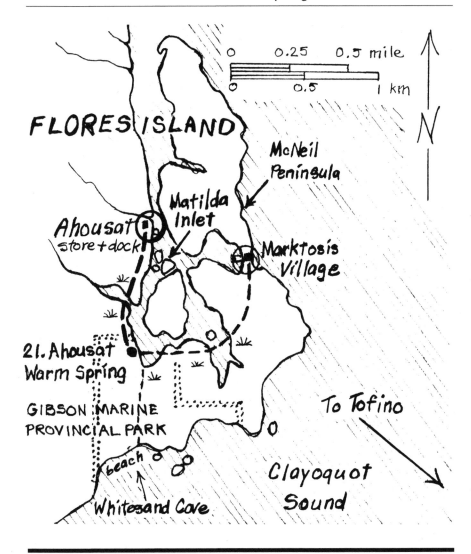

0   0.25   0.5 mile

0   0.5   1 km

FLORES ISLAND   N

McNeil
Peninsula

Matilda
Inlet

Ahousat
store + dock

Marktosis
Village

21. Ahousat
Warm Spring

GIBSON MARINE
PROVINCIAL PARK

To Tofino

beach

Whitesand Cove

Clayoquot
Sound

The hike: Charter boats to Flores Island normally drop people off at Ahousat, where there's a dock and a tiny general store. Trails are poorly defined, but one can follow the B.C. Hydro power poles south from along the shoreline of Matilda Inlet to the spring. A small bay mentioned has to be skirted or cut across, depending on the tide. Private boats can cruise right by Ahousat and head for the dock (if it's still afloat) on the tidal flat by the pool.

Visitors can also be deposited at Marktosis. A faint trail heads south, through a dense ground cover of salal, salmonberry bushes, and ferns, towards a line of power poles at Matilda Inlet. At the halfway point, it reaches the bay and follows the poles and shoreline west to the spring. At low tide the water is only six in/fifteen cm) deep, and you can cut across the head of the inlet. The distance is the same from either trailhead.

The warm spring: A concrete swimming pool, about eight-by-twenty ft and four foot deep/2.4-by-six-by-1.2 m, collects the flow. The pool has a magnificent setting on a beach at the southwest tip of Matilda Inlet in tiny Gibson Marine Park. The only drawback is a soaking temperature that hovers around 77 degrees F/25 degrees C, well below the optimum range except during hot weather.

With a bit of time to spare, there's an outstanding side trip nearby. As you near the spring, an old boardwalk path branches south. The scenic route leads to a sandy beach on the south end of the island at Whitesand Cove. Tiny islands dot the ocean view, and Vargas Island is visible to the southeast across Clayoquot Sound.

Just for the record, infrared scanning has detected several thermal ponds along the shore about 0.5 mi/.8 km north and along the south edge of a small bay opening onto Matilda Inlet. But the ponds are stagnant and full of rotting vegetation. They're even cooler than the Ahousat spring and are in a logged-off area.

22 Meager Creek Hot Springs

General description: A "Shangri-la" of cedar soaking pools below a remote road in the upper Lillooet River Valley, northwest of Pemberton. Swimwear seems the norm. Elevation 2,400 ft/732 m.
Map: Squamish Forest District.

Finding the hot springs: From Vancouver, take scenic Highway 99 north past Whistler (see following hike) and on to Pemberton. Go north to Pemberton Meadows, about seventeen mi/twenty-seven km up the Lillooet River. Beware of log trucks, and turn right on Hurley River Road.

The gravel road bridges the river and comes to a fork in five mi/eight km where it turns uphill. Bear left on the rougher Lillooet River Road and continue to the Mile-24 log truck sign.

Take the left fork here and cross the river. Follow Meager Creek Road seven miles (eleven km) upstream on another logging road ending by the springs. Meager Creek Hot Springs, a total of forty-seven mi/seventy-five km from Pemberton, are signed on the ground and prominently named on the forest map.

The way it was: Logging opened the way to Meager Creek in the late 1970s and brought with it a few hardy hot springers. B.C. Hydro took an active interest for a time, exploring the springs' potential as an alternate energy resource. The specs were impressive: the largest springs in the province, a temperature range of 101-129 degrees F/38-54 degrees C, and a volume of 347 gal/min/1,526 l/min. But the project was eventually abandoned as unfeasible and the springs left to nature.

The upper pool at Meager Creek Hot Springs features a submerged bench for relaxed soaking.

The lower pool at Meager is a unique example of a primitive spring that's been developed to the nth degree.

Then, on Thanksgiving weekend of 1984, Nature stepped in and dealt a harsh blow. Heavy rains brought down a monstrous mud slide that covered the valley floor and flooded areas as far away as Pemberton. The hot springs were demolished, vehicles buried, and the surviving bathers evacuated by helicopter.

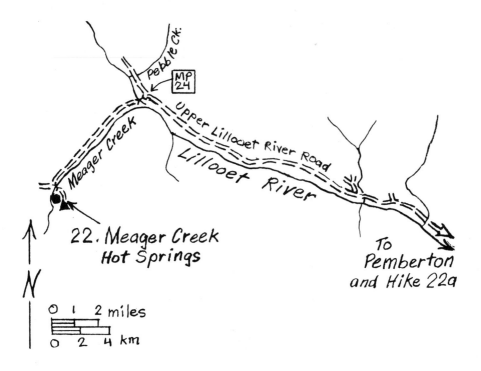

22. Meager Creek
Hot Springs

To
Pemberton
and Hike 22a

N

0   1   2 miles

0   2   4 km

The hot springs today: The Squamish Forest District, after years of hard work mending the damage, has developed the area into a designated recreation site. The grounds, maintained by a cheerful caretaker working on contract with the Forest Service, were planned to accommodate large numbers.

Tastefully designed to blend into the environment, two huge cedar pools have been constructed—along with ample decks and cabanas for clothes. The parking lot and camping area now sit on terraces high up the bank, and stairways ease the descent. An age-old forest spreads a green canopy, and fern-bordered causeways span marshy spots below.

The uppermost pool measures a full fifteen by twenty ft/4.5 by six m and has a submerged bench along one side. Clocking in at 110 degrees F/43.3 degrees C at the time I was there, it sorely needed some means of channeling cold water from the creek. The lower gem, known as "sky pool," is even longer and about neck deep when standing up. It registered just 90 degrees F/32.2 degrees C, but was definitely a five-star soak on a midsummer day.

In addition, there's a creekside pool built of mortared rock. This one's easy enough to cool with a few splashes from the glacier-fed stream. Also nearby is a small rock pool beside a sauna shed. Winding paths connect all the soaks, and the forest provides both shade and privacy.

Meager Creek Hot Springs has indeed come a long way. Nowadays, visitors are said to pour in by the hundreds on long weekends. Let's just pray the numbers don't grow too much larger and bring problems so common to overused hot springs in the states, or the Forest Service may live to regret the paradise they've developed here.

HIKE 22a *Singing Pass via the "Musical Bumps"*

General description: A moderate 10.5-mi/seventeen-km, point-to-point hike featuring alpine views and a flower-meadowed pass in the heart of Garibaldi Park, between Vancouver and Pemberton en route to Meager Creek Hot Springs.
Elevation gain and loss: +1,640 ft/500 m, -3,770 ft/1,150 m.
Trailhead elevation: 5,900 ft/1,800 m at the Round House.
High point: 6,720 ft/(2,050 m.
Low point: 3,770 ft/1,150 m at Fitzsimmons Creek trailhead.
Hiking quads: Cheakamus and Fitzsimmons Garibaldi Park 92J/2E or Whistler 92J/2 NTS.
Road map: Garibaldi Provincial Park brochure or Squamish Forest District.

Finding the trailheads: Take Highway 99 to Whistler Village and go east following signs toward Blackcomb Mountain Ski Area. Watch for a dirt road veering right, signed "to Singing Pass." Drive three mi/4.8 km uphill to Fitzsimmons Creek trailhead and leave a car here.

Return to Highway 99, and hop south to the Gondola exit. Drop a second vehicle off at the Gondola Base parking lot and ride the gondola, followed

At Singing Pass, hikers look across flowered meadows to a skyline of snowcapped peaks.

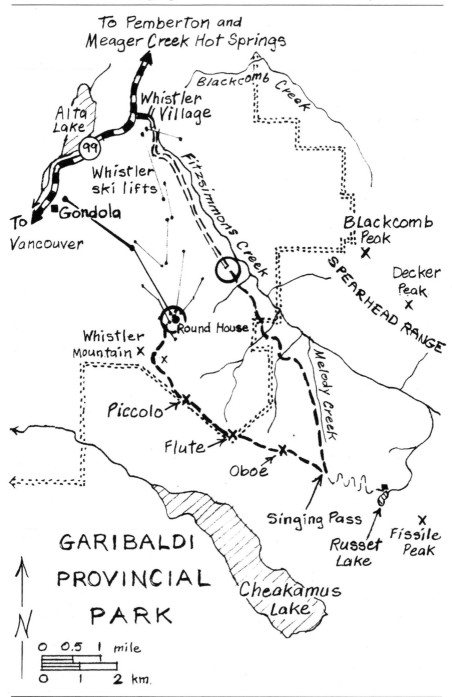

To Pemberton and
Meager Creek Hot Springs

Blackcomb Creek

Whistler
Village

Alta
Lake

99

Whistler
ski lifts

To
Vancouver

Gondola

Fitzsimmons Creek

Blackcomb
Peak
X

Decker
Peak
X

SPEARHEAD RANGE

Round House

Whistler
Mountain X   X

Melody Creek

Piccolo

Flute

Oboe

Singing Pass

Russet
Lake

X
Fissile
Peak

GARIBALDI

PROVINCIAL

PARK

Cheakamus
Lake

N

0   0.5   1   mile

0   1   2 km.

by Red Chair, to the "high start" trailhead at the Round House on the north side of Whistler Mountain. The trails aren't marked on the Whistler quad.

The hike: The high route to Singing Pass is a favorite among connoisseurs of alpine vistas. After a brief initial climb, it glides along a ridge capped by three knolls: Piccolo, Flute, and Oboe. Hikers ride the "musical bumps," as they're affectionately called, on a descending scale (each bump lower than the last) to Singing Pass. Here, the Fitzsimmons Creek Trail lets you continue the downhill glide back to the shuttle car.

The advantages of the point-to-point route vs. a round trip on Fitzsimmons Creek Trail are the nonstop panoramic views plus a good 330 ft/100 m less gain. The only drawbacks are the required car shuttle between trailheads and the need to take ski lifts. Call the Whistler Infocentre (604/932-5528) to make sure the lifts are running.

From the Round House, an unofficial path works its way south to the top of the T-bar, then on up a narrow basin found between the summits of Whistler and Little Whistler. Try to avoid the ice fields near the lower summit as you traverse steep slopes to the crest. The climb places you 820 ft/250 m above the Round House, encircled by lofty views of Garibaldi Park.

Here you'll turn your back on Whistler Mountain and begin a southeasterly course along the knobby spine. Sail over 6,560-ft/2,000-m Piccolo Summit, dip and rise over Flute, then bob to Oboe. Look straight down at Cheakamus Lake ahead to nearby Fissile Peak, and across Fitzsimmons Valley to a multitude of peaks in the Spearhead Range to the northeast.

Coast down flowered slopes to Singing Pass, nearly 500 ft/150 m below Oboe, where tiny wildflowers blanket broad subalpine meadows. From Singing Pass itself, a side trip beckons. The 1.2-mi/two-km path to Russet Lake crosses a ridge that adds an extra 820-ft/250-m gain to the hike but offers yet another horizon of snow-clad peaks.

The route down Fitzsimmons Creek begins with a brief view of mountains on the west side of the main valley below, seen from the head of Melody Creek, then drops into old-growth forest. You'll be continuing down the musical scale as you skirt the side canyons of Oboe and Flute Creeks, then finally cross Harmony Creek a short way from the trail's end.

23 St. Agnes Well

General description: Roadside hot tanks by the Lillooet River, seasonally frequented by locals and man-eating mosquitoes, southeast of Pemberton. Keep swimwear handy. Elevation 400 ft/122 m.
Map: Squamish Forest District.

Finding the hot spring: From Vancouver, take Highway 99 north to Pemberton (the turnoff to Meager) and go east to Lillooet Lake. The paved road soon branches up and away to Duffey Lake (see following hike) and Lillooet. Bear right on the gravel Pemberton-Douglas Forest Road, keeping an eye peeled for logging trucks. Follow it the length of the lake and down the east side of the Lillooet River past Rogers Creek.

HOT SPRINGS 23 *St. Agnes Well*
HIKE 24a *To Sloquet Creek Hot Springs*

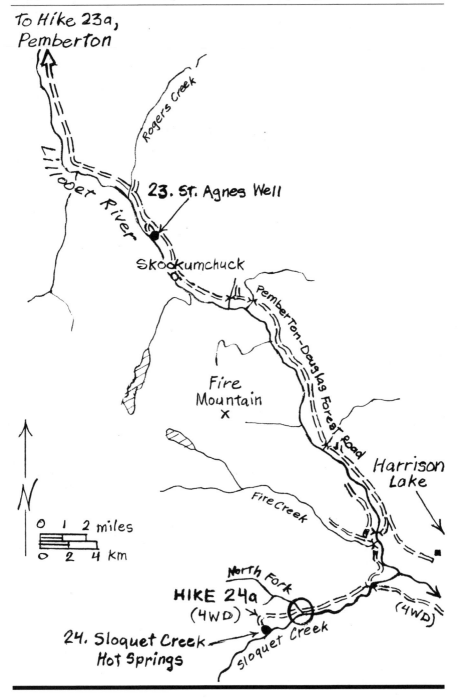

To Hike 23a, Pemberton

Rogers Creek

Lillooet River

23. St. Agnes Well

Skookumchuck

Pemberton-Douglas Forest Road

Fire Mountain X

Harrison Lake

N

0 1 2 miles
0 2 4 km

Fire Creek

North Fork

HIKE 24a (4WD)

24. Sloquet Creek Hot Springs

Sloquet Creek

(4WD)

Soakers at St. Agnes Well must choose between two halves of a fiberglass tank (one half is hidden under the A-frame shack).

Start watching number plates on the B.C. Hydro towers hang a right at Tower 682. A short track heads past a wooded camping area to the spring. St. Agnes Well, forty mi/sixty-four km from Pemberton, is named on the forest map but misplaced across the road.

The hot spring: Users have cut a fiberglass septic tank in half to create two oval-shaped soaking tanks here. The spring bubbles up at 129 degrees F/54 degrees C and is fed into the tubs, along with a cold water source, by sections of PVC pipe. One tank is squeezed inside a ramshackle shelter, and the other sits across a small clearing in the woods.

The land around St. Agnes Well, located near the nearly-deserted village of Skookumchuck, was once a large homestead. The property is still privately owned but is open to the public. The name Skookumchuck means "good water" in Chinook Indian language.

The best part about St. Agnes (called Skookumchuck by some) is that it breaks the long drive to Sloquet Creek Hot Springs (see 24 below). Popular with folks from as far off as Vancouver, it periodically gets some heavy-handed treatment. Piles of empty beer cans and other garbage greeted my visit, and clouds of hungry mosquitoes kept it short!

HIKE 23a *Joffre Lakes*

General description: A moderate seven-mi/eleven-km round-trip day hike or overnighter to glacier-fed lakes and alpine views in Joffre Lakes R.A., east of Pemberton on the way to St. Agnes Well.
Elevation gain and loss: 1,200 ft/366 m.
Trailhead elevation: 4,100 ft/1,250 m.
High point: 5,300 ft/1,615 m at Upper Joffre Lake.
Hiking quad: Duffey Lake 92J/8 NTS.
Road map: Squamish Forest District.

Finding the trailhead: Follow the directions above to Duffey Lake Road, found eleven mi/eighteen km east of Pemberton or twenty-nine mi /forty-seven km north of St. Agnes Well. Signed to Lillooet, the recently paved road climbs to tiny Joffre Lakes Recreation Area in another eight mi/thirteen km. The signed trail, not shown on the NTS quad, starts off from the campground.

The hike: Good things come in small packages, and the short climb to Upper Joffre Lake opens into a world of tiny wildflowers backed by snow and ice. Climbers' tents are dwarfed by the broad snout of a glacier hanging over the blue-green surface, and white peaks cast shimmering reflections on the water.

Joffre Lakes Trail begins in deep woods but soon emerges to a magnificent view of the glacier from the lower lake. Continuing in forest through a thick growth of ferns and berry bushes, the improved track does its best to skirt muddy areas around the lake.

Beyond, the route climbs steeply for the next mi/1.6 km, zigzagging high above Joffre Creek in the shade of tall cedars and Douglas fir. Next comes a boulder field to cross before the path drops to bridge the creek and circle the small middle lake.

A final short pitch brings you to beautiful Upper Joffre. The size of the two lower lakes combined, its roughly triangular shape is convoluted with tiny inlets and peninsulas. Clusters of subalpine fir dot the rocky slopes, and a wall of scree and talus rises above the far shore to the ragged tongue of the glacier, backed by Mount Matier.

For a head-on confrontation, take the rocky path beyond the lake and follow the inlet stream to the camping area. A cairned route rises over talus to a ridge overlooking the lake and mountains beyond, and the short climb adds a gain of around 700 ft/213 m to the hike. Look directly across the lake to Joffre Peak. A few more steps brings you face to face with the icefalls of the Matier Glacier.

"In the dark": Planning an early start for the climb, I broke camp and started morning coffee in the dark, disdaining the aid of a flashlight. Who needs light to do a simple task performed every day? Not me. No problem finding the pot and the water bottle. No problem filling the pot and starting up the stove. The problem came a few minutes later when the horrible smell of burning plastic told me the one item I hadn't found—my breakfast bowl stashed inside the pot!

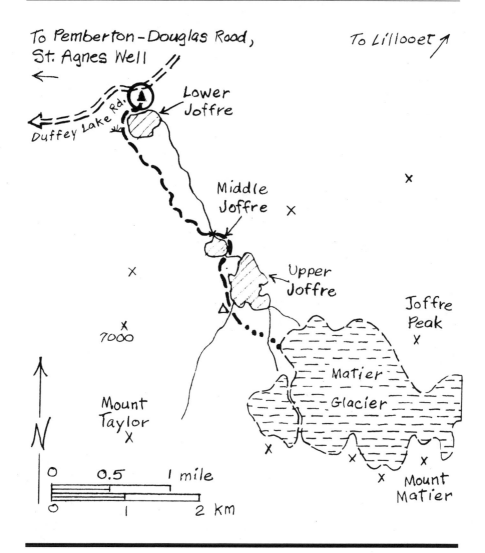

To Pemberton-Douglas Road,
St. Agnes Well

To Lillooet ↗

←

Duffey Lake Rd.

Lower
Joffre

Middle
Joffre ✕

✕

Upper
Joffre

Joffre
Peak
✕

✕
7000

Matier

Glacier

Mount
Taylor
✕

N

✕

✕   ✕

✕

Mount
Matier

0   0.5   1 mile

0   1   2 km

Joffre Lakes Trail starts with a preview of the Matier Glacier seen from the lower lake.

24 Sloquet Creek Hot Springs

HIKE 24a *To Sloquet Creek Hot Springs*

General description: A major stream ford plus an easy four-mi/6.4-km round-trip walk (vs. a bumpy jeep ride) to remote creekside hot pools in the lower Lillooet River Valley, southeast of Pemberton. Swimwear advised if others present.
Elevation gain and loss: +200 ft/61 m, -60 ft/18 m.
Trailhead elevation: 560 ft/171 m at the North Fork crossing.
High point: 760 ft/232 m.
Hiking quads: Glacier Lake 92G/16 and Stave River 92G/9 NTS (optional).
Road map: Squamish Forest District.

Finding the trailhead: Follow the directions to 23 and continue down the Lillooet River. At a "Y" in twenty mi/thirty-two km, bear right and cross the river then go left to bridge Fire Creek. Drive two mi/3.2 km down the west side of the river to a rough road on the right just before the bridge over Sloquet Creek.

The narrow Sloquet Creek Road has some rocky spots that demand a high clearance vehicle and very few places to park—much less turn around. If in doubt, you can park below and walk the final 5.5 mi/8.8 km.

At 3.5 mi/5.6 km, the road dives beneath the North Fork Sloquet Creek. There's ample room to park (or pitch a tent) nearby. The pullout is a grand total of 63.5 dusty mi/102 km from Pemberton. The springs are marked without a name on the forest map and omitted on the Stave River quad.

The hike: Fording the North Fork Sloquet Creek would be suicide during the spring runoff, and it's still a good two feet deep (0.6 m) in midsummer. The water's icy cold and the current moves along at a good clip. Beyond, a jeep track continues two mi/3.2 km west through deep woods well up the bank, finally dropping down to end beside the stream. There's a good tentsite or two in the grassy clearing, and a short path leads downstream to the pools.

The hot springs: The main spring, one of the hottest in B.C. at 154 degrees F/68 degrees C, cascades into a pool hot enough to cook eggs. Downstream, steamy water from other springs flows through a chain of shallow pools in the bedrock bank. Closest to the source, the largest pool registers nearly 113 degrees F/45 degrees C. The temperature drops to a toasty 105 degrees F/40.5 degrees C in the creekside pools, and cold water can be admitted for a cooler dip.

The soaking pools are enclosed on one side by a tangle of undergrowth and overhanging trees and hemmed in on the other by the rushing torrent of Sloquet Creek. Shafts of sunlight filter through the treetops, and the stream ripples right past your nearly submerged nose. How close to heaven can you get?

Road note: Just for the record, the river road does continue down the west

Sloquet Creek Hot Springs offers the ultimate in secluded soaking close to nature.

side of Harrison Lake all the way south to Highway 7, but it's reported to be quite rough—for 4WD vehicles only. The sixty-mi/ninety-seven-km drive is said to take six to ten hours. So, unfortunately, there's no easy link between the hot springs here and those down at Clear Creek (see below).

25 Clear Creek Hot Springs

HIKE 25a *To Clear Creek Hot Springs*

General description: An easy five-mi/eight-km round-trip walk, or a rough jeep ride, to hot tubs in the backwoods above the east side of Harrison Lake, north of Kent. Swimwear anyone's guess.
Elevation gain and loss: About 1,000 ft/305 m.
Trailhead elevation: About 1,500 ft/457 m.
High point: Hot springs, 2,500 ft/762 m.
Hiking quad: Mount Urquhard 92H/12 NTS (optional).
Road map: Chilliwack Forest District.

Finding the trailhead: From Vancouver, take Highway 7 east to the Kent district. Go north on Highway 9, passing Harrison Hot Springs Resort and Sasquatch Provincial Park. Beware of log trucks as you continue on the gravel Harrison Forest Road up the east side of Harrison Lake.

HIKE 25a *To Clear Creek Hot Springs*

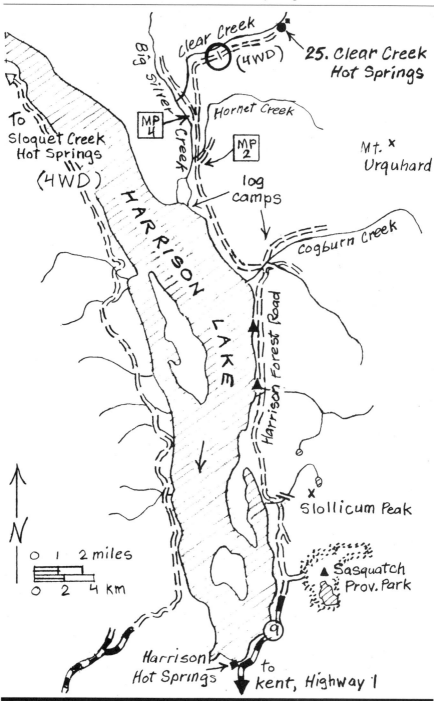

Clear Creek

Big Silver Creek

(4WD)

25. Clear Creek Hot Springs

Hornet Creek

To Sloquet Creek Hot Springs (4WD)

MP 4

MP 2

Mt. x Urquhard

log camps

HARRISON LAKE

Cogburn Creek

Harrison Forest Road

Slollicum Peak

N

0   1   2 miles

0   2   4 km

Sasquatch Prov. Park

Harrison Hot Springs

to kent, Highway 1

Take the left fork at Cogburn Creek, where the main road accesses a logging camp, and in another few miles pass Silver Creek log camp. Mile signs for the log trucks currently begin here. Bear left at Milepost 2, then make a right turn near Milepost 4 on an old mining road.

The 6.5-mi/10.5-km Clear Creek Road has been improved somewhat in the last few years. When the surface is dry, passenger cars now manage to get about four mi/6.5 km up—a total drive of around forty-one mi/(sixty-six km from Harrison Hot Springs. The springs aren't marked on either map.

The hike: Park wherever you can find room and dig out your walking shoes. The final 2.5 mi/four km aren't worth the wear and tear even on a jeep. The track is bordered by stately trees, and it's a pleasant walk. A few primitive campsites can be found near both the "trailhead" and the tubs.

The hot springs: At last count, Clear Creek sported four soaking tubs perched on rocks at the water line—a wooden tub six ft/1.8 m in diameter, a plywood box that would hold about the same volume if it didn't leak, and two garden variety bathtubs. The spring bubbles out of the bank at 95 degrees F/35 degrees C, and lengths of PVC pipe transport water to the tub of your choice.

Nearby, there's a cabin and a swimming pool built of cedar logs by a woman prospector back when the road was first opened. The pool wastes away collecting silt and algae. Although she still has mining claims, the land is publicly owned.

You'd expect this far-flung spot to be one of the quieter soaking grounds in the province, but unfortunately this isn't the case. Remote as it may be, Clear Creek is still the closest wild dip to the metropolitan Vancouver area. It's normally reachable and usable from April through September, but visitors on summer weekends must come prepared to wait awhile for a tub.

B. THE KOOTENAY REGION

Hot springs and hikes

In the West Kootenays, Highway 23 north of Nakusp leads to easy-access yet secluded soaks at St. Leon, Halfway, and Halcyon (26-28) near Upper Arrow Lake in the Selkirk Mountains; hiking options include a climb to an overlook of the lake. In the East Kootenays, the remaining four springs fan out north of Cranbrook. A remote road northwest of town accesses a trek to Dewar Hot Springs (29a) in the Purcell Wilderness. North of town, a loop drive combines roadside soaks at popular Ram Creek and Lussier (30, 31) with hikes in nearby parks in the Rockies. To the northeast, logging roads access a stroll to Fording Mountain Warm Springs (32a).

Season

Although early summer through fall is the best time, the soaks in the West Kootenays can be reached from the highway in winter by X-C skiers and shouldn't be affected by the spring runoff. In the East Kootenays, access to all but Lussier hinges on seasonal road closures.

The hiking season is normally late July through mid-September for high routes such as Saddle Mountain and the viewpoints above Fish Lake. Prime time for the trek to Dewar is mid-August. Summer weather generally brings hot days with occasional thunderstorms, and you can expect cold nights at higher elevations.

26 St. Leon Hot Springs

General description: A unique soaker in a cedar forest well hidden below a dirt road in the Selkirk Mountains, north of Nakusp in the West Kootenay region. Keep swimwear handy. Elevation 2,200 ft/670 m.
Map: Arrow Forest District.

Finding the hot springs: From Nakusp, take Highway 23 north about fourteen mi/twenty-three km up the east side of Upper Arrow Lake. Turn right 1.5 mi/2.4 km past a rest area onto St. Leon Forest Road (south of the bridge over St. Leon Creek) and climb two mi/3.2 km to a pullout. A path plunges downhill and reaches the pool in about 0.25 mi/0.4 km. St. Leon isn't marked on the forest map.

The hot springs: A clearing in the forest reveals a concrete pool with free-flowing curves and a smoothly sloped bottom. The kidney-shaped pool, built by a highway crew, is a good fifteen ft/4.6 m long and 2.5 ft/.8 m deep in the center. The springs emerge from fractures in nearby rocks and are piped into the pool to provide a blissful soak at around 103 degrees F/39 degrees C. There's also a small pool in the rocks above.

St. Leon Hot Springs is on private property but open to the public. A hotel dating back to gold rush days once stood nearby, as at nearby Halcyon, but

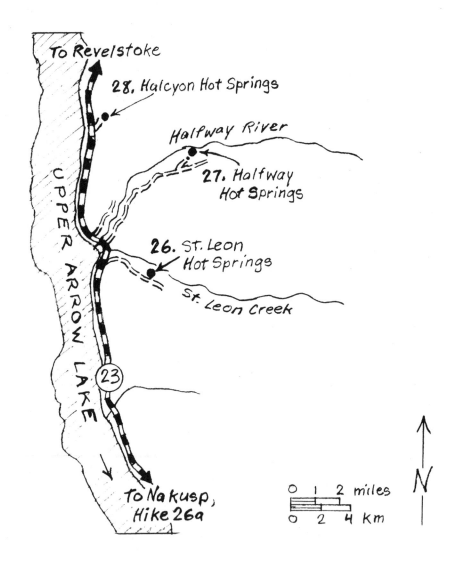

To Revelstoke

28. Halcyon Hot Springs

Halfway River

27. Halfway Hot Springs

26. St. Leon Hot Springs

St. Leon Creek

UPPER ARROW LAKE

23

To Nakusp, Hike 26a

0 1 2 miles
0 2 4 km

N

The unique pool at St. Leon, with curves in the shape of a guitar, sets a new standard in creative design.

both hotels burned down in the 1950s and no trace remains today. The forest is magnificent, and the gourmet sampler of wild dips would be hard pressed to improve on the present user-built pool.

HIKE 26a *Saddle Mountain Lookout*

General description: A strenuous six-mi/9.7-km round-trip climb to a lookout tower with sweeping views of the Arrow Lakes and surrounding mountains, not far from St. Leon Hot Springs.
Elevation gain and loss: 2,243 ft/684 m.
Trailhead elevation: 5,400 ft/1,646 m.
High point: 7,643 ft/2,330 m.
Hiking quad: Nakusp 82K/4 NTS.
Road map: Arrow Forest District.

Finding the trailhead: From Nakusp, drive about twelve mi/twenty km south on Highway 6 and take the ferry across Arrow Lake. Turn right on Saddle Mountain Road and drive six mi/ten km up the far shore. Take a left on the lookout road and climb five mi/eight km to the road-end parking area. The trailhead is around twenty-three miles/thirty-seven km from Nakusp.

The hike: Saddle Mountain Trail begins near the top of a large clearcut but is soon wrapped in a forest of hemlock and cedar as it climbs the east-facing flank. You'll pass an old cabin on the way, then travel past stands of spruce and balsam, and finally reach alpine meadows dotted with tiny wildflowers giving way to rocky slopes near the summit.

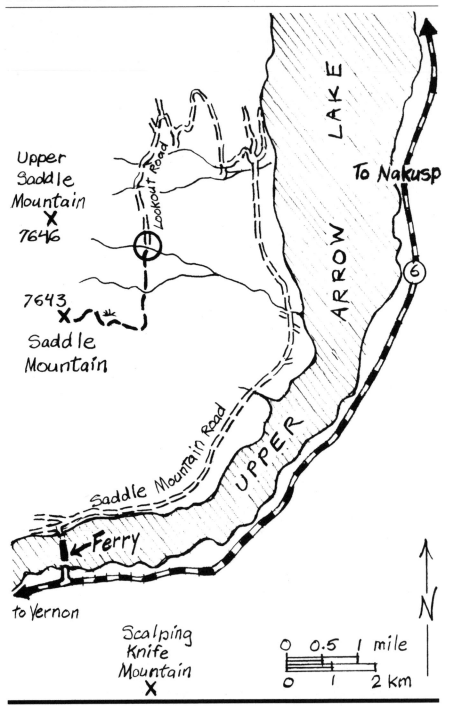

Upper
Saddle
Mountain
X
7646

7643
X

Saddle
Mountain

Lookout Road

Saddle Mountain Road

To Nakusp

6

ARROW LAKE

UPPER

Ferry

to Vernon

Scalping
Knife
Mountain
X

N

0   0.5   1 mile

0   1   2 km

From Saddle Mountain Lookout, the view across Upper Arrow Lake includes Nakusp.
Arrow Forest District, BC, photo.

The lookout is a great spot to enjoy the sight of Upper and Lower Arrow Lakes stretched out below. Look west to views of the Monashee Range and east to the southern Selkirks. Scalping Knife Mountain looms across the lake canyon to the south. But don't lose track of time, or you'll find yourself watching the last ferry of the day leave without you.

27 Halfway Hot Springs

General description: Steamy soaking boxes hiding in the woods below a dirt road in the Selkirk Mountains, north of Nakusp in the West Kootenay region. Skinnydippable with discretion. Elevation 2,000 ft/610 m.
Map: Arrow Forest District.

Finding the hot springs: From Nakusp, drive north about fifteen mi/twenty-four km up the east side of Upper Arrow Lake on Highway 23, past the St. Leon Creek bridge. Turn right on an old logging road just south of the Halfway River bridge and follow it 6.5 mi/10.4 km uphill. Drop over the edge on a

At Halfway Hot Springs, you can start the day out right with a cup of coffee and a toasty soak.

track that ends at a fire ring. A path plunges down the bank to reach the springs in 0.25 mi/0.4 km. The springs aren't marked on the forest map.

The approach: The first clue is a small sign nailed to a tree that reads: "There's no place anything like this place anywhere near this place, so this must be the place!" Thanks to the volunteer work of Peter Roulston and the Arrow Lake Naturalists of Nakusp, the site is now complete with a secluded camping area and outhouse in addition to the soaking boxes.

The next sign welcomes the visitor, gives a bit of background, and provides a few pointers on enjoying a comfortable soak. A notice warns about poison ivy—which flourishes along the path and surrounds the springs.

The hot springs: Around the bend is the coup de gras—a plywood soaking box about seven ft/two m square with an adjoining box half the size. A pipe channels water from the 141-degree F/60.5-degree C spring, and a valve regulates the flow. The recommended technique is to leave it at just a trickle, otherwise it gets far too hot. A bucket has been provided for adding river water.

The three-sided shed offers a dry spot for clothes, and decking spans the muddy ground around the springs. A path leads to the nearby river where those so inclined can take an ice-cold plunge between soaks. A lush cedar forest wraps the area in total privacy.

Just for the record: A second hot spring on the Halfway River was discovered by the Forest Service in 1973 while fighting a forest fire; it's said to lie another seven mi/eleven km upstream in a rocky gorge. Unfortunately, the terrain isn't conducive to making a pool, as the spring flows down a rockslide of boulders. Logging roads follow both sides of the river, and the road on the north bank continues up the broad valley into the high country.

*"**Mirage**": After an afternoon of bushwhacking up both sides of the river with friends from Cranbrook, we found the path and decided on one last try. Expecting an algae-coated puddle at best, we were dumbfounded to find the user-built facilities, and*

stood gawking at a group in the pool sipping wine from long-stemmed glasses and nibbling snacks from a well stocked cooler.

If we'd only known in advance, we could have saved ourselves the effort and stopped at the Travel Infocentre in Nakusp. It seems they have an album on display with color photos, full specs, and directions to all three "wild" dips in the area.

28 Halcyon Hot Springs

General description: Roadside hot soaks overlooking a lake in the Selkirk Mountains, north of Nakusp in the West Kootenay region. Nudity common despite heavy use. Elevation 2,000 feet (610 m).
Map: Arrow Forest District.

Finding the hot springs: From Nakusp, follow Highway 23 north about 20.5 mi/thirty-three km up the east side of Upper Arrow Lake, or six mi/9.6 km north of the Halfway River bridge (see 27 above). A dirt road on the right goes uphill and soon reaches the springs. Folks camping overnight usually park above the springs. Neither Halcyon nor the turnoff are marked on the forest map.

The hot springs: Three patched-together soaking boxes lined with plastic nestle into a grassy hillside a short distance apart. The springs range from 116-123 degrees F/46.5-50.5 degrees C. Lengths of pipe carry water from the source to the tubs, and the pipes can be diverted for a cooler soak. The springs have a high lithium content, and many visitors fill bottles of the stuff to take home.

Halcyon is on private land but open to the public. Like St. Leon, it's the site of a hotel dating back to gold rush days. No sign remains of past use, but there's talk of possible future development. The soaking boxes here are frequently filled to capacity, and the area shows some signs of abuse. The best feature at Halcyon is the sweeping view of the Monashee Mountains across the long expanse of Upper Arrow Lake.

HIKE 28a *Trails in the Western Kootenays*

Travelers heading farther north could try the 1.5-mi/2.5-km stroll to tiny Pingston Lake or climb the steep 3.7-mi/six-km Mount Begbie Trail to the toe of the glacier. Crossing the icefall to the summit requires mountaineering skills. A chain of lakes west of the peak are reached by an alpine route.

Both of these hikes are found near Highway 23 on the stretch between Shelter Bay and Revelstoke and are administered by the Revelstoke Forest

Visitors enjoy breakfast with a view at Halcyon Hot Springs.

District. Or you could save your energy for a choice of hikes in Mount Revelstoke or Glacier National Park.

Those traveling south could drive up to Nakusp Hot Springs (a city-owned plunge) and take either a scenic 0.5-mi/.75-km loop stroll on the Cedar Trail or a strenuous 2.5-mi/four-km trek to Kimbol Lake. A good option farther south is the climb to Saddle Mountain (Hike 26a).

The Arrow Forest District in Castlegar administers this area. The Travel Infocentre in Nakusp, open on weekends, can also shed light on local trails as well as all three hot springs.

CRANBROOK AREA MAP

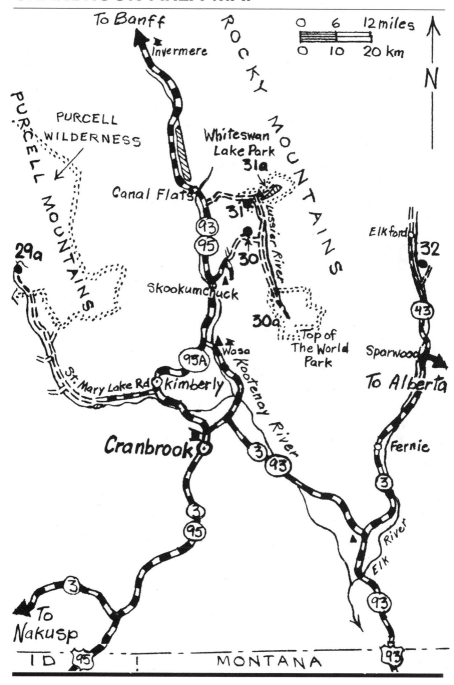

To Banff

Invermere

ROCKY MOUNTAINS

0 6 12 miles
0 10 20 km

N

PURCELL WILDERNESS

PURCELL MOUNTAINS

Whiteswan Lake Park
31a

Canal Flats

31

Lussier River

Elkford
32

93
95

30

29a

Skookumchuck

30a

Top of The World Park

Sparwood

95A
Wasa

Kootenay River

To Alberta

43

St. Mary Lake Rd Kimberly

Cranbrook

3
93

Fernie

3

3

95

Elk River

To Nakusp

3

93

ID 95 ! MONTANA 93

29 Dewar Hot Springs

HIKE 29a *To Dewar Hot Springs*

General description: A trek of around twelve mi/19.3-km round-trip, leading to geothermal wonders and a dicey dip in the Purcell Wilderness, northwest of Cranbrook in the East Kootenay region. Highly skinnydippable.
Elevation gain and loss: 200 ft/61 m.
Trailhead elevation: 4,600 ft/1,402 m.
High point: Hot springs, 4,800 ft/1,463 m.
Hiking quads: Kaslo 82F/15 and Dewar Creek 82F/16 NTS.
Road map: Cranbrook Forest District.

Finding the trailhead: From Cranbrook, take Highway 95A north to Marysville (one stop before Kimberly). Turn left on St. Mary Lake Road and head west past the lake, where pavement turns to gravel. The main road follows the St. Mary River, curving northwest past a side road at Redding Creek.

When you reach another road branching left signed "West Fork St. Mary Road," about thirty-five mi/fifty-six km from Marysville, bear right on Dewar Creek Road. Head northward up the main valley on a deteriorating surface that peters out in five mi/eight km in a meadowed camping area. Neither the path nor the hot springs are marked on the maps.

The challenge: The geothermal display at Dewar Creek is guaranteed to take your breath away—both the steaming springs and the wild setting are visually stunning. But the access to this remote fairyland can be a different story, as is the problem of blending temperatures for a proper soak.

Both the roads and the trail are subject to spring washouts, and visitors should check with the Park Service before setting out. The roads get progressively rougher even when intact; it's also a bit of a navigational challenge to follow them. The path isn't too difficult in dry weather but becomes a quagmire when damp.

There's an intriguing discrepancy regarding trail length. The trailhead register gives a round-trip figure of eleven mi/eighteen km. BC Parks say they've consistently told people it's twelve mi/19.3 km. The high bid, excluding one at sixteen mi/twenty-six km from an unofficial source, comes from the Ministry of Forests in Cranbrook, which claims it's a total of fourteen mi/22.5 km round trip. Take your pick!

The hike: The Dewar Creek Trail into the Purcell Wilderness Conservancy can be found west of the clearing. The path plunges into a twilight forest of Douglas-fir and Engelmann Spruce dotted with stands of aspen and birch.

You'll soon cross a major stream on a footbridge, then continue through woods along the east bank of Dewar Creek. Many small side streams intersect the route, and the ground tends to stay damp. Huge puddles of ankle-

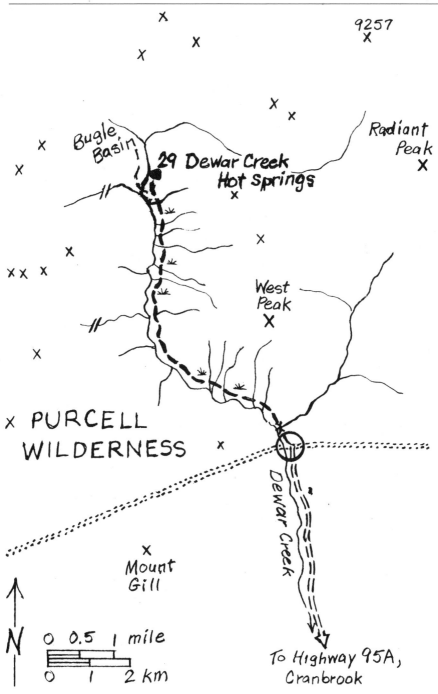

Bugle Basin

29 Dewar Creek Hot Springs

Radiant Peak
X

9257
X

West Peak
X

X PURCELL
WILDERNESS

Dewar Creek

X
Mount
Gill

N

0   0.5   1 mile

0   1   2 km

To Highway 95A,
Cranbrook

The scalding source pools on the travertine bluff at Dewar are for display purposes only.

deep mud alternate with meadows laced with blue lupine and pale pink paintbrush. The path eventually emerges onto a broad promontory opposite the climbers route to Leaning Towers.

Camping isn't allowed at the hot springs, but there's a campsite at Bugle Basin on a bench above the creek, just a five-minute walk upstream. A rock outcrop there is a good spot to observe wildlife in the early mornings.

The hot springs: The bluff is shrouded by billowing clouds of steam. Tendrils of 180-degree F/82-degree C water issue from a multitude of fractures in the travertine and drop over the rocky bank into a small pool at the base. Meanwhile, ice-cold creek water enters between the rocks that dam the outer edge. As a consequence, one side of you will be roasting while the other side freezes, and the hot and cold currents don't stay blended without constant stirring. There's no siesta time in this pool—staying comfortable is a full-time job!

In winter, thermal heating around the springs creates a hole in the surrounding blanket of deep snow, and special plants and lichen keep the area green all year. Deer and elk are attracted to the tender shoots, and an occasional mountain goat scrambles by to sample the mineral licks.

The springs are spectacular any time of year, but the prime time for a soak is around mid-August. Before then the streamside soaking pool might still be partly submerged, and by September it could be high and dry. With an icy torrent on one side and a waterfall of scalding water on the other, there's not much room for error!

30 Ram Creek Hot Springs

General description: Warm pools on a hillside above a dirt road in the East Kootenay region, north of Cranbrook. Swimwear advised. Elevation 4,800 ft/1,463 m.

Map: Invermere or Cranbrook Forest District.

Finding the hot springs: From Cranbrook, take Highway 93/95 about thirty mi/forty-eight km north to Skookumchuck. Turn right just past town on Premier Lake Road and bear left in about five mi/eight km. Turn right in another mile/1.6 km and cross the Lussier River bridge.

At a cattleguard, turn right on a dirt road signed "White-Ram" and follow it 6.7 mi/10.8 km, or a total of thirteen mi/twenty-one km from the highway, to a pullout at a sharp turn. Park here and follow the track uphill to the pools. Those wishing to camp nearby will find a clearing in the woods on either side of the road a few bends back downhill. The hot springs, designated an ecological reserve, aren't marked on the forest map.

Daisies speckle the hillside above the soaking pool at Ram Creek.

The hot springs: Users have dug out a waist-deep pool around twenty ft/six m in diameter in a grassy slope by the springs. The pool is dammed with rocks and has a sandy bottom. Water emerges at 94 degrees F/34.6 degrees C from several fissures along the bank above and fills the main pool as well as a smaller one attached to the upper end. Poison ivy thrives on the slopes above the springs, and daisies carpet the landscape.

Road note: White-Ram Road continues to an intersection. The right fork goes to Top of the World Park (see following hike), and the left fork goes north to Whiteswan Park and Lussier Hot Springs before returning to the highway near Canal Flats. A loop drive can thus be made combining the two roadside dips with a hike in both parks, with a total driving distance of about seventy-seven mi/123 km, mostly on gravel. The loop to just the hot springs would total about fifty-eight mi/ninety-three km.

HIKE 30a *Fish Lake*

General description: An easy, 7.5-mi/twelve-km round-trip day hike or over-nighter to a popular lake in a park high in the Kootenay Ranges of the Rocky Mountains, near Ram Creek Hot Springs.
Elevation gain and loss: +700 ft/212 m, -250 ft/76 m.
Trailhead elevation: 5,450 ft/1,661 m.
High point: 5,800 ft/1,768 m at Fish Lake.
Hiking quads: Queen Creek 82G/14 NTS or Top of the World Park brochure.
Road map: Cranbrook Forest District or park brochure.

Finding the trailhead: Follow the directions above to Ram Creek Hot Springs and continue 3.5 mi/5.6 km to the upper end of White-Ram Road. Turn right on the gravel Lussier River Road and drive 9.3 mi/fifteen km south to the parking lot and trail sign in Top of the World Provincial Park. The current trails aren't marked on the NTS quad.

The hike: Whether it was the vaguely fish-shaped outline on the map that inspired the name or the abundance of Dolly Varden and cutthroat trout, Fish Lake it became. Popular with anglers and hikers alike, it offers scenic tent-sites along the shore and a log cabin for overnight rental. Alpine peaks encircle the small lake, and side trips lead to higher viewpoints.

Two paths follow the Lussier River upstream to Fish Lake. The hiker's route parallels the west bank and a horse/ski trail takes the east bank. The latter, although muddy and rough, has one major drawing card—a short side trip to Crazy River and Crazy Creek, two streams that bubble up from subterranean channels.

One can follow the hiker's path to the midway point near Sayles Meadow, then bridge the river and take the horse/ski trail to pass "the Crazies" on the final stretch. The paths merge just below the lake, and the 1.2-mi/two-km Lakeshore Trail circles the shoreline, offering a variety of views across the lake, glimpses of peaks beyond, and other routes to explore.

HIKE 30a *Fish Lake*

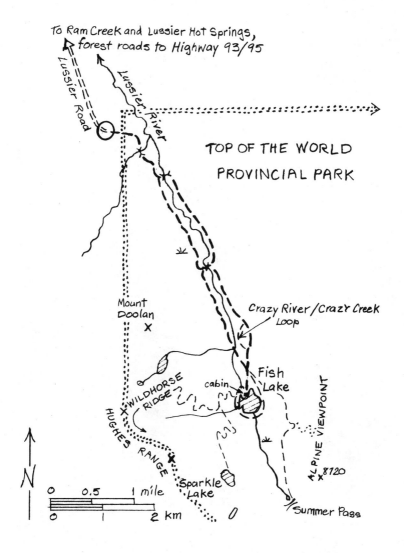

To Ram Creek and Lussier Hot Springs, forest roads to Highway 93/95

Lussier Road

Lussier River

TOP OF THE WORLD PROVINCIAL PARK

Mount Doolan X

Crazy River/Crazy Creek Loop

WILDHORSE RIDGE

cabin

Fish Lake

ALPINE VIEWPOINT

HUGHES RANGE

N

0   0.5   1 mile

0   1   2 km

Sparkle Lake

Summer Pass

X 8120

The shoreline at Fish Lake offers glimpses across the silvered surface.

Options: From the south shore, one 2.5-mi/four-km trail climbs alpine meadows to Summer Pass with a gain of 1,410 ft/430 m. Nearby, a two-mi/3.2-km scramble on scree slopes gains nearly 2,000 ft/600 m to Alpine Viewpoint and offers panoramic views of the Lussier Valley as well as Mount Morro. The 9,554-ft/2,912-m peak (the highest point in the park) dominates the Van Nostrand Range to the east.

From the west shore, a 1.7-mi/2.8-km path climbs to Sparkle Lake with a

HOT SPRINGS 30 *Ram Creek Hot Springs*
HOT SPRINGS 31 *Lussier Hot Springs*
HIKE 31a *Whiteswan Lake*

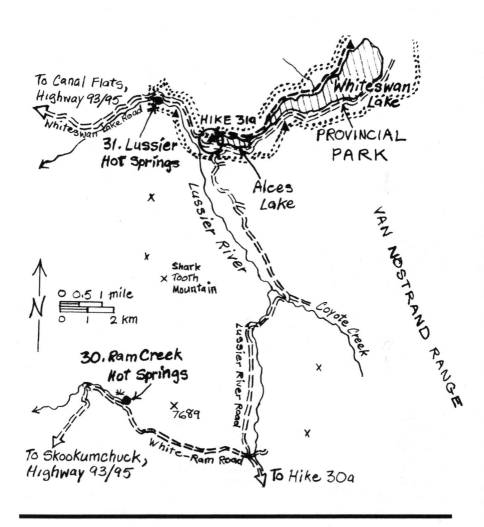

To Canal Flats,
Highway 93/95

Whiteswan Lake Road

31. Lussier
Hot Springs

HIKE 31a

Whiteswan
Lake

PROVINCIAL
PARK

Alces
Lake

Lussier River

VAN NOSTRAND RANGE

Shark
x Tooth
Mountain

N

0 0.5 1 mile

0   1   2 km

Lussier River Road

Coyote Creek

30. Ram Creek
Hot Springs

x
7689

x

x

x

To Skookumchuck,
Highway 93/95

White-Ram Road

To Hike 30a

gain of 1,148 ft/350 m, while an offshoot zigzags two mi/3.2 km up to Wildhorse
Ridge. The stiff 3,000-ft/640-m gain is offset by views of nearby Dolomite Lake
backed by Mount Doolan to the north plus jagged peaks of the Hughes Range
to the west.

31 Lussier Hot Springs

General description: Easy-access riverside soaks in the East Kootenay region, north of Cranbrook in Whiteswan Lake Provincial Park. Swimwear required by park rules. Elevation 4,000 ft/1,219 m.
Map: Cranbrook Forest District.

Finding the hot springs: The most direct route to Lussier is to take Highway 93/95 north from Cranbrook to Whiteswan Lake Road, located about nineteen mi/thirty km past Skookumchuck (the turnoff to Ram Creek Hot Springs) and three mi/4.8 km south of Canal Flats. Drive 10.5 dusty mi/seventeen km east into tiny Whiteswan Lake Provincial Park. The signed parking turnout is just inside the park boundary, and a covered stairway drops down the steep bank to the riverside pools.

The alternate route, a loop drive combining Ram Creek and Lussier Hot Springs, can be found by following the directions and road note in 30 above past Ram Creek to the Lussier River Road. Turn left and follow the gravel logging road 9.5 mi/15.2 km north, passing extensive clearcuts, to Whiteswan Lake Road. You'll find several developed campgrounds in the park. Go left for two mi/3.2 km to Lussier. The springs aren't marked on the forest map.

The hot springs: A chain of rock-lined soaking pools can be found along a gravel beach on the scenic Lussier River. All have comfortable sandy bottoms and are kept clean by the ample flow of the springs. The popular pools are

At Lussier Hot Springs, a chain of pools emerges through the summer months as the river level drops.

accessible all year thanks to the logging trucks, and the uppermost pool should normally be above water even during spring runoff.

The springs bubble first into a small wooden hot tub that registers 110 degrees F/43.3 degrees C, then flow beneath a deck into a large 106-degree F /41-degree C soaking pool. The outflow, tempered by a trickle from a cold spring, fills another large soaker just below. Succeeding pools, each slightly cooler than the one above, emerge as the river recedes through the summer.

HIKE 31a *Whiteswan Lake*

General description: An easy lakeshore stroll, up to seven mi/11.2 km round-trip, in a tiny park in the Kootenay Ranges of the Rocky Mountains, near Lussier Hot Springs.
Elevation gain and loss: Minimal.
High point: 4,000 ft/1,219 m.
Hiking quads: Canal Flats 82J/4 and Mount Peck 82J/3 NTS or Whiteswan Lake Park printout.
Road map: Cranbrook Forest District.

Finding the trailhead: Follow the directions above to Lussier and drive two mi/3.2 km east to the junction of Whiteswan Lake and the Lussier River Road. The trailhead is located in nearby Alces Lake Campground.

Moose can often be seen browsing at Whiteswan Lake.

The hike: Whiteswan Lake nestles in a small but popular provincial park that offers pleasant mountain scenery and excellent fishing. The 2.5-mile /four-km long lake, together with tiny Alces Lake, are stocked annually with 30,000 rainbow trout. Several family campgrounds accommodate the weekend crowds, and a fisherman's path skirts the north shores of both lakes.

The lakeshore route begins at the west end of Alces Lake and hugs the rocky shore to a picnic site at the far end, then follows the meadowed inlet stream to the larger lake. One can look back past Alces to rugged Shark Tooth Mountain and other peaks across the Lussier Valley.

Whiteswan Lake sits just below White Knight Peak, but the upper slopes can't be seen from the trail. Looking south, the route offers increasing glimpses of the Van Nostrand Range. You'll pass a boater's camp about midway along, and the path ends at Home Basin Campground at the northeast tip of the lake.

32 Fording Mountain Warm Springs

HIKE 32a *To Fording Mountain Warm Springs*

General description: An easy two-mi/3.2-km, round-trip walk to a thermal pond in the Elk River Valley, northeast of Cranbrook in the East Kootenay region. Swimwear advised if others present.
Elevation gain and loss: Minimal.
Warm Springs: 4,100 ft/1,250 m.
Hiking quad: Tornado Mountain 82G/15 NTS (optional).
Road map: Cranbrook Forest District.

Finding the trailhead: From Cranbrook, take Highway 3 about seventy- eight miles/125 km to Sparwood and continue on Highway 43. Make a right turn about midway between Sparwood and Elkford and bridge the confluence of the Elk and Fording Rivers. The final approach up the Elk River Valley is via a series of active and inactive logging roads. Contact the Forest Service in Cranbrook or the logging camp in Sparwood regarding the current route. The maps can't keep pace with the changing roads, and the springs aren't marked either.

The hike: The last one-mi/1.6-km stretch is over an old road that's now closed to motor vehicles. It leads through an evergreen forest to meadowed slopes above the Elk River. The route emerges near the springs at the upper end of a clearing. There's a small campground just beyond the springs and a view across the river valley to mountain ranges farther west.

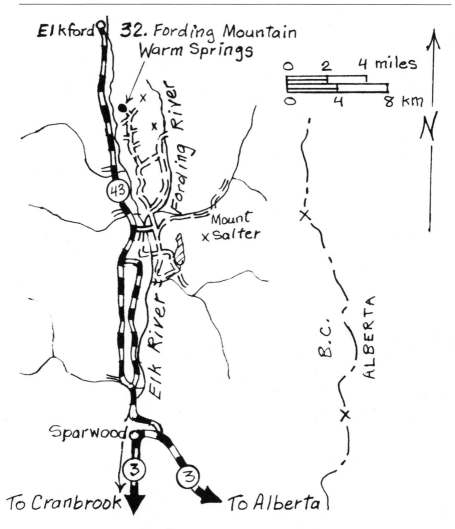

The warm springs: One spring emerges from at least two outlets at the bottom of a large oval-shaped pond. Unfortunately, the temperature hovers around 76 degrees F/24.4 degrees C, but the pond looks like a classic swimming hole and even sports a diving board. The outflow snakes across the meadow, and a second spring bubbles to the surface at 78 degrees F/25.5 degrees C two bends downstream.

Fording Mountain Warm Springs (known locally as Sulphur Springs) has a very high sulphur content and the associated smell of rotten eggs. The highly mineralized water attracts a variety of wildlife, and one can sometimes see moose, deer, and elk grazing nearby. The poplar-lined meadow, a pleasant spot to pitch a tent, doesn't see many visitors.

HOT SPRINGS IN IDAHO

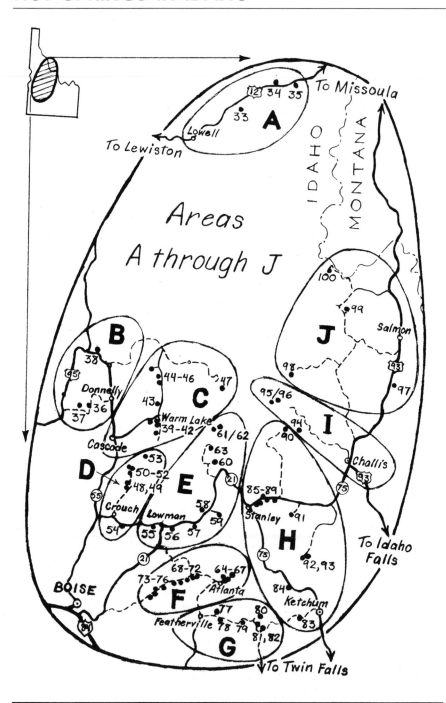

IDAHO

An Overview

It just so happens that the state of Idaho contains more than twice the number of geothermal gems than the thirty-two described in Oregon, Washington, and British Columbia put together! The sixty-eight shown on the Idaho Locator Map are all located in prime hiking areas in national forests. Nearly a third lie either near the edge or well within the boundaries of protected wilderness areas. And yet, surprisingly few backcountry buffs visit the "Potato State." Even the spectacular Sawtooths, congested by Idaho's standards, seem deserted to hikers accustomed to fighting the summer crowds in the Cascades or Olympics.

Compared to Oregon and Washington, the backcountry of Idaho is far less developed. Few forest roads are paved, many involve the time-consuming process of skirting rocks and potholes, and most cover vast distances in an endless cloud of dust.

Campgrounds are mostly undeveloped and still free. The hikes often involve wading, log balancing, or rock hopping across unbridged streams. But Idaho's hot springs make up for any minor inconvenience. Most get relatively little use or abuse, and those reached by the longer access roads or located a few miles up a trail see few visitors at all.

Access Areas A through J

Idaho's best bubblies are found in the central mountain ranges. They're grouped here by similar road access into the ten sections shown on the locator map. These sections are defined by approach routes rather than by political or wilderness boundaries so that the greedy gourmet with limited time may sample several on the same trip.

A tiny north-central area, covered in the first section of text (A), is found between Lewiston and Missoula via U.S. Highway 12. It lies along the Lochsa River in Clearwater National Forest. One of the three hot springs here is tucked away in the Selway-Bitterroot Wilderness.

A west-central area, covered in the next six sections (B through G), is reached north and northeast of Boise, respectively, via State Routes 55 and 21, and northeast of Mountain Home by U.S. Highway 20. It includes all of the backcountry west of the Sawtooth crest and extends north into the southwestern quarter of the River of No Return Wilderness. Outside of the two wildlands, the hot soaks and hikes are found in the rolling mountains of Payette, Boise, and Sawtooth national forests.

An east-central area, covered in the final three sections (H through J), is accessed north of Twin Falls via State Route 75 and northwest of Pocatello and Idaho Falls by U.S. Highway 93. It consists mainly of the eastern side of the Sawtooth range and the Sawtooth National Recreation Area (Sawtooth NRA), plus the eastern half of the River of No Return Wilderness and adjacent mountains. This rugged country is administered by Sawtooth, Challis, and Salmon national forests.

At the beginning of each of the ten sections, you'll find a summary of the hot springs, the hikes, and the season. Here you'll also find an Area Map marking all the hot springs and hikes as well as the back roads, ranger stations, land features, etc.

Wilderness hot springs and hikes

Central Idaho is composed of a mountainous mass, fully 100 miles wide and 300 miles long, etched by deep river canyons. The Selway-Bitterroot Wilderness forms the northern third of this spine, and the vast River of No Return fills in most of the remainder. The combined wildland is among the most pristine areas left in the lower forty-eight states. Whitewater float trips are the main drawing card, and the hiking trails are scarcely touched outside of hunting season. The scenery for the most part is subtle compared to the jagged Sawtooths to the south. The canyons are dotted with sagebrush and ponderosa pine up to around 7,000 feet, while forests of spruce and fir dominate the higher elevations.

The Selway-Bitterroot Wilderness, with over 1.3 million acres, covers four national forests. From the adjacent River of No Return to the south, it stretches north almost to U.S. Highway 12. Hikes 33a-b climb to steamy pools and remote lakes in the northwestern corner, and Hikes 35a-c lead to easy-access soaks farther east plus a dip into the wilderness beyond.

The 2.3-million acre Frank Church-River of No Return Wilderness spreads out through six national forests and forms the largest designated wildland in the lower forty-eight states. Near the northern boundary, the mountains are bisected by the Salmon River Canyon—the second deepest gorge in North America (Hells Canyon is the deepest). It was dubbed "The River of No Return" by a National Geographic party in 1935 because of its steep walls and many rapids. Farther south, the 100-mile long Middle Fork Salmon River carves the third deepest gorge, bisecting the wilderness in its journey northward to the Main Salmon.

A surprising number of virtually unknown hot springs lie concealed along the Middle Fork and its many tributaries. As the few access roads are far apart, the trips are grouped for the traveler's convenience into separate sections. Only one of these far-flung gems (63) can be found near a road; the other nine are reached by the following hikes: 47a, 60a, 61/62a, 90a, 94a, 95/96a, and 98a. With few exceptions, they exact their toll in the form of long dusty roads and lengthy "upside-down" treks that start on top of a mountain and wind up at the bottom.

Just south of the canyon country of the River of No Return rise the alpine peaks of the Sawtooth Wilderness, filling 217,000 prime acres of the Sawtooth NRA. The Sawtooths draw hikers along 300 miles of well tended paths through an intricate landscape of colorful granite shaped into countless needle-edged spires, peaks, and ridges. Small lakes and streams are fringed with postage stamp meadows lush with wildflowers and forests of spruce, fir, and pine. The area boasts more than forty-two peaks reaching over 10,000 feet.

The Sawtooths contain only one known hike-in hot spring (67a). But they also offer several roadside ones not far from major trailheads. On the east side of the range, hot dips found in the Sawtooth NRA (85-89) may be alternated with popular hikes into the high country (85a-c). On the west side, trailhead bubblies and less congested paths out of Grandjean (59a-b) and Atlanta (66a-c) do much to make up for the extra mileage on both tires and boots.

FOR MORE INFORMATION

Visitors should contact the following Forest Service district offices for updates on hot springs, road and trail conditions, stream crossings, etc. If the receptionist can't answer your questions, ask for the recreation officer. Maps may be purchased here, and most districts offer free trail printouts.

Hot Springs 33 and Hikes 33a,b: Lochsa Ranger District, Clearwater National Forest, Route 1, P.O. Box 398, Kooskia, ID 83539; 208/926-4275.

Hot Springs 34,35 and Hikes 35a-c: Powell Ranger District, Clearwater National Forest, Highway 12 at Powell Junction, (mail): Lolo, MT 59847; 208/942-3113.

Hot Springs 36,37 and Hike 37a: Council Ranger District, Payette National Forest, P.O. Box 567, Council, ID 83612; 208/253-4215.

Hot Spring 38: New Meadows Ranger District, Payette National Forest, New Meadows, ID 83654; 208/347-2141.

Hot Springs 39-43 and Hike 42a: Cascade Ranger District, Boise National Forest, P.O. Box 696, Cascade, ID 83611; 208/382-4271.

Hot Springs 44-46 and Hikes 44a,b; 46a: Krassel Ranger District, Payette National Forest, P.O. Box 1026, McCall, ID 83638; 208/634-0600.

Hot Spring 47 and Hike 47a: Middle Fork Ranger District, Challis National Forest, P.O. Box 750, Challis, ID 83226; 208/879-5204.

Hot Springs 48-54 and Hikes 51/52a; 53a,b: Emmett Ranger District, Boise National Forest, 1648 North Washington, Emmett,ID 83617; 208/365-4382. Or check at the Garden Valley Ranger Station.

Hot Springs 55-59 and Hikes 56a,b: Lowman Ranger District, Boise National Forest, HC-77, P.O. Box 3020, Lowman, ID 83637; 208/259-3361.

Hikes 59a,b: Sawtooth NRA, Star Route (Highway 75), Ketchum, ID 83340; 208/726-7672. Or check at the Stanley Ranger Station south of town.

Hot Springs 60 and Hikes 60a,b: Middle Fork District (see 47 above).

Hot Springs 61-63 and Hike 61/62a: Middle Fork District (see 47 above). Or check at the Boundary Creek Guard Station at the trailhead.

Hot Springs 64-66: Boise Ranger District, Boise National Forest, 5493 Warm Springs Ave., Boise, ID 83712; 208/343-2527.

Hikes 66a-c: Sawtooth NRA (see Hike 59 above).

Hot Spring 67 and Hike 67a: Sawtooth NRA (see Hike 59 above).

Hot Springs 68-76: Boise District (see 64-66 above).

Hot Springs 77-82 and Hikes 79a; 80a: Fairfield Ranger District, Sawtooth National Forest, P.O. Box 189, Fairfield, ID 83327; 208/764-2202.

Hot Springs 83 and Hikes 84a, b: Ketchum Ranger District, Sawtooth National Forest, Sun Valley Road, P.O. Box 2356, Ketchum, ID 83340; 208/622-5371.

Hot Springs 84-89 and Hikes 85a-c: Sawtooth NRA (see Hike 59 above).

Hot Springs 90 and Hike 90a: Middle Fork District (see 47 above).

Hot Springs 91-93 and Hikes 91a;93a: Sawtooth NRA (see Hike 59 above).

Hot Springs 94-96 and Hikes 94a; 95/96a: Middle Fork District (see 47 above).

Hot Springs 97 and Hike 97a: Salmon Ranger District, Salmon National Forest, P.O. Box 729, Salmon, ID 83467; 208/756-3724.

Hot Springs 98,99 and Hikes 98a,b: Cobalt Ranger District, Salmon National Forest, P.O. Box 729, Salmon, ID 83467; 208/756-2240. Or check at the Cobalt Guard Station on the way in (208/756-3221).

Hot Spring 100: North Fork Rnager District, Salmon National Forest, P.O. Box 180, North Fork, Id 83466; 208/865-2383.

A. OUT OF LOWELL

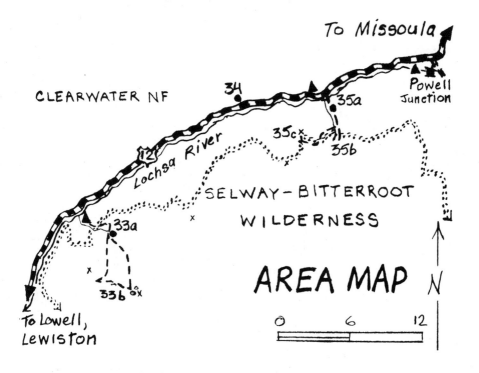

Note: Lowell offers only the most basic services to travelers.

Hot springs and hikes

U.S. Highway 12 bisects north-central Idaho between Lewiston, on the west edge, and Missoula, across the Montana border to the east. It follows the Lochsa River through lush Clearwater Forest to an area spanning the sixty-five miles between Lowell and Powell Junction. A quiet trail in the Selway-Bitterroot Wilderness leads to hot soaks at Stanley (33a) and continues with a rugged backcountry loop. Twenty miles up the highway comes a toasty soak at Weir Creek (34). And ten miles on up the road, a stroll to the ever-popular Jerry Johnson (35a) mixes well with hikes into the wilderness beyond.

Hot soaks at Stanley are best on cooler days from late spring through fall. The streamside path to Weir Creek limits access during spring runoff. Jerry Johnson, however, has easy access on packed snow through the winter and the uppermost pools are usable year around. The hiking season is normally late July through September for the high-elevation climbs beyond the hot springs. Summer weather tends to be hot, and thunderstorms are fairly common.

---

33 Stanley Hot Springs

HIKE 33a *To Stanley Hot Springs*

General description: A moderate eleven-mile, round-trip day hike or overnighter featuring secluded soakers in an age-old forest, east of Lewiston in the Selway-Bitterroot Wilderness. Swimwear superfluous baggage.
Elevation gain and loss: +1,620 feet, -120 feet.
Trailhead elevation: 2,100 feet.
High point: Stanley, 3,600 feet.
Hiking quad: Huckleberry Butte USGS or Selway-Bitterroot Wilderness (Forest Service).
Road map: Wilderness quad or Clearwater National Forest.

Soaking pools at Stanley offer hikers a quiet retreat from the cares of the world.

Finding the trailhead: Drive twenty-six miles northeast of Lowell on U.S. Highway 12 to Wilderness Gateway Campground. Go past Loops A and B, and the amphitheater, to Trail 211 parking area. The springs are marked on the forest and USGS maps but not on the wilderness map.

The hike: The well-tended path climbs a few switchbacks and then traverses a hillside well above Boulder Creek to enter the Selway-Bitterroot Wilderness in about two miles. The elevated route provides a number of pleasant views up and down the wide valley. Bracken fern and thimbleberries line the path and cover the surrounding slopes between islands of Douglas-fir and pines.

At a signed trail junction in five miles, take the right fork (221) marked "to Maude and Lottie Lakes". The path drops downhill to cross Boulder Creek on a rustic but sturdy log pack bridge and enters a dark forest with a plush green carpet. Continue south along the edge of Huckleberry Creek and you'll find the soaking pools in a large clearing above the trail just beyond a couple of campsites.

The hot springs: Water steams out of a canyon bank, tumbles through a chain of delectable hot pools lined with giant logs, then continues down past the trail to the creek below. The bubblies come in all sizes and shapes and range in temperature from 90 to 110 degrees. Spacious campsites tucked into the nearby woods make this an inviting overnight stay or a good base camp for the Seven Lakes Loop (Hike 33b).

HIKE 33b *Stanley Hot Springs to the Seven Lakes Loop*

General description: A rugged eighteen-mile, loop backpack from the hot springs to a group of lonesome lakes in the rugged backcountry of the Selway-Bitterroot Wilderness.
Elevation gain and loss: 3,880 feet.
Trailhead elevation: 3,600 feet at Stanley Hot Springs.
High point: 6,800 feet.
Maps: Same as Hike 33a plus Greenside Butte USGS.

Finding the trailhead: Follow Hike 33a to Stanley Hot Springs.

The hike: A group of "sister" lakes clusters together in a remote neighborhood of wooded ridges and peaks at the end of a lengthy side trip from the hot springs. Included in the family are lovely-but-lonesome Lottie, misunderstood Maude (left without a name when hers was given by mistake to another), and a clinging group of spinster sisters called The Seven Lakes. They don't get much company out here and welcome overnight guests with open-meadowed arms.

To pay them a call, walk south a short distance from Stanley to a junction. Take the right fork (221), a seldom maintained path signed "to Lottie and Maude Lakes." The route zigzags south up a densely forested ridge with a steady gain of 2,800 feet in eight miles, then drops 280 feet in the last 0.25 mile to a second junction.

Turn left (east) and follow a main trail (220) that skirts sky-blue Lottie Lake in 0.5 mile followed shortly by the real Maude Lake. The lake misnamed

HIKE 33a   *To Stanley Hot Springs*
HIKE 33b   *Stanley Hot Springs to the Seven Lakes Loop*

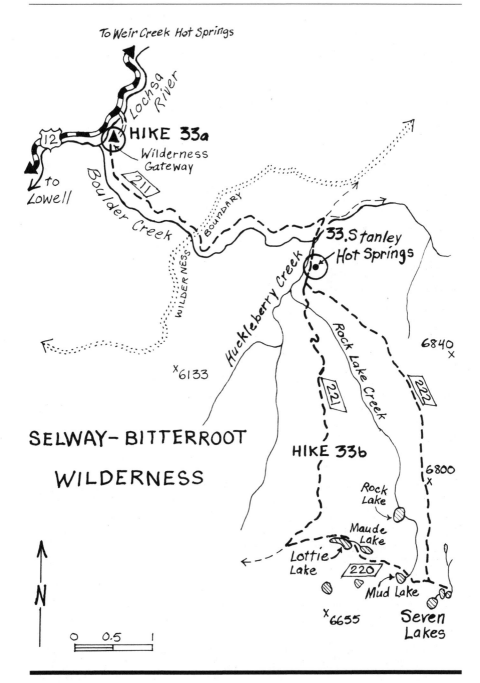

To Weir Creek Hot Springs

Lochsa River

12

to Lowell

HIKE 33a

Wilderness Gateway

211

Boulder Creek

WILDERNESS BOUNDARY

33. Stanley Hot Springs

Huckleberry Creek

X 6133

Rock Lake Creek

6840 X

221

222

SELWAY- BITTERROOT

WILDERNESS

HIKE 33b

6800 X

Rock Lake

Maude Lake

Lottie Lake

220

Mud Lake

X 6655

Seven Lakes

N

0   0.5   1

Maude on all the maps hides her face beneath a 6,655-foot peak south of Lottie. Climb over a low saddle to pass Mud Lake (stuck with an unenviable name) in a shallow basin off to the right. A short distance beyond the outlet comes another junction. Bear right here to reach the Seven Lakes in a total of ten miles.

Two of the lakes lie alongside the trail. Low ridges and rocky knolls separate the smaller lakes and ponds in the group and conceal a variety of attractive campsites. The largest lake (at 6,484 feet) is tucked away a quarter-mile to the south. A tiny island breaks the surface, and high walls rim the southern edge of the wide basin.

For the third leg of the loop, retrace your steps to the last junction. Take the right fork (222) following a seldom used route due north. As the path climbs high above Rock Creek Canyon, the views get broader and broader. You'll pass Rock Lake 600 feet below and finally reach the highest point on the hike (a crest at 6,800 feet with a 360-degree panorama of lakes and mountains) two miles above the Seven Lakes.

The path continues north and then northwest, mostly through dense woods, with a punishing plunge of 3,200 feet in the final six miles back to Stanley. Enjoy a well earned soak before retracing the 5.5 miles back to the trailhead at Wilderness Gateway Campground.

34 Weir Creek Hot Springs

General description: A quiet soaking pool cloaked in greenery at the end of a 0.5-mile creekside path, east of Lewiston. Swimwear optional. Elevation 2,900 feet.
Map: Clearwater National Forest.

Finding the hot springs: Drive about forty-five miles northeast of Lowell on U.S. Highway 12. Park in a pullout along the Lochsa River just east of Milepost 142 at the bridge over Weir Creek. Follow a twisting and sometimes slippery path up the west side of the creek to reach the pool, staying on the route closest to the creek. The springs are marked on the forest map, but the path isn't shown.

The hot springs: A delightful bather-built pool, bordered by split logs, sits under a canopy of evergreens above a lively creek. The water is constantly cleaned by an ample flow from the 117-degree springs, and the temperature can be fine tuned with the aid of a removable wooden gutter. There's a second pool nearby, and the runoff flows down the steep rocks through a third pool and from there to one or more shallow dips by the edge of the creek. A hot springer's dream come true!

"Key-note": I returned to my locked car after a dip to discover the key still hanging in the ignition! No way in short of breaking a window, eighty miles from the nearest town, the sun sinking fast, and my camping gear in plain view but out of reach. Just when I'd absorbed these cold facts, a passing motorist came to the rescue. With a piece of fence wire bent into a loop, he fished for the doorlock-pull through a slit in the window while I pulled down on the glass. He managed to ring it after several misses, but the loop slid off the slick-

Couples can enjoy quiet moments to themselves by the secluded pool at Weir Creek Hot Springs.

sided pull as soon as he tugged, thanks to modern burglarproof engineering. By this time I'd lost all hope, but not so my determined new friend. He eventually succeeded in hooking the key ring itself, maneuvered it out of the ignition, and inched it out through the slit in the window! We drank an immediate toast to success with the cold beer liberated from my cooler.

35 Jerry Johnson Hot Springs

HIKE 35a *To Jerry Johnson Hot Springs*

General description: An easy two-mile round-trip stroll to soaker-full pools in a scenic valley, east of Lewiston. A skinnydipper's delight.
Elevation gain and loss: 150 feet.
Trailhead elevation: 3,050 feet.
High point: Jerry Johnson, 3,200 feet.
Hiking quad: Selway-Bitterroot Wilderness (Forest Service).
Road map: Same or Clearwater National Forest.

Finding the trailhead: Take U.S. Highway 12 about fifty-five miles northeast of Lowell (or 10.5 miles southwest of Powell Junction) to Warm Springs Pack Bridge, which spans the Lochsa River 0.5 mile west of Milepost 152. There's ample parking nearby, but make sure to get your gear out of sight

At Jerry Johnson, social animals often debate the issues of the day over a morning soak.

and lock up. "Car clouting" has long been a problem here. The springs are marked on the forest map but not on the wilderness quad.

The hike: Three separate hot springs, each with two or more soaking pools, lie near a creek in a broad valley forested with stately old-growth cedar and grand fir. Cross the pack bridge to the sign for Warm Springs Creek Trail (49). A second sign posted on a nearby tree states a warning that unclothed bathers or hikers may be found beyond this point. And such is indeed the case at "J.J." Follow the sneaker-worn path a short mile upvalley to the springs.

The hot springs: The first batch of rock-lined soakers, known to many as "the waterfall pools," are down the bank from the trail right at waterline. These are easy to miss if unoccupied. They need a creek water mix to drop into the comfort zone, as 115-degree water gushing from holes in the steep bank pours directly into one after the other.

You can't miss the next user-friendly group of pools. The broad outflow from the second spring crosses right over the trail en route to the creek. The hottest pool sits just above the path, and steamy rivulets lead over the rocks to more dips by the creek. These rocky pools vary in size and temperature, and it isn't hard to find one that's just right.

The third spring, a short way beyond the others in a grassy meadow above the trail, has two rock and mud soaking pools. One is over knee deep and large enough to float several cozy bodies; it maintains a steady 106 degrees without a mix from the creek. However, the silty bottom is easily stirred up. If you plan on climbing out clean, you'll have to find some means of doing it without standing up. Lots of luck!

Nighttime closure: Due to a variety of overuse and abuse problems arising from the year-round popularity of the springs, the Forest Service has been forced to turn Jerry Johnson into a day use area. Nocturnal visits and overnight camping are no longer permitted. The new rules, posted at the trailhead, are strictly enforced.

HIKE 35b *Jerry Johnson Hot Springs to The Falls*

General description: A moderate five-mile, round-trip day hike from the hot springs up the creek canyon on a quiet trail in Clearwater National Forest.
Elevation gain and loss: 800 feet.
Trailhead elevation: 3,200 feet at the hot springs.
High point: The Falls, 4,000 feet.
Maps: Same as Hike 35a.

Finding the trailhead: Follow Hike 35a to Jerry Johnson.

The hike: The valley bordering Warm Springs Creek rises to a modest overlook. The Falls are a chain of small dropoffs and pools—don't expect a classic waterfall. The view is obscured by trees and too distant to be impressive, but the route is a pleasant climb through old-growth woods.

Stroll a mile south from the hot springs on Warm Springs Creek Trail past a junction. Beyond this point the valley begins to narrow and the path switchbacks well above the east bank through deep forest. A brief detour around one side canyon adds a little variety. You'll reach the best overlook about 0.25 mile beyond the wilderness marker.

HIKE 35c *Jerry Johnson Hot Springs to Bear Mountain*

General description: A strenuous twelve-mile, round-trip day hike or overnighter from the hot springs to a mountaintop overlooking the Selway-Bitterroot Wilderness.
Elevation gain and loss: +4,160 feet, -200 feet.
Trailhead elevation: 3,200 feet at the hot springs.
High point: Bear Mountain Lookout, 7,184 feet.
Maps: Same as Hike 35a, or Bear Mountain and Tom Beal Peak USGS.

Finding the trailhead: Follow Hike 35a to Jerry Johnson.

The hike: A bird's-eye view of the Lochsa River canyon to the north and the Selway-Bitterroot Wilderness backcountry to the south is the reward for a nonstop uphill grind to the lookout tower capping Bear Mountain.

From the hot springs, walk a mile south on Warm Springs Creek Trail to a signed junction with McConnell Mountain Trail (213). Turn west, cross a pack bridge and zigzag up the ridge above Queen Creek. The route contours around

A short side trip from Jerry Johnson follows the creek to a series of drop-offs called the Falls.

an unnamed peak and then follows the wilderness boundary westward. It dips across a rocky saddle and rises to a junction at 7,000 feet just below the summit.

McConnell Mountain Trail drops south at this point, and a 0.5-mile spur covers the final, tapering stretch to the summit. There's a campsite near the junction, and a short path leads from the lookout spur to a spring with good water on the west side of Bear Mountain.

HIKE 35a *To Jerry Johnson Hot Springs*
HIKE 35b *Jerry Johnson Hot Springs to The Falls*
HIKE 35c *Jerry Johnson Hot Springs to Bear Mountain*

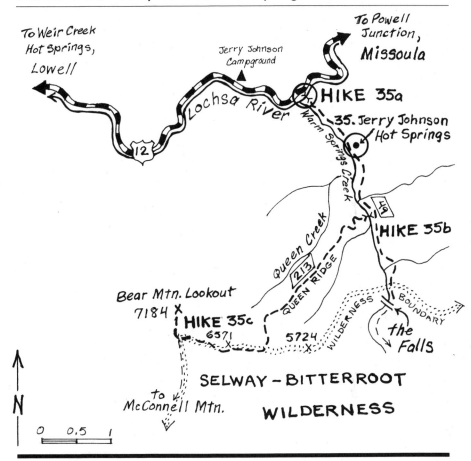

B. OUT OF DONNELLY

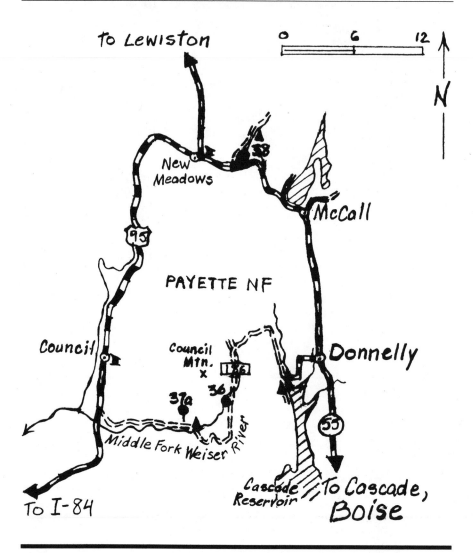

to Lewiston

0   6   12

N

New Meadows

95

PAYETTE NF

McCall

Council

Council Mtn. x

36

37a

36

Donnelly

55

Middle Fork Weiser River

To I-84

Cascade Reservoir

To Cascade, Boise

Hot springs and hikes

State Route 55 speeds north from Boise past Cascade (Section C) to the small town of Donnelly. To the west, a seasonal road along the Weiser River passes roadside baths at White Licks (36) and accesses a hike-in soak at Council Mountain (37a). North of town, a dirt road between McCall and New Meadows hits a soak at popular Krigbaum (38). All three reside in Payette National Forest.

Season

Winter road closures are the limiting factor on these springs. Soaks at Council

Mountain are best in cooler weather (as is the hike in) while bathing at White Licks is good any old time. Krigbaum's pool escapes spring runoff and can be reached in winter on cross-country skiis. The hiking season varies with elevation, and summer weather is generally warm to hot with scattered thundershowers.

36 White Licks Hot Springs

General Description: Roadside bathhouses in a popular camping area on the Middle Fork Weiser River, west of Donnelly. Wear what you normally bathe in. Elevation 4,900 feet.
Map: Payette National Forest.

Finding the hot springs: From Boise, take State Route 55 north to Donnelly, where seasonal roads cross the mountains to U.S. Highway 95. Head west on Roseberry Road, signed to Rainbow Point Campgrounds, then left on Norwood and right on Tamarack. Cross a bridge at Cascade Reservoir in four miles, where pavement ends. Turn right on a gravel road signed Council—34, then left in a mile on Forest Road 186. The route goes north, then west and south along the river, reaching White Licks four miles past Forest Road 245. The springs, signed by the road and named on the forest map, are about fifteen miles west of Donnelly or eighteen miles east of U.S. Highway 95.

The hot springs: Two small shacks, each housing a concrete bathing tub, sit in a grassy flat bordered by riverside woods. Each tub has two inlet pipes fed by the springs—one at 110 degrees and the other at 80 degrees. The bath temperature can be adjusted by plugging either pipe, and the tubs can be drained after use. The rustic bathhouses and primitive campground, on a parcel owned by Boise Cascade, are free of charge and maintained by users.

37 Council Mountain Hot Springs

HIKE 37a *To Council Mountain Hot Springs*

General description: A moderate four-mile round-trip day hike to hidden pools in a wooded ravine, west of Donnelly. Swimwear superfluous.
Elevation gain and loss: 720 feet.
Trailhead elevation: 3,760 feet.
High point: 4,480 feet at the hot springs.
Hiking quad: Council Mountain USGS.
Road map: Payette National Forest.

Finding the trailhead: Follow the directions above to White Licks and continue nine miles (two miles past Cabin Creek Campground). At Milepost

The highlight at Council Mountain is a bubbly Jacuzzi built for two.

9, you'll reach the trail sign by a small pullout. The springs, marked without a name on both maps, are a total of twenty-four miles west of Donnelly or nine miles east of U.S. Highway 95.

The hike: Warm Springs Trail (203) is a steep and steady climb above the east bank of Warm Springs Creek, but a canopy of ponderosa and Douglas-fir shades the way. Keep an eye out for rattlesnakes in the summertime. The creek forks two miles upstream, and here the path drops to cross and continue up the other side. The hot springs, with a telltale border of orange algae, cascade down the rocky bank at the crossing.

The hot springs: There's a choice of two pools in the bed of the creek. A shallow steamer at the base of the cascade checks in at 106 degrees, and the springs above are so hot that my digital thermometer stopped registering. A few yards downstream, the combined flow of hot and cold currents swirls down a slick waterslide into a bubbly Jacuzzi. This little gem registers around 92 degrees—just the ticket on a hot summer day.

38 Krigbaum Hot Spring

General description: A secluded soak above a forest road, north of Donnelly. Skinnydippable with discretion. Elevation 4,100 feet.
Map: Payette National Forest.

Finding the hot spring: From Donnelly, take State Route 55 twelve miles north to McCall and continue seven miles to Forest Road 453, signed to Last Chance Campground. Follow the dirt road for 0.5 mile or so up Goose Creek. Park by the bridge and take a short path up the east bank to the pool. Krigbaum

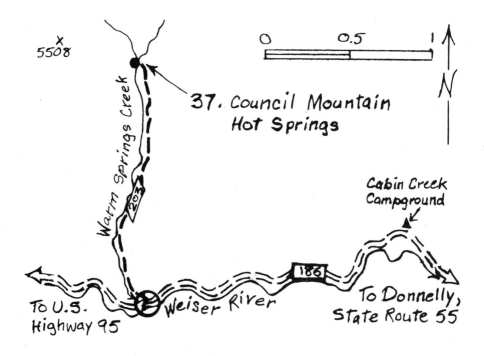

37. Council Mountain
Hot Springs

(also known as Last Chance) isn't marked on the forest map.

The hot spring: A curtain of creekside trees hides Krigbaum's soaking pool from the road. Spring water gushes from an overhead pipe into the rocky pool, and the ample flow keeps it clean. The soaker, enclosed between boulders on the bank above Goose Creek, is big enough to pack maybe half a dozen human sardines side by side. The temperature runs around 95-100 degrees.

This idyllic retreat gets heavily used through the summer months and sometimes shows signs of abuse. It's on a private plot surrounded by national forest. The pool can be reached and enjoyed virtually year around, and chances for a quiet soak are better in the off-season months. Please respect the land-owner's rights and pack out what you pack in.

Note to hikers: For a pleasant half-day outing, drive up to Last Chance Campground and take the Goose Creek Trail upstream to The Falls. It's a round trip of four miles that's easygoing except for a few stream fords.

C. OUT OF CASCADE & WARM LAKE

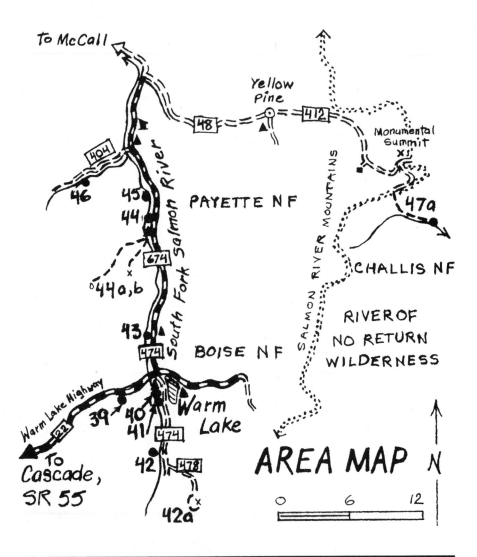

Hot springs and hikes

State Route 55 climbs north from Boise to Cascade. To the northeast, a paved road leads to a variety of easy-access soaks (39-43) on the South Fork Salmon River and a hike to Rice Peak, all in the Warm Lake area of Boise Forest. To the north are roadside hot pools (44-46) together with quiet trails in Payette Forest. And northeast of this area, a mad expedition into the River of No Return Wilderness plunges down a canyon to Kwiskwis Hot Spring (47a).

Season

The dips in the Warm Lake area can be reached by cross-country skiers from the Warm Lake Highway and should escape the river's grasp at high water, making them usable year-round. Penny's best before the river's too low, while Darling's Cabin requires a late-season ford. The remainder can be enjoyed whenever road access allows. The hiking season stretches from around mid-July through mid-October. Summer weather is generally hot with occasional thunderstorms.

39 Trail Creek Hot Spring

General description: Peekaboo pools and a bathtub in a wooded canyon below a highway, northeast of Cascade. Keep cutoffs handy. Elevation 5,900 feet.
Map: Boise National Forest.

Finding the hot springs: From State Route 55 at Cascade, take the Warm Lake Highway about nineteen miles northeast. Watch for a large pullout on your right at 0.4 mile east of Milepost 61. Slide down a slippery sixty-yard path from the west end to the canyon floor and up Trail Creek to the soaking pools. The spring isn't marked on the forest map.

The hot spring: A 115-degree spring spreads rivulets down a creek bank into

Trail Creek has acquired a bathtub set between the creek bottom pools. It's a welcome addition and hopefully will survive spring runoffs.

a few shallow pools. Between them perches a bathtub filled with steaming water fed in by a pipe. The temperature can be lowered by adding creek water, and a handy bucket (sometimes) sits nearby. The spot is visible from the west side of the pullout but just out of sight from passing motorists.

40 Molly's Tubs

General description: A bevy of bathtubs on the South Fork Salmon River hidden below a dirt road, northeast of Cascade. A swimsuit/birthday suit mix. Elevation 5,200 feet.
Map: Boise National Forest.

Finding the hot springs: From State Route 55 at Cascade, take the Warm Lake Highway about twenty-three miles northeast (3.7 miles past Trail Creek Hot Spring) to graded Forest Road 474. Drive south for 1.3 miles to a small pullout on your right and follow a short path down to the tubs. The spring isn't shown on the forest map.

The hot spring: Five brightly painted bathtubs lined up side by side, plus three more sitting just below, collect the flow from this spring with the aid of hoses which the user can move from one to another. River water may be added for a cooler soak. The tubs sit on raised platforms that span the muddy channel running from the spring to the nearby river. How civilized can a primitive hot spring get?

41 Molly's Hot Spring

General description: A soaker-friendly pool above the South Fork Salmon River located 0.25 mile from a dirt road, northeast of Cascade. Bathing suits optional. Elevation 5,300 feet.
Map: Boise National Forest.

Finding the hot springs: Follow the directions above to Forest Road 474 and go south 1.9 miles (0.6 mile past Molly's Tubs) to a junction. Park here and walk west on a road closed to motor vehicles that leads to the river and soon bridges it. Immediately past the bridge, hang a right on an overgrown path that meanders back downstream and up a short slope to the pool. Molly's isn't marked on the forest map.

The hot spring: Molly hides out behind a wall of evergreens far enough above the river to escape the spring runoff. Her 120-degree spring streams down the hillside past a square soaking box built directly over the flow, and the tub temperature can be lowered by diverting incoming pipes.
The soaking box is lined with plastic but, at last tally, the liner sadly needed

replacing and the box needed some TLC. There's a plywood platform to dry off on and a pleasant river view through the trees. Molly's has great potential—she just needs a helping hand!

Molly's "short cut": While enjoying a pleasant soak, I was joined by a friendly young couple. In the course of conversation, it turned out that the lady was a professional barber who just happened to have all the tools of her trade in their camper! An hour later, wrapped in a plastic apron with a towel around my neck, shears clicking and hair flying to the winds, I sat on a handy stump at their camp in a nearby meadow while she treated me to an expert trim.

Molly's Tubs, at last count, had five new bathtubs in addition to the three shown here.

HOT SPRINGS 39 *Trail Creek Hot Spring*
HOT SPRINGS 40 *Molly's Tubs*
HOT SPRINGS 41 *Molly's Hot Spring*
HOT SPRINGS 42 *Vulcan Hot Springs*
HOT SPRINGS 43 *Penny Hot Spring*

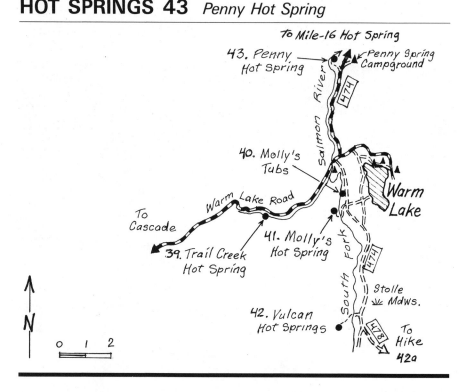

The hot spring that fills the pool at Molly's was once used to supply a nearby swimming pool, now in ruins, called the South Fork Plunge.

42 Vulcan Hot Springs

General description: A popular creek-wide soaker at the end of a 0.75-mile path, northeast of Cascade. Swimwear optional despite heavy use. Elevation 5,600 feet.
Map: Boise National Forest.

Finding the hot springs: Follow the directions to Forest Road 474 given in 40. Drive south about 6.5 miles (4.6 miles past Molly's and shortly beyond Stolle Meadows). A spur on your right ends at an unofficial camping area by the river and a split-log footbridge at the trailhead. The unsigned path crosses two more logs and soon reaches a creek littered with fallen trees, then follows the warming stream uphill to the pool. Just beyond lies the spectacular source of the now-steaming creek. Vulcan is named on the forest map.

The hot springs: Many bubbling springs join forces to form a hot creek which cools as it flows down a wooded hillside toward the South Fork Salmon River. The creek has been dammed with logs at the point of optimum soaking temperature (around 105 degrees) to form an emerald-green soaking pool about thirty feet across with a sand and mud bottom. This is a heavily used spot that shows some signs of abuse. Please treat it with care.

HIKE 42a *Rice Peak*

General description: A strenuous three-mile, round-trip day climb to a peak in Boise National Forest with distant views, near Vulcan Hot Springs.
Elevation gain and loss: 1,300 feet.
Trailhead elevation: 7,400 feet.
High point: Rice Peak Lookout, 8,700 feet.
Hiking quad: Rice Peak USGS.
Road map: Boise National Forest.

Finding the trailhead: Follow the road access above to Vulcan. Continue south for just under a mile and bear left on Rice Peak Road (478). The six-mile road gradually deteriorates, and you may be better off walking the final two-mile stretch unless you have a 4WD. Check with the ranger in Cascade for current conditions; mud often makes access impossible before July. If you hike the last two miles up Rice Creek to the trailhead, you can tack on an extra 1,000-foot gain.

The hike: Warm Lake is a better area for geothermal gems than for interesting hikes, the climb to Rice Peak being one of the few exceptions. The 360-degree view from the lookout reveals an expanse of distant peaks ranging from the Salmon River Mountains to the double silhouette of the Sawtooths backed by the White Clouds, around to the wooded mountains above Cascade and McCall.

Rice Peak trail (103) continues up Rice Creek where the road leaves off and soon reaches tiny Rice Lake. Cross the outlet on logs and circle the north shore past some grassy campsites. Now the path climbs a long, steep mile to a saddle just south of the peak, takes a short break, then zigzags up the last 0.5 mile to the summit. On the return trip, many hikers take a short cut by boulder hopping straight down the west side of the mountain to Rice Lake.

The steamy pool at Vulcan seems to be getting a tad hotter every year. If this trend keeps up, a new soaker may have to be built somewhere downstream.

HOT SPRINGS 42 *Vulcan Hot Springs*
HIKE 42a *Rice Peak*

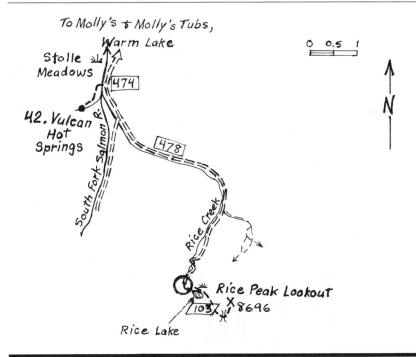

43 Penny Hot Spring

General description: A lonesome spring in the South Fork Salmon River Canyon reached by a 0.25-mile path, northeast of Cascade. Naked bodies welcome. Elevation 4,800 feet.
Map: Boise National Forest.

Directions: Follow the directions to Forest Road 474 given in 40 but also refer to Road Update in 44 below. Drive 4.4 miles north, then turn left just past the Nickel Creek sign near Penny Spring Campground. The overgrown road soon transforms into a path that shows more sign of deerprints than footprints. The route curves north around a hill above the river, then drops sharply beside a cliff to the pools at the bottom. The spring isn't marked on the forest map or even the state geothermal.

The hot spring: Steaming water flows down the side of a cliff into a few rock and sand pools along a scenic bend in the river. (You can spot several other hot springs on the opposite bank by the telltale orange slime). Penny gets very little use or upkeep, and the fragile pools swamp during high water. There's plenty of hot water just waiting for some energetic soul to rebuild a proper

At Penny Hot Spring, river water at your elbow can be channeled into the pools to produce whatever temperature you prefer.

soaking pool, so if you're intent on a bath, bring a shovel and plenty of elbow grease!

For "what it's worth", the road from Warm Lake to Penny Hot Spring passes Two-bit and Six-bit Creeks on one side, then Dime and Nickel Creeks on the other. Dollar Creek lies just beyond. To sum it up: A penny's just a penny, but this one's got potential.

44 Mile-16 Hot Spring

General description: A sylvan soaker in the South Fork Salmon River Canyon hidden below a dirt road, northeast of Cascade. Highly skinnydippable. Elevation 4,150 feet.

Maps: Boise and Payette National Forests.

Finding the hot spring: Follow the directions to Forest Road 474 given in 40. Drive north past Penny into Payette National Forest (where the road number changes to 674) to Poverty Flat Campground, a total of about 14.5 miles. Continue about 1.25 miles north to a small pullout and walk the final 0.25 mile down the road. Hunt for an unmarked path that drops over the steep bank to the riverside pool. Mile-16 isn't marked on the forest map.

Road update: The South Fork Road (474/674) is closed for construction

This five-star delight at Mile-16 is a prime example of how to design and build a proper soaking pool.

through late 1994. It's being paved all the way from Warm Lake downstream to the East Fork Road (48). This major undertaking is an effort to reduce sedimentation to protect native chinook and steelhead runs. All roadside parking will end up designated sites only, and the official pullout for Mile-16 will be signed for day use only. When completed, the road may be kept open year-round. In the meantime, the closure lasts from June 1 through early September. Check with the Forest Service regarding access in the spring and fall.

The hot spring: A crystal-clear soaking pool, well concealed from the nearby road, sits at the base of a steep bank on the river's edge. It's enclosed by attractive chunks of stream rock mortared tightly in place. A large slab at one end makes a perfect backrest for enjoying the view up the tree-studded canyon. Spring water, cooling from 115 degrees as it trickles down the bank, can be diverted by means of a long pipe coupled to a hose, and the temperature seems to stay a steady perfect.

Referred to locally as Mile-16 Hot Spring because of its strategic location on the road, it's also known as Fire Crew and Holdover. Whatever it's called, this is a top notch, tastefully designed pool in a great setting. Please don't abuse the privilege of using it—remember, no soap or shampoo.

HIKE 44a *Blackmare Lake*

General description: A moderate eighteen-mile, round-trip overnighter to a remote lake in Payette National Forest, near Mile-16 Hot Spring.
Elevation gain and loss: +3,100 feet, -500 feet.
Trailhead elevation: 4,200 feet.
High point: Blackmare Lake, 7,040 feet.
Hiking quads: Blackmare and White Rock Peak USGS.
Road maps: Boise and Payette National Forests.

Finding the trailhead: Follow the directions above to Poverty Flat Campground and park at the south end by the pack bridge.

The hike: Sapphire-blue Blackmare Lake, lying in a basin flanked by granite walls, makes a pleasant overnight trip. Half a dozen 8,000-foot peaks rim the basin, and narrow bands of trees mark the ridges with diagonal stripes. The isolated lake nestles at the head of a glacial valley that provides access for the lightly used trail.

Turn right across the bridge onto Blackmare Trail (100). You can count on wet feet fording Blackmare Creek (treacherous during high water). The wooded route then climbs the north bank and follows the creek up the steep-walled valley. At a branch in just under four miles, bear left to a second junction.

Take the right fork along the South Fork of Blackmare Creek (302). This stretch has a fairly gentle grade. After crossing a few side streams and then the creek itself, you'll pass the South Fork Cutoff in seven miles. Turn back across the creek and climb 1,360 feet in the final two-mile stretch upvalley to Blackmare Lake.

HOT SPRING 44 *Mile-16 Hot Spring*
HIKE 44a *Blackmare Lake*
HIKE 44b *White Rock Peak*

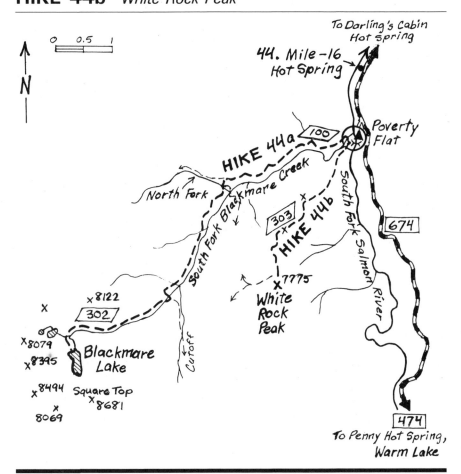

HIKE 44b *White Rock Peak*

General description: A strenuous ten-mile, round-trip day climb to a mountaintop in Payette National Forest, near Mile-16 Hot Spring.
Elevation gain and loss: 3,575 feet.
Trailhead elevation: 4,200 feet.
High point: White Rock Peak, 7,775 feet.
Hiking quad: White Rock Peak USGS.
Road map: Same as Hike 44a.

Finding the trailhead: Follow the road access for Hike 44a.

The hike: If you're more in the mood for a backbreaking climb than a creekside stroll, this scramble up a seldom used trail will fit the bill! There are glimpses between trees of the surrounding hills as you climb the ridge and a modest view from the summit.

Turn left across the bridge onto White Rock Peak Trail (303). Switchbacks drag the rough path up the ridge through a forest of pine and Douglas fir to reach the summit in five grueling miles. Watch your footing—the track is eroded and slippery in many spots. Be sure to drop in for a relaxing soak at "Mile-16" after the hike.

45 Darling's Cabin Hot Spring

General description: A secluded hot tub on the wrong side of the South Fork Salmon River, northeast of Cascade. Naked bodies welcome. Elevation 4,000 feet.
Map: Payette National Forest.

Finding the hot spring: Follow the directions to Forest Road 474 given in 40 but refer also to Road update in 44 above. Drive north on Forest Road 474/674 about eighteen miles (2.5 miles past Mile-16 Hot Spring). Watch for abandoned cabins on a flat by the river and park in the closest turnout. In late season, you can ford near the cabin and follow a faint path up the bank to the tub. The spring is unmarked on the forest map and omitted on the state geothermal.

The hot spring: Spring water is piped into a galvanized stock tank hidden in the woods above the river. The tank measures four feet in diameter, and the soaking temperature runs around 92 degrees. It's located on a (currently) unpatented mining claim and appears to be rarely visited. Unknown even to the Forest Service, this obscure spring is nevertheless worth wading the river to check out.

46 Buckhorn Hot Spring

General description: A steamy shower pool misplaced on the maps and well concealed from a dirt road, northeast of Cascade. A skinnydipper's fantasy. Elevation 4,920 feet.
Map: Payette National Forest.

Finding the hot spring: Follow the directions to Forest Road 474 given in 40 but also refer to Road Update in 44 above. Drive north on 474/674 about twenty-five miles to Buckhorn Creek Road (404). (Just for the record, you passed Teapot Hot Springs a mile back—several hot seeps and shallow pools, but no pullout and much too visible).

Cross the river bridge and drive six dusty miles west to a pullout and trail sign at the road end. Now, back up 0.1 mile and find the path in the woods going down to the creek. Cross on a nearby log and head thirty yards

HOT SPRING 46 *Buckhorn Hot Spring*
HIKE 46a *To "Buckhorn the Second"*

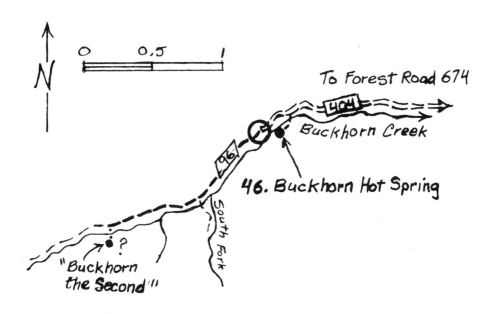

upstream over a gravel bar to the spring. Buckhorn is misplaced on both the forest map and the USGS quad and omitted altogether on the state geothermal.

The hot spring: A steamy channel flows down a wooden gutter and splashes into a shallow rock-lined pool just above Buckhorn Creek. The temperature range at the source checks in at a toasty 106-112 degrees, and there's no way to lower the setting—except to divert the gutter and wait for the pool to cool.

The real Buckhorn nestles in a mountain meadow bordered by forest. It's out of sight from the road and offers total privacy. All in all, it's not bad for a hot spring that doesn't belong where it ended up. If you're curious about where it's supposed to be, you might try the following hike.

Above the shower pool at Buckhorn Hot Spring you can see channels flowing into other potential dips.

HIKE 46a *To "Buckhorn the Second"*

General description: A moderate three-mile round-trip wild goose chase up a forested canyon, near the real Buckhorn Hot Spring. No need whatsoever to pack a swimsuit.
Elevation gain and loss: 500 feet.
Trailhead elevation: 4,900 feet.
High point: 5,400 feet.
Hiking quad: Fitsum Peak USGS.
Road map: Payette National Forest.

Finding the trailhead: Follow the directions above to Buckhorn Creek Trailhead. The hot spring is clearly (mis)marked on both maps and missing on the state geothermal.

The hike: What have you got to lose? Maybe there really are two Buckhorns? Go left at the trail sign onto Buckhorn Creek Trail (96), a route that crosses a summit beside Rapid Peak and tiny Summit Lake. A sign in 0.5 mile points left to the South Fork Buckhorn Creek Trail (which soon peters out) and another states "Buckhorn Hot Spring—1." Aha, you're on the right track?

The trail climbs a bit, passes a second canyon, and opens into an occasional meadow. All well and good. But no sign to greet you in the allotted mile. Not even a ghost of a path down the brushy slope. Not a good omen at all. Next, a rushing creek to balance across on slippery rocks followed by a bushwhack with a 200-foot gain up the opposite wall through solid brush. Visibility zero when you reach the target area.

Why, that needle in a haystack routine would be child's play compared to this hunt! You know, on second thought, maybe that counterfeit Buckhorn back by the trailhead will still be there waiting.

The hot spring: The old saying about "a bird in the hand" sure fits this situation to a tee. To enjoy what's at hand, just head down the trail to 46 above.

47 Kwiskwis Hot Spring

HIKE 47a *To Kwiskwis Hot Spring*

General description: A wild and woolly thirteen-mile, round-trip day hike or overnighter to an isolated hot spring on a creek above the Middle Fork Salmon River, buried in the River of No Return Wilderness southeast of Yellow Pine. Swimwear totally nonfunctional here except for sun protection factor.
Elevation gain and loss: +340 feet, -2,780 feet.
High point: Trailhead, 8,120 feet.
Low point: Kwiskwis, 5,680 feet.
Hiking quads: Big Chief Creek and Big Baldy USGS, or River of No Return Wilderness, south half (Forest Service).
Road map: Wilderness quad or Boise and Payette National Forests.

Warning: This somewhat crazy expedition is for wilderness buffs and hot springs fanatics only! The trailhead at Mule Hill, on the brink of the vast River of No Return Wilderness, is over seventy miles from Warm Lake. The final twenty-three teeth-jarring miles of corrugated and rocky dirt from the closest town, Yellow Pine, are enough to test the mettle of the most determined adventurer (not to mention his or her vehicle). The primitive trail plunges downhill to a creek valley that reaches a hot spring few folks have ever heard of and fewer still have ever visited.

If you decide to brave the trip in, you'll be rewarded with views of undulating mountains and gentle valleys, acres of solitude in a lovely creekside meadow with idyllic camping, and a money-back guarantee that you won't have to wait in line for a soak at Kwiskwis Hot Spring.

Finding the trailhead: Follow the directions to Forest Road 474 given in 40 but refer also to Road Update in 44 above. Drive north about thirty-four newly paved miles to the upper end. Turn right on the East Fork Road (48) and proceed fifteen dusty miles to Yellow Pine. (Last chance to buy gas—or anything else!) Check with the sheriff on the status of Meadow Creek Lookout Road. Continue the grind east for fourteen miles on Forest Road 412, an active mining road, to an eye-catching four-way stop sign at Stibnite.

A tiny gold mining settlement during the 1930s, Stibnite mushroomed to a population of over a thousand during World War II when it became the country's biggest producer of tungsten. When the war boom ended, it dwindled into a ghost town. But Stibnite has recently sprung back to life once again as the home of an ambitious new gold mining venture.

Climb five rocky and serpentine miles on Forest Road 375 to Monumental Summit (open from July 1 to November 15) and watch for a primitive road (641) signed "to Meadow Creek Lookout" dropping off to your right. The ridge road winds out to the trailhead on Mule Hill. Drivers of low clearance vehicles will have to skirt a few rocks (if the width of the road allows) or stop to toss them over the edge, but the road is usually passable.

Keep your eyes peeled in four miles for signs of an old horse camp in a clearing on the ridgetop. This is the "certified trailhead" at 8,120 feet. Park here and walk back to the woods. Search for U.S. Forest Service Trail 219 on

Kwiskwis Hot Spring spreads out a feast of hot water and Indian Creek supplies the cold. The rare guest must furnish the only thing missing—a proper soaking pool.

HIKE 47a *To Kwiskwis Hot Spring*

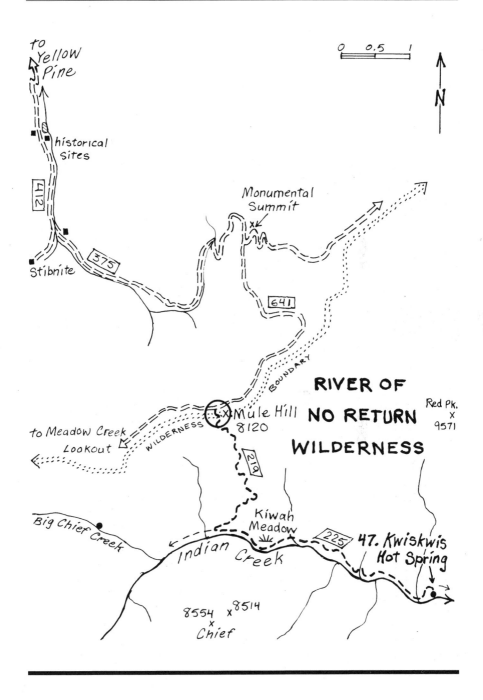

to Yellow Pine

historical sites

412

375

Stibnite

Monumental Summit
x

641

BOUNDARY

WILDERNESS

RIVER OF

NO RETURN

WILDERNESS

Red Pk.
X
9571

x Mule Hill
8120

to Meadow Creek
Lookout

219

Kiwah Meadow

Big Chief Creek

225

47. Kwiskwis
Hot Spring

Indian Creek

8554 x 8514
x
Chief

your right (south), and you'll find an overgrown path marked by a faded sign that simply says "Primitive Area." This is it—last chance to change your mind!

The hike: The track drops down the flank of Mule Hill, passes the crumbling remains of an old log cabin, then plunges in earnest down a twisting ridge. In one or two places it snakes down sloping meadows with wall-to-wall views, but for most of the 2.5-mile, 2,000-foot drop, the route is engulfed in virgin forest.

The path finally comes to rest in a peaceful valley at the junction of Indian Creek Trail (225). The creek flows southeast to join the Middle Fork Salmon River in about fifteen miles; Kwiskwis, named on the maps, lies four miles downstream.

Just for the record: Upstream on Big Chief Creek lurks another hot spring marked on the wilderness map but not on the state geothermal. And several miles downstream, on the Middle Fork Indian Creek, are two springs reported by the state geothermal to have the highest surface temperature range (161-190 degrees) of any in the wilderness! No reports on usability—anyone care to check them out?

You'll soon reach broad Kiwah Meadow—a delightful spot to settle down for a lunch break or a week's retreat from the cares of the world. The path is hard to see through the knee-high grass but picks up again beyond this point.

After crossing the first side creek, the route climbs the north bank to traverse a precipitous talus slope. It's hard to be sure of the "official" trail as there are a maze of game paths crisscrossing at varying heights. Most are badly eroded and hard to cling to but all lead in the same direction—downstream. You'll know you're on the right track at the third stream crossing (Kwiskwis Creek) if you see a faded sign that labels it "Quis Quis." A short way beyond, you should intersect the upper springs.

The hot spring: Scalding water emerges from the ground at up to 156 degrees but drops into the comfort zone by the time it reaches Indian Creek below. More springs appear as you follow the broad flow downhill. The shallow pool(s) at the bottom fill in with creek gravel and will need some excavation work, but that's just the price you pay for "the wilderness experience" and a steamy soak at the end of the trail. There's a small campsite across the creek, but the best camping by far is back at Kiwah Meadow.

An element adding even more spice to the adventure is the fact that the Forest Service has little firsthand information to help the hiker. This remote area is a slice of the Frank Church-River of No Return "wilderness pie" held by Boise National Forest but administered, at least in theory, by Challis National Forest. However, the District Office sits roughly seventy air miles across the state map from Mule Hill.

By a series of roundabout roads, a trail crew based in Challis would have to drive a staggering 180 miles to reach the trailhead, and only 115 of them would be on pavement. The final forty miles of dirt get progressively worse over potholes and rock. As a result, this is one piece of wilderness that seems more than likely to remain just that!

D. OUT OF CROUCH

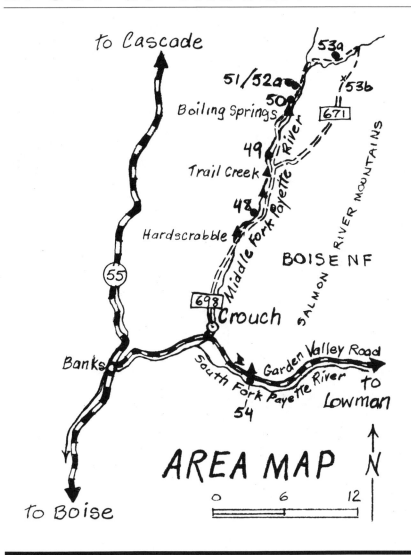

to Cascade

53a

51/52a
53b
50
Boiling Springs
671
49
Trail Creek
48
Hardscrabble
Middle Fork Payette River

BOISE NF

SALMON RIVER MOUNTAINS

55

698
Crouch

Banks
Garden Valley Road
South Fork Payette River
to Lowman
54

AREA MAP N

0   6   12

to Boise

Hot springs and hikes

Midway between Boise and Cascade on State Route 55, the paved Garden Valley-Lowman Road shoots eight miles east at Banks to the tiny town of Crouch. A dirt road in Boise National Forest follows the Middle Fork Payette River northeast of town to roadside hot dips (48-50) followed by a batch on a river trail upstream—notably, Moon dipper and Pine Burl (51/52a). East of town comes Hot Springs Campground (54) en route to Lowman (Section E).

To reach Rocky Canyon Hot Spring, the user must ford the river and scramble up the opposite bank.

Season

Low elevation promoates a long soaking season limited only by winter road closure and spring runoff on the riverside pools. Fire Crew and Moondipper are best in early summer while Rocky Canyon, Boiling Springs, and Pine Burl are usable well into the fall. The pool at Hot Springs Campground can be enjoyed all year. The hiking season for the trek to Bull Creek has a narrow window—while the river's low and before the pool's left stranded. Summer weather runs hot and dry, but thunderstorms aren't uncommon.

48 Rocky Canyon Hot Spring

General description: Highly visible hot pools on the wrong side of the Middle Fork Payette River, northeast of Crouch. Swimwear essential. Elevation 3,440 feet.
Map: Boise National Forest.

Finding the hot springs: From State Route 55 at Banks, take the Garden Valley Road about eight paved miles east to Crouch. Follow graded Forest Road 698 northeast about 12.5 miles (1.5 miles past Hardscrabble Campground) and park in a pullout on your left. You'll have to wade the wide river, which could be dangerous during high water. The spring is marked on the forest map.

The hot spring: Near the mouth of Rocky Canyon, a spring flows at 120 degrees down a slope to the river. Bathers have carved out a family sized soaker and a few smaller pools dropping step-by-step down the rocky ledges, and each pool is slightly cooler than the one above. Take your pick!

The water-level pools at Fire Crew are swamped in the spring runoff and landlocked by midsummer.

49 Fire Crew Hot Spring

General description: Roadside hot dips screened by woods on the Middle Fork Payette River, northeast of Crouch. Keep cutoffs handy. Elevation 3,600 feet.

Map: Boise National Forest.

Finding the hot springs: Follow the directions above to Forest Road 698. Drive about 15 dusty miles (2.5 miles past Rocky Canyon Hot Spring) to a junction at Trail Creek Campground. Take the left fork (still 698) for 0.3 mile, then bear left on a spur ending at the river. A loop encircles an unofficial camping area; the pools are out on a gravel bar to your right. Fire Crew isn't shown on any map—not even the state geothermal.

The hot spring: A few pools framed by sun-warmed rocks are concealed from the road just upstream from Rocky Canyon. Also at the river's edge but luckily on the near side, these little known dips are frequented chiefly by (you guessed it) the local fire crew. Early in the season, the hot flow through the pools can be fine tuned by adjusting a rock or two around the edges. It's an attractive spot and sometimes a pleasant surprise.

50 Boiling Springs

General description: Easy-access hot springs and soaks on the Middle Fork Payette River, northeast of Crouch. Nudity is a no-no if you're over five. Elevation 4,000 feet.
Map: Boise National Forest.

Fihding the hot springs: Follow the directions to Forest Road 698 given in 48. Drive about twenty-three miles (past Rocky Canyon and Fire Crew Hot Springs) to the road-end campground and trailhead (see Hikes 51/52a and 53a). Stroll 0.25 mile north to find the springs flowing down a bank beside a cabin. The cabin, formerly a Forest Service guard station, is now rented to the public for recreational use. Please ask permission before entering and try to avoid the cabin area as much as possible. Boiling Springs is named on the forest map.

The hot springs: Steaming water emerges at over 130 degrees from fissures in a cliff at Boiling Springs Guard Station and flows through a small pool hidden halfway up the rocks. The water gradually cools as it runs through a ditch across a wide meadow. A few rock-lined pools at the river's edge are usually filled on weekends with kids from the nearby campground. River water can be added for a cooler soak.

This tiny pool at Boiling Springs, hidden between boulders just below the source, is far too hot for soaking.

51/52 Moondipper and Pine Burl Hot Springs

HIKE 51/52a *To Both Hot Springs*

General description: An easy four-mile, round-trip "double feature" not to be missed, playing near the Middle Fork Payette River northeast of Crouch. A bathing suit/birthday suit mix.
Elevation gain and loss: 80 feet.
Trailhead elevation: 4,000 feet.
High point: Hot springs, 4,080 feet.
Hiking quads: Boiling Springs and Bull Creek Hot Springs USGS.
Road map: Boise National Forest.

Finding the trailhead: Follow the directions above to Boiling Springs and take your pick of two routes upstream. The springs are marked on the forest map but not on the USGS quad.

The hike: Moondipper and Pine Burl enjoy a setting worthy of their captivating names. Two separate springs checking in at 120 degrees flow down the banks of a creek just above the river into a pair of scenic soakers spaced 200 yards apart along the tree-studded canyon. Both get swamped during high water, but are well worth a bit of annual maintenance.

An unmarked path, steep and slippery in spots, hugs the west side of the river all the way; this is the safer route when the water level is high (usually until August). The Middle Fork Trail (33) is more direct, but you'll have to ford twice in the two-mile hike upstream. If in doubt, check with the ranger at Garden Valley.

The hot springs: When you reach Dash Creek, the first side stream on the west side, you'll soon find Moondipper spread out against a rocky bank. The large, sandy-bottomed pool can hold quite a few happy soakers and offers a lovely view up the canyon. It's usually landlocked by midsummer and can get a mite too hot for comfort by then without some means of transporting cold water from the creek.

Pine Burl, a tiny gem tucked out of sight just a few bends upstream, is a hot springer's fantasy of the perfect spot for a quiet party for two. The name is proudly inscribed, along with those of its four volunteer builders, on a small masonry dam at the downstream end. If the water gets too hot, the rocks at the other end can be shifted to let creek water trickle in.

The soaking pool at Moondipper requires some remodeling every year, but the setting makes up for the effort.

53 Bull Creek Hot Springs

HIKE 53a *To Bull Creek Hot Springs*

General description: A slightly insane twenty-two-mile, round-trip backpack up the Middle Fork Payette River to a far-flung hot dip on Bull Creek. No need whatsoever to pack a swimsuit.
Elevation gain and loss: 1,200 feet.

Trailhead elevation: 4,000 feet.
High point: Bull Creek Hot Springs, 5,200 feet.
Maps: Same as Hike 51/52a.

Finding the trailhead: Follow the directions above to Boiling Springs. The springs are named on both maps.

The hike: This trip combines the two-mile stroll to Moondipper and Pine Burl (Hike 51/52a) with a nine-mile extension upstream to reach Bull Creek Hot Springs in a total of eleven miles. The path snakes back and forth across the swift-moving Middle Fork Payette River an exhausting total of twelve times en route to Bull Creek. See Hike 51/52a for a choice of routes from the trailhead to Dash Creek.

Immediately after passing Moondipper at two miles, the Middle Fork Trail (33) begins crossing the wide stream at almost every bend in its convoluted course. In the next few miles, you'll pass several minor hot springs and seeps marked on the maps. The condition of whatever pools they may have depends on how many flocks of sheep have plodded through them en route to or from their summer pastures. One local ranger calls them all "hog wallows", but he's obviously not a true fanatic dedicated to the cause of investigating every hot puddle no matter how remote. Unlike some of us, he's a man of common sense!

The route climbs briefly away from the river, then continues up the west bank for a mile or so. Two more wet fords and you'll reach a welcome camping area near the mouth of Bull Creek at 7.5 miles, 4,400 feet. Best to camp here—there aren't any good campsites at the hot springs.

Wade the Middle Fork one last time to pick up Bull Creek Trail (102) on the north bank of the creek. Follow the faintly-blazed path 3.5 miles east to find the hot springs on a bluff near a small stream. See below for a much less difficult route from a different direction.

The hot springs: The remote springs overlooking Bull Creek may or may not have a bather-friendly pool to greet you just when you really need a hot soak. Too late in the season, when a nearby side creek dries up, the stranded pool(s) grow hot enough to boil eggs and hikers alike; too early, you'll freeze more than your toes in the cold river en route. This venture would be sheer madness when the water level is high; be sure to check with the ranger at Garden Valley before setting off.

HIKE 53b *Bull Creek Hot Springs via Silver Creek Trail*

General description: A relatively easy eighteen-mile, round-trip backpack to the bubblies on Bull Creek from an alternate trailhead.
Elevation gain and loss: +1,540 feet, -1,280 feet.
Trailhead elevation: 4,940 feet.
High point: Silver Creek Summit, 6,240 feet.
Hiking quads: Bull Creek Hot Springs and Wild Buck Peak USGS.
Road map: Boise National Forest.

HOT SPRINGS 50 *Boiling Springs*
HIKE 51/52a *To Moondipper & Pine Burl Hot Springs*
HIKE 53a *To Bull Creek Hot Springs*
HIKE 53b *Bull Creek Hot Springs via Silver Creek Trail*

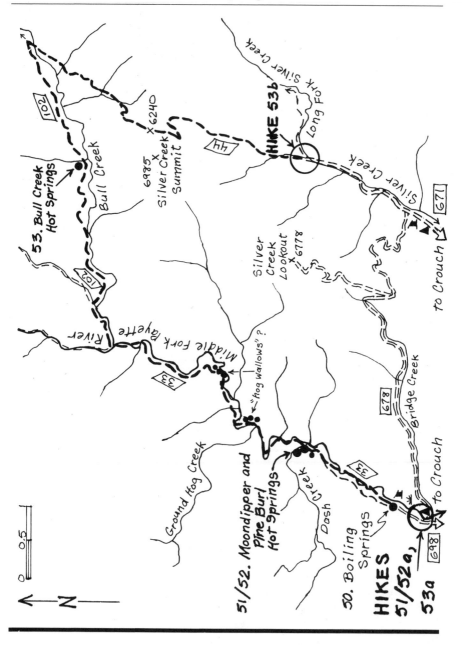

Finding the trailhead: Follow the directions to Trail Creek Campground given in 49. Bear right on Silver Creek Road (671) and drive to the road-end parking area and trail sign (about two miles beyond the guard station).

The hike: Silver Creek Trail offers a far drier, more scenic, and slightly shorter approach to Bull Creek than the wet trek up the Middle Fork described above—minus the hot springs en route. You'll gain an extra 1,300 feet climbing over Silver Creek Summit, but the views along the trail make up for it.

Two trails begin here. Be sure to take Silver Creek Trail (44) and not the one branching off to your right. Follow the route over Silver Creek Summit at 6,240 feet, enjoy the broad views and maybe a nice dry lunch, then drop down the far side to reach Bull Creek in about six miles—a pleasant spot to spend the night. Cross the creek and watch for the Bull Creek Trail (102) in about 0.25 mile. Turn left onto the blazed path and follow it three miles downstream above the north bank of Bull Creek to reach the hot springs (at 5,200 feet) on a bluff overlooking the canyon.

54 Hot Springs Campground

General description: A popular soaking pool on a bank between a highway campground and the South Fork Payette River, east of Crouch. Swimwear strongly recommended. Elevation 3,100 feet.
Map: Boise National Forest.

Finding the hot spring: From State Route 55 at Banks, take the paved Garden Valley-Lowman Road east to Hot Springs Campground (a mile inside the forest boundary and six miles east of Crouch). There's a pullout on the bank, and steps lead down to the pool. The campground is named on the forest map.

The hot spring: A comfortable soaker big enough for a family group has been dug out of the bank above the river. The shallow pool, dammed with rocks and logs, offers a toasty soak year-round courtesy of a pipe that transports the flow from the springs. At the river's edge, you'll also find one or more seasonal dips not far from a concrete slab that once supported a public bathhouse.

Hot springers en route between Crouch and Lowman can make a convenient stop at Hot Springs Campground.

E. OUT OF LOWMAN

Note: The only services at Lowman are the district ranger station and the all-in-one-stop South Fork Lodge, restaurant, post office, store and gas pump.

Hot springs and hikes

State Route 21, the Ponderosa Pine Scenic Route, runs northeast of Boise to easy-access soaks on the South Fork Payette River at Pine Flats and Kirkham (55, 56) near Lowman, and on to Tenmile and Bonneville (57, 58); these combine well with a trek to Red Mountain and points beyond. Next, Sacajawea's roadside pools (59) mark the Grandjean trailhead into the western Sawtooths. Finally, hot springs in the River of No Return Wilderness to the north are reached by a hike to Bear Valley (60a) and a backpack to Trail Flat and Sheepeater (61/62a) on the Middle Fork Salmon River, with a bonus dip at Dagger Creek (63) near the trailhead. *Note:* Lowman can also be reached from Crouch, Atlanta, and Stanley (Sections D, F and H).

Season

Although early summer through fall is prime time, the uppermost soaks at Pine Flats, Kirkham, and Bonneville are usable all year. Spring runoff buries Tenmile and Sacajawea, and prevents access to Bear Valley before late summer. The rest can be enjoyed whenever the roads are open, but the trek down the Middle Fork is best after mid-August. The hiking season in the high Sawtooths generally runs from late July through mid-September. Summer weather tends to be hot with occasional thunderstorms, with cold nights at higher elevations.

E. OUT OF LOWMAN

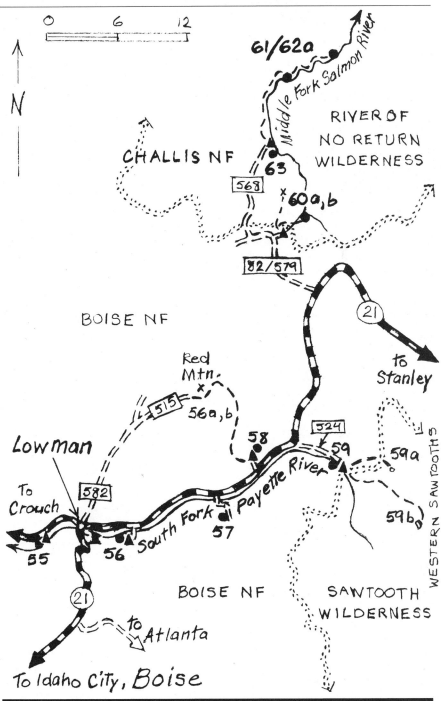

Scale: 0 6 12

N

61/62a

Middle Fork Salmon River

RIVER OF
NO RETURN
WILDERNESS

CHALLIS NF

63

568

X 60a,b

82/579

BOISE NF

21

to
Stanley

Red
Mtn.
X

515

56a,b

524

WESTERN SAWTOOTHS

58

59

59a

Lowman

To
Crouch

582

South Fork Payette River

59b

55

56

57

21

BOISE NF

SAWTOOTH
WILDERNESS

to Atlanta

To Idaho City, Boise

55 Pine Flats Hot Spring

General description: Hot dips and a built-in cliffside shower on the South Fork Payette River, west of Lowman. Bathing suits required. Elevation 3,700 feet.
Map: Boise National Forest.

Finding the hot springs: From Boise, take State Route 21 about seventy miles northeast to Lowman. Turn left on the newly-paved road to Garden Valley and drive five miles to Pine Flats Campground. From the west end, follow an unmarked path .3-mile downstream to a wide gravel bar; look for the hottest pool up the rocky cliff. The spring isn't marked on the forest map.

The hot spring: A hot shower pouring over a cliff decorates one side of a pool hidden twenty feet above the river. This one's big enough to pack maybe half a dozen human sardines side by side and hot enough to turn them into lobsters. Cooler pools at the bottom collect the runoff from the showerbath above, and a large swimming hole at the river's edge adds the final touch. Those who prefer more privacy can wade along the base of the cliff to find yet another hot pool with shower hidden in the rocks.

56 Kirkham Hot Springs

General description: Hot waterfalls and body-full bubblies on the South Fork Payette River below a highway campground, east of Lowman. Swimwear a must. Elevation 3,900 feet.
Map: Boise National Forest.

Finding the hot springs: Drive four miles east of Lowman on State Route 21. Cross the bridge to Kirkham Campground and park at the west end. Follow a short path down to the river. The springs aren't marked on the forest map.

The hot springs: In plain view below the highway, these popular pools are frequently filled with boisterous teenagers and large family groups. The rock and sand pools, interspersed with steaming showers, come in all sizes, shapes, and temperatures. Kids of all ages love to leap off the rocks into deep holes in the river, and older folks can be seen scattered about on boulders dozing in the sun. The adjacent campground adds to the congestion here, and it's usually Winnebago City on summer weekends. Try early mornings or the off-season months—it's worth it.

The upper pool at Pine Flats features a steamy hot shower at one end.

Sun worshippers at Kirkham enjoy a simultaneous soak and hot shower.

HIKE 56a *Red Mountain Loop*

General description: A strenuous ten-mile, round-trip day climb (including a 4.5-mile, partially cross-country loop) to a viewpoint and off-trail lakes below, not far from Kirkham Hot Springs.
Elevation gain and loss: 2,560 feet (1,180 feet to start of loop; loop, 1,380 feet).
Trailhead elevation: 6,280 feet.
High point: Red Mountain Lookout, 8,722 feet.
Hiking quads: Cache Creek and Miller Mountain East USGS.
Road map: Boise National Forest.

Finding the trailhead: Take State Route 21 to Lowman and turn north on Forest Road 582. Drive twelve dusty miles toward Bear Valley, then turn right on Clear Creek Road (515) and go six bumpy miles to a roadblock with grassy space nearby for horses and a few cars. The trailhead is a mile back from the end of the road.

The hike: A brisk climb up a mountainside carpeted with wildflowers leads to a lookout crowning the rocky summit of Red Mountain. Look straight down on three lakes and out across a sea of green ridges and valleys to the Salmon River Mountains and the Sawtooths. The bird's-eye view is worth the climb, and a cross-country scramble down past the Red Mountain Lakes loops back to a connecting trail. With time to spare, you could continue from this point along a scenic ridge route ending at Bonneville Hot Springs in twenty miles (see below).

Walk the last road-mile to the register box and Clear Creek Trail. The route soon crosses Rough Creek and follows a second creekbed up a wooded slope,

Three of Red Mountain's small lakes are visible to the east beneath the 8,722-foot summit.

then veers away to climb through chaparral followed by open meadows. Turn left onto the lookout spur and switchback north toward the summit. In early summer, you'll pass patches of flaming Indian paintbrush, Red Mountain heath, and Mariposa lilies along the way. Take a break to enjoy the broad view from the lookout at 8,722 feet, four miles from the new trailhead.

To reach the nearest lake, just east of the summit, pick your route carefully down the precipitous slope past a small pond on your left. Circle the blue-green lake, rimmed by tall trees, on a faint path along the north shore and hop across its outlet. Next, scramble east down a wooded gulley to reach the largest of the Red Mountain Lakes at 7,850 feet. The deep green surface mirrors a wall of pines and firs.

Angle due south through a rocky cleft and pass a long pond on your right. Next, turn southeast to pass one more lake on your left (last chance to fill your canteen). Pick the easiest route south down a grassy slope to intersect Kirkham Ridge Trail two miles below the summit. Unless you plan to continue the fourteen scenic miles from here to Bonneville, turn right for 0.5 mile on Kirkham Ridge Trail (145) and right again on Clear Creek Trail. Follow it west past the lookout spur, then back out the way you came in.

HIKE 56b *Red Mountain to Bonneville Hot Springs*

General description: A strenuous twenty-mile, one-way overnighter linking the climb over Red Mountain with overviews of the Sawtooths en route to hot dips farther up the highway.

Elevation gain and loss: +4,480 feet, -6,080 feet.

Trailhead elevation: 6,280 feet.

High point: Red Mountain Lookout, 8,722 feet.

Hiking quads: Same as Hike 56a plus Bull Trout Point and Eightmile Mountain USGS.
Road map: Same as Hike 56a.

Finding both trailheads: Drive about nineteen miles northeast of Lowman on State Route 21 and leave a car at Bonneville Campground. Shuttle a second car about thirty-seven miles to the trailhead on Clear Creek Road. See Hike 56a for road access.

The hike: The Link Trail may well provide not only the most spectacular views of any hike in Boise Forest but also the best vantage point for seeing the entire length of the Sawtooth Range. The route parallels these jagged peaks from just enough distance for the hiker to absorb their full impact. For mile after mile along the sharp crest, the trail offers breathtaking views as it winds south toward State Route 21.

This hike combines the climb over Red Mountain with a trek along the Link Trail ending in a total of twenty miles at Bonneville Campground and Hot Springs. It's suggested as a one-way trip as the gain is much more gradual in this direction. (There's a grueling gain of 2,920 feet in the first four miles when hiked from the lower end.) The only drawback is the car shuttle involved. See Hike 56a for the route over Red Mountain from Clear Creek Trailhead.

When you drop south from the Red Mountain lakes, you'll intersect Kirkham Ridge Trail (145) at six miles, 7,680 feet. Turn left for another two miles to reach the Link Trail. There's a campsite with a broad view but no water by the junction of Clear Creek and Kirkham Ridge Trails, at 7,600 feet, and a few more grassy spots in the area where Eightmile Creek crosses Kirkham Ridge Trail.

Turn south onto the upper end of the Link Trail (148) at eight miles, 7,480 feet. Climb the ridge above Eightmile Creek and enjoy the views over your shoulder of the many small lakes fanning out beneath the rugged east face of Red Mountain. The high point on the trail (8,120 feet) traverses the side of an unnamed peak. Soon, you'll reach a narrow saddle with the first view to the Sawtooths.

The next stretch crosses the shady side of another peak that may still have snow patches in late July. The path then drops 760 feet down a canyon to reach Castro Creek at eleven miles, 7,360 feet. Cross on logs to a large camping area in a clearing—the best on the Link Trail and the only year-around water source.

The trail continues south along Castro Creek and then climbs to a knoll with another vista. For the next few miles, it dips and rises along the crest at around 7,300 feet. Near a sign marked "East Fork," you'll pass a few campsites with access to early-season creek water.

This prime stretch offers magnificent panoramas as it slowly winds south to pass beneath the 7,871-foot summit of Eightmile Mountain at 15.5 miles. You'll get a close-up look up Grandjean Canyon (Hikes 59 a, b) before plunging a nonstop 2,920 feet in four miles to the base of the mountain.

When you reach the register box at the lower end of the Link Trail, you'll be just 0.5 mile from your car. Cut left through the woods on a faint path that leads down a gulley and intersects the dirt road to reach Bonneville Campground and Hot Springs at twenty miles, 4,680 feet.

HIKE 56a *Red Mountain Loop*
HIKE 56b *Red Mountain to Bonneville Hot Springs*
HOT SPRINGS 58 *Bonneville Hot Springs*

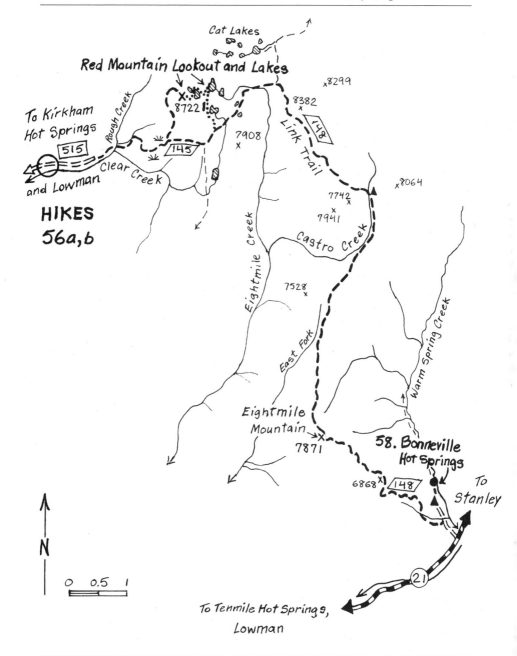

"Rain-check": *The first time I was here, it started spitting rain as I arrived at the Link Trail. By the time I reached the top, there was almost zero visibility. A cold wind seemed to be gusting from all directions at once, and the drizzle increased to a driving downpour. The trail turned into a creek that flowed past me as I sloshed up every hill. It reversed direction on the downhill stretches, and ponds formed on the level spaces between grades. I could barely make out my wet running shoes, much less the sweeping vistas I'd been anticipating.*

When I reached the campsite on Castro Creek, I found to my horror that everything in my pack was soaked—even my sleeping bag! This left me no choice but to hike on out. I splashed uphill, downhill, across a pond only to repeat this dreary sequence mile after mile as the cold rain turned to sleet and hail. I reached the dry refuge of my car just after dark and the warm haven of Bonneville shortly thereafter—determined to try again for the gold next season!

57 Tenmile Hot Springs ·

General description: A quiet creekside soak near a dirt road off the highway and the South Fork Payette River, east of Lowman. Highly skinnydippable.
Elevation: 4,500 feet.
Map: Boise National Forest.

Finding the hot springs: Take State Route 21 about thirteen miles east of Lowman (8.5 miles past Kirkham) to a sign for Tenmile trailhead between Mileposts 85 and 86. Bridge the river onto Forest Road 531. The dirt road follows the river upstream past a road branching right and a spur on the left in a mile (signed to Tenmile Trail and Camp) followed by a road forking right. It then turns south and tracks Tenmile Creek a mile upstream to a bridge washout. Ford the creek (an easy crossing after spring runoff) and walk 0.3 mile upstream to an old corral by the springs. Tenmile can't be found on any ·map—not even the state geothermal.

The hot springs: A steamy soaker, ten feet in diameter and knee deep, nestles among sun-warmed rocks between the abandoned road and the stream. Bubbles percolate up through the algae at 118 degrees, and visitors should come prepared for a bit of restoration work. In early season, creek water can be channeled in as coolant, but the spring is left stranded on the bank after runoff. As the creek level drops, small pools can be dug at waterline, allowing the creek to mix with the overflow from the source pool. A spring downstream flows through a meadow to a dip by the creek, and another soaker is reported to be farther upstream.

Tenmile Hot Springs offers users a challenge in the art of creative plumbing.

58 Bonneville Hot Springs

General description: Private bathing and communal soaking in a wooded canyon near a family campground, northeast of Lowman. Nude bathing allowed in bathhouse only. Elevation 4,700 feet.
Map: Boise National Forest.

Directions: Follow State Route 21 about nineteen miles northeast of Lowman (six miles past Tenmile) to Bonneville Campground and park at the far end. Follow a creekside path 0.25 mile north to the springs. (See Hike 56b for a ridgeline trip ending up here.) The springs are marked on the forest map.

The hot springs: There is no time a hot soak is more welcome than right after a cold hike (see "Rain-check" above). The relief is immediate and the contrast unforgettable! Bonneville is a haven on such a day. A rustic bathhouse straddles the outflow, and hoses channel 103-degree water into a knee-deep wooden tub which can be drained and refilled after each use. Your clothes stay dry while your tired body gets wet. Sheer luxury!

The springs flow past the bathhouse and tumble directly over a rocky cliff into a soaking pool that spans one arm of Warm Spring Creek. It's a clear, sandy-bottomed gem that measures a good twenty five by thirty feet. Users have built a masonry dam from boulders edged with a driftwood log. More hot water flows down the bank into a chain of smaller pools downstream as well as a secluded waterfall pool upstream. Bonneville is said to be usable year-round and reached in winter by cross-country skiers. The off-season months are indeed the only time for a quiet soak at this popular retreat.

These creek-wide soakers at Bonneville are well engineered and a major improvement to an already great spot.

59 Sacajawea Hot Springs

General description: Roadside hot dips on the South Fork Payette River, near the Grandjean trailhead into the Sawtooths, northeast of Lowman. Nudity is a no-no. Elevation 5,000 feet.
Map: Boise National Forest.

Finding the hot springs: Drive about twenty-one miles northeast of Lowman on State Route 21 (two miles past Bonneville) and turn right on the graded forest road to Grandjean (524). Drive 4.6 miles to Waipiti Creek junction and continue 0.6 mile. Park wherever you can find space and climb down the rocks to the pools. Sacajawea isn't shown on the forest map.

The hot springs: A large number of soaker-friendly pools of all sizes and shapes line a beach along the scenic river. The outflow from many springs, at temperatures up to 108 degrees, cools as it fans out down the bank, and the pool temperatures can be fine-tuned by adding river water. Another welcome refuge for weary hikers, Sacajawea is found just a mile from one of the principal gateways into the Sawtooths. You couldn't ask for a nicer finish to any hike.

The riverside pools at Sacajawea take on a new look every summer.

HIKE 59a *Trail Creek Lakes*

General description: A strenuous twelve-mile, round-trip day hike or over-nighter climbing to timberline meadows and lakes in the Sawtooth Wilderness, near Sacajawea Hot Springs.
Elevation gain and loss: 3,085 feet.
Trailhead elevation: 5,160 feet.
High point: Upper Trail Creek Lake, 8,245 feet.
Hiking quads: Grandjean and Stanley Lake USGS.
Road map: Boise National Forest.

Finding the trailhead: Follow the directions above to Sacajawea and continue another mile southeast to the end of the road. The trailhead for both Trail Creek and Baron Lakes is at the east end of Grandjean Campground.

The hike: Each of these small glacial lakes has a character all its own. As the route rises closer to timberline, rocky knolls and basins of pink Sawtooth granite gradually replace tree-studded lower slopes, and tight clusters of subalpine fir reluctantly give way to a land of stark rock.

Walk east through woods for the first 0.25 mile and bridge Trail Creek to a junction. The right fork heads south to Baron Lakes (Hike 59b), and the left fork (453) climbs Trail Creek. You'll have to cross five times on logs or rocks on the way up the narrow V-shaped canyon. This could be dangerous during high water. The route enters the wilderness just before the fourth ford, then snakes up a steep slope to the Trail Creek junction with a 2,400-foot gain in four miles.

Turn right on Trail 483, cross the creek one last time in a boggy patch, then climb a ridge to a viewpoint looking down the precipitous canyon. The final piece of eroded track zigzags over a rocky bench, passes some creekside camp-sites in a grove of tall trees, then tops a last short pitch to come to rest by the first of the lakes at 4.75 miles, 8,000 feet.

Lower Trail Creek Lake has a waterfall at its far end. Level campsites at the outlet look out across the blue-green water to granite walls rimming the thickly wooded basin. A conical peak juts up from the southeast shore, and brook trout ripple the surface late in the day. Circle the northern shore on a fisherman's path to a flat with a few more campsites in the woods.

The path climbs a slope just beyond the clearing to reach the second lake at 8,225 feet. The wide basin here has fewer tall trees, and small meadows are interspersed with outcrops of rock. Mount Regan stands out at 10,190 feet a mile to the east. Follow the north shore and, as you near the end, pick a cross-country route heading north. Scramble up a talus slope and work your way through a maze of granite knolls and small ponds to reach the third lake at six miles, 8,245 feet.

A moonscape of boulders and granite slabs rims the shoreline of Upper Trail Creek Lake, and tiny wildflowers dot the subalpine meadows. A scree slope tails out across the shallow center of the lake; from the last stone you can see every detail on the rocky bottom.

"Slip-sliding away": When I reached the uppermost lake, I slithered down the talus to fill my canteen at the deep end. Just as I leaned forward with bottle in hand, all the rocks around me suddenly started to move. Before I had time to react, the rocks and I were sliding together into the lake! I didn't really object to the unexpected swim, although I would rather have had time to leave my clothes, boots, and lunchbag behind. The thought foremost in my mind as the cold water engulfed me was of my poor camera. This trusty old Olympus, which had survived untold watery adventures in our travels together, had finally met its Waterloo.

HIKE 59b *Baron Lakes*

General description: A moderate 21.5-mile, round-trip overnighter featuring alpine lakes and panoramic views in the Sawtooth Wilderness, near Sacajawea Hot Springs.
Elevation gain and loss: +3,440 feet, -100 feet.
Trailhead elevation: 5,160 feet.
High point: Upper Baron Lake, 8,505 feet.
Maps: Same as Hike 59a plus Warbonnet Peak USGS.
Road map: Same as Hike 59a.

Finding the trailhead: Follow the road access for Hike 59a.

The hike: The name "Sawtooths" conjures up images of sharp craggy peaks rising above serrated ridges. The Baron Lakes country is the Sawtooths at their best. The two deep-blue upper lakes lie in glacial bowls hemmed in by peach and rose-hued walls of Sawtooth granite. Stands of fir thin out as you climb from one lake to the next, with colorful rock becomimg ever more dominant. The view back across the lakes from Baron Divide takes in countless rocky spires and peaks.

This is the quieter of two equally scenic routes to the popular Baron Lakes. It travels up the U-shaped glacial canyon of Baron Creek to reach Upper Baron Lake in 10.75 miles. The east-side trailhead at Redfish Lake is three miles shorter. You could see the best of both routes by entering at Grandjean, crossing over Baron Divide, and exiting at Redfish Lake in 18.5 miles (see Hike 85c).

Stroll east for the first 0.25 mile to a junction. The left fork climbs to Trail Creek Lakes (Hike 59a), and the right turns south to Baron Lakes. Follow the level South Fork Payette River (Trail 452) 1.5 miles southeast, then turn east onto Baron Creek Trail (101) and climb two miles along the grassy slope above the wide canyon. Just beyond a creek ford that can be difficult in early summer, North Baron Trail branches off to the left, climbing to Sawtooth Lake in six miles (see Hike 85a). The main canyon veers southeast for several miles as the rocky walls slowly converge.

Ford Moolack Creek at five miles, 6,200 feet. This major stream, set in a grove of cottonwoods, is followed by several tiny creeks lined with wildflowers and quaking aspen. The grassy slopes between fords are brushed with stands of spruce and fir. As the walls finally close in, you'll have a good view of Tohobit Falls and Peak on the opposite bank at seven miles. Next in line are Warbonnet Falls and Peak. The trail then hairpins 800 feet up the headwall

HOT SPRINGS 59   *Sacajawea Hot Springs*
HIKE 59a   *Trail Creek Lakes*
HIKE 59b   *Baron Lakes*

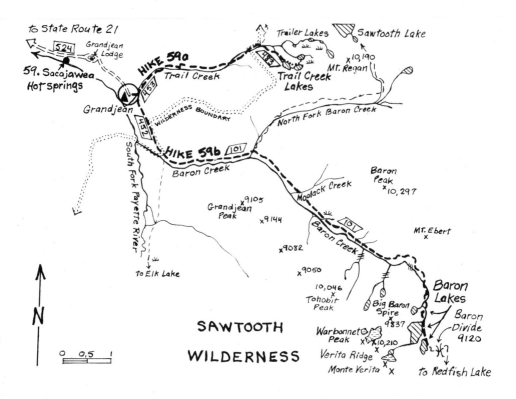

alongside the roaring Baron Creek Falls. Above, the trail crosses the first bridge after the one at Trail Creek nine miles back.

Little Baron Lake lies in a shallow basin off the trail a short hop west of the third stream crossing. It has several uncrowded campsites in the trees near the outlet. Subalpine firs ring the small lake and give it acres of privacy but limited views.

Baron Lake is the next stop, at 10.25 miles, 8,312 feet. A jagged wall of granite across the lake is mirrored in the sapphire-blue water. The most level campsites lie on the west side of the outlet facing the view. If these are full, try the west shore across from the trail.

The two lower lakes are bordered to the west by 9,837-foot Big Baron Spire. Just south of this flat faced peak, the sawtoothed silhouette of Verita Ridge parallels Baron Lake to the west and eclipses 10,210-foot Warbonnet Peak. Southwest of the halfmile-long lake rise the two towering crests of Monte Verita.

The short trail to Upper Baron climbs the ridge that separates them, and the only semi-level campsite is right beside the path where you first drop into the rocky basin at 10.75 miles, 8,505 feet. The continuing trail over the divide climbs sharply above the east shore, with a broader view at every switchback, and Baron Lake becomes more visible just below the upper lake. From Baron Divide, at a skyscraping 9,120 feet, the Sawtooths seem to stretch out forever!

Upper Baron Lake reflects a clear image of 9,837-foot Big Baron Spire.

60 Bear Valley Hot Springs

HIKE 60a *To Bear Valley Hot Springs*

General description: An almost easy seven-mile, round-trip day hike or over-nighter to a chain of pearls locked up in the River of No Return Wilderness, northeast of Lowman. Swimwear superfluous baggage.
Elevation gain and loss: +160 feet, -320 feet.
High point: Trailhead, 6,360 feet.
Low point: Hot springs, 6,200 feet.
Hiking quads: River of No Return Wilderness, South half (Forest Service) or Blue Bunch Mountain and Cape Horn Lakes USGS.
Road map: Wilderness quad or Boise National Forest.

Finding the trailhead: On State Route 21, drive about thirty-seven miles northeast of Lowman or twenty-one miles northwest of Stanley. Turn west on Forest Road 82/579 signed to Bruce Meadows and Boundary Creek. At about eight miles, a small sign marks the turnoff to Marsh Creek Trail and Fir Creek Campground (if you pass the airstrip you've gone too far). Park at Fir Creek Pack Bridge, the trailhead. The springs are marked only on the USGS map.

The hike: Bear Valley Creek has a claim to fame apart from its hot springs. It joins Marsh Creek just downstream to become the headwaters of the Middle Fork Salmon River—one of the star attractions in the River of No Return Wilderness (see Hike 61/62a). The trail was used heavily at one time by salmon fishermen but has seen little use in the last ten years due to a closure designed to protect the spawning salmon. Chances are good that you'll have the hot pools to yourself.

Turn right across the bridge onto Marsh Creek Trail (12). Follow the creek east for the first easy 1.5 miles, then watch for a spot in a large meadow where the trail crosses it and disappears into the woods. This ford would be suicidal during high water; the stream is a good twenty yards wide and often knee-deep through mid-August. Next, the path winds through a tangle of lodgepole pines strewn about on the ground like an oversized child's game of pick-up sticks.

Watch closely for a tree on your left in 3.5 miles that bears the message "HS." Take your choice of faint paths winding down a geothermal slope. Don't be discouraged when you reach the bottom and find only one murky, ankle deep pool filled with algae. Stroll downstream to a larger flow and track it past a grassy campsite to a chain of five-star gems dropping step by step to the creek's edge.

It should be mentioned that there's an alternate route that saves fording the creek as well as 0.5 mile of walking. It's a primitive path that follows the south bank from Fir Creek Campground to where the Forest Service trail crosses over. The catch is that it erodes away traversing a slippery stretch well up the steep bank. It's not a route for small children or anyone afraid of heights. The prudent choice would be to hold off until late August and take the official trail.

This creekside dip is the last link in the chain at Bear Valley Hot Springs.

The hot springs: Imagine a string of clear pools of perfect soaking temperature drawing you from one to the next down to the edge of a lively creek. The uppermost and largest is sheltered under a canopy of evergreenery, while the creekside dips, lined with sun warmed rocks, give a feeling of openness and contact with the stream. The setting is as close to perfection as nature allows.

HIKE 60a *To Bear Valley Hot Springs*
HIKE 60b *Blue Bunch Mountain*

HIKE 60b *Blue Bunch Mountain*

General description: A moderate ten-mile, round-trip day climb to a mountaintop in the River of No Return Wilderness, near Bear Valley Hot Springs.
Elevation gain and loss: +2,480 feet, -100 feet.
Trailhead elevation: 6,360 feet.
High point: Blue Bunch Mountain, 8,743 feet.
Hiking quads: Same as Hike 60a minus the Cape Horn Lakes USGS.
Road map: Same as Hike 60a.

Finding the trailhead: Follow the road access for Hike 60a.

The hike: The serious hiker with a day to spare and energy to burn might consider a second outing from the same trailhead. This brisk climb has a gain of 2,480 feet in five miles but tops off with views of Red Mountain to the southwest (see Hikes 56a,b) and Cape Horn Mountain to the southeast.

Turn left across the bridge onto Blue Bunch Mountain Trail (13). The path climbs north through wooded slopes scarred by a recent fire to reach Blue Bunch Ridge in about four miles. Beyond a sheepherder's cabin and spring, the route becomes hard to trace in spots. Continue north along the tapering ridge for the final two miles and enjoy glimpses of the valleys below. The trail peters out, along with the weary hiker, at the viewpoint on the summit.

61/62 Trail Flat & Sheepeater Hot Springs

HIKE 61/62a *To Trail Flat & Sheepeater Hot Springs*

General description: A moderate twenty six-mile round-trip backpack to a "double bubble" known only to river rats, in the Middle Fork Salmon River Canyon of the River of No Return Wilderness, northeast of Lowman. "Naked bodies welcome" seems the tradition.
Elevation gain and loss: +500 feet, -1,100 feet.
High point: Trailhead, 5,800 feet.

Late summer is the perfect time for backpackers to visit Trail Flat Hot Springs.

Low point: Sheepeater, 5,200 feet.

Hiking quads: Middle Fork of the Salmon or River of No Return Wilderness, south half (both Forest Service).

Road map: Wilderness quad or Boise National Forest.

Finding the trailhead: Follow the road access for Hike 60a above but continue past the landing strip. Turn right (north) on Forest Road 568 and drive about fifteen miles to a junction near the end. The right fork goes to Dagger Creek Hot Spring (see 63), and the left fork goes to Boundary Creek Campground and trailhead, twenty-three dusty miles from State Route 21. There's a ranger on duty there all summer. Sheepeater is shown on all but the Boise Forest map; Trail Flat is marked only on the Middle Fork map and omitted even on the state geothermal.

The hike: Two remote hot springs lie six miles apart near the upper end of the Middle Fork Salmon River. The streamside soaks at Trail Flat are submerged at high water but should be fine by midsummer, while Sheepeater's secluded dips lie on a rocky terrace well above the river's grasp. The 100-mile-long river (the only navigable stream of such length in the northwest where powerboats are banned) lies within the National Wild and Scenic Rivers system of the River of No Return Wilderness.

The route to both springs follows the west side of the river downstream from Boundary Creek, a launch site where rafts splash down over a 100-foot-high ramp. By around mid-August, the rafts are flown to a lower put-in at

The Middle Fork Trail between Trail Flat and Sheepeater Hot Springs offers many views up and down the rugged canyon.

HIKE 61/62a *To Trail Flat and Sheepeater Hot Springs*
HOT SPRINGS 63 *Dagger Creek Hot Spring*

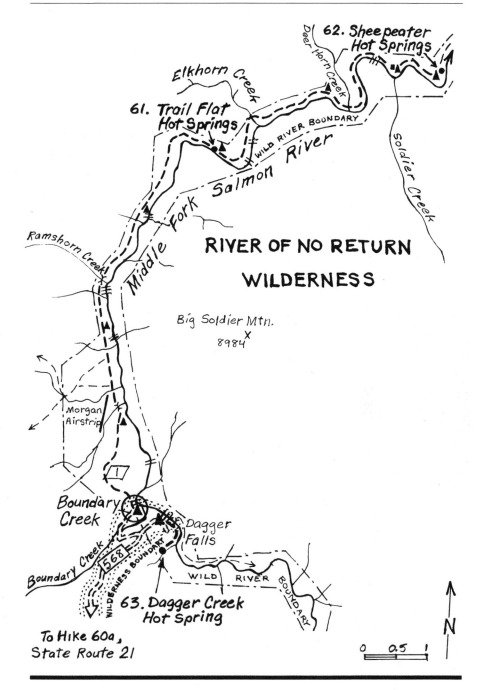

62. Sheepeater Hot Springs

Deer Horn Creek

Elkhorn Creek

61. Trail Flat Hot Springs

WILD RIVER BOUNDARY

Middle Fork Salmon River

Soldier Creek

RIVER OF NO RETURN

WILDERNESS

Ramshorn Creek

Big Soldier Mtn.
8984 X

Morgan Airstrip

Boundary Creek

568

Dagger Falls

Boundary Creek

WILDERNESS BOUNDARY

WILD RIVER BOUNDARY

63. Dagger Creek Hot Spring

To Hike 60a, State Route 21

0   0.5   1

N

Indian Creek. From this time on, the hot pools and nearby campsites should be less congested, the side creeks safe to ford, and the trail high and dry above the river. The access road is open until mid-October.

The Middle Fork Trail (1) follows an abandoned road for the first mile or so over wooded hills, passing a private airstrip and side trails at Sulphur and Prospect creeks; it reaches the river at four miles, near a point overlooking a turquoise pool by the bridge over Ramshorn Creek.

The path briefly hugs the river, then climbs well up the bank. Traversing this slope, it seems to drape loosely from the base of one anchoring tree to the next like a Christmas tree chain drooping from bough to bough. There are no views until you reach an open hill above Trail Flat. Once you spot the gravel bar, you can usually make out the steam rising from the pools.

Drop down a rocky slope to reach the campground at seven miles, 5,400 feet. The pools are found along the beach just below. (Check out the two-sided outhouse hiding behind a tree just off the trail—the odd shape seems to be quite the fashion in camps along the Middle Fork.)

The twelve-mile round trip from Trail Flat to Sheepeater is the most scenic stretch of the hike; it can be done in one long day with ample time to enjoy the soaking pools at both ends. The route stays close to the river much of the way, and when it climbs it keeps the river in sight. Hills wooded with tall ponderosas alternate with boulder-strewn slopes, and there are many pleasant views up and down the canyon.

About a mile below Trail Flat, the path drops down to ford Elkhorn Creek, which may be impassable at high water. It climbs and then dips again to cross Deer Horn Creek on an upstream log at ten miles.

When you pass Joe Bump's log cabin, followed by a grave marked "Elmer Set Trigger Purcell, prospector/trapper, 1936," you'll be in the home stretch. Watch for steam from Sheepeater's springs in a clearing off to your left at thirteen miles. There's a large camping area by the river and another in a clearing just above.

The hot springs: Trail Flat has one large, very hot source pool midway along the gravel beach. The steamy outflow runs through several increasingly cooler soaking pools fanning out to the river's edge. The sizes and shapes vary, as users have to scoop out new pools each year after the spring runoff.

At Sheepeater, you'll find a square soaking box lined with split logs. Big enough to house a small army, the semi-landlocked pool makes a cozy (though a bit cloudy) cocoon. Shortly beyond it are three tiny pools tucked up against the bank. These hotter dips have an ample flow to keep them clean but no handy means of lowering the temperature. You can track the broad outflow down the hill to two slightly cooler pools hidden in the woods.

Tired feet come out like new after a soak at Dagger.

63 Dagger Creek Hot Spring

General description: A peaceful soak near the trailhead to Trail Flat and Sheepeater hot springs, northeast of Lowman in the River of No Return Wilderness. Swimwear optional. Elevation 5,800 feet.
Map: Same as road map above.

Finding the hot spring: Follow the road access for Hike 61/62a to the junction near the end of Forest Road 568. The right fork will take you to Dagger Falls. Park at the tiny campground and follow a fisherman's path along the Middle Fork Salmon River. Go past the falls 0.5 mile upstream to the mouth of Dagger Creek and then follow the creek a short way upstream to the pool. The spring isn't marked on the forest map.

The hot spring: This little dip has a double distinction. It's the only hot spring in the River of No Return Wilderness that doesn't require a rugged hike to reach. It's also the only one you can plop your tired body into right after a lengthy hike to other geothermal delights. It lies just within both the wilderness and the Wild and Scenic River boundaries less than a mile from a quiet backwoods campground.

Dagger Creek Hot Spring perks up through the sand and mud bottom of a rock-lined pool in the grass along the creek bank. The soaking pool is shallow and barely big enough for a cozy couple to stretch out in, but the temperature at a toasty 103 degrees is hard to beat. It offers a handy remedy for stiff muscles after the trek to Trail Flat and Sheepeater.

F. OUT OF ATLANTA

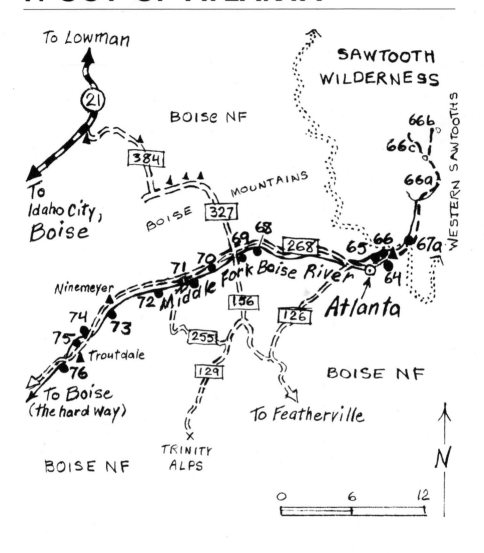

Note: Atlanta offers no services except the Whistle Stop cafe/bar, a small lodge, post office, and public phone.

Hot springs and hikes

The Atlanta trailhead into the western Sawtooths, ninety miles northeast of Boise, is accessed by forty-five miles of dirt roads from State Route 21. Trailhead soaks add much to the appeal as does the tiny backwoods town. From the hot springs (64-66), wilderness buffs can trek to panoramic views around

Spangle Lakes or day hike to Lynx Creek—the uppermost soak on the Middle Fork Boise River (67a). West of town, collectors can drive downstream to tally up nine more (68-76), with five-star soaks at Granite Creek and Loftus. Hikers will enjoy the nearby Trinity Lakes centered around 10,000-foot Trinity Mountain.

Season

The main road(s) to Atlanta are kept open all year. All soaks but Atlanta, Phifer, and Loftus are submerged during spring runoff. Weatherby, Brown's Creek, and Ninemeyer require a river ford (the window is usually mid-August through early October). The hiking season in the high Sawtooths and Trinity Alps doesn't get underway until late July and usually runs through mid-September, while the foothills downstream enjoy a longer season. Summer weather can be hot with cold nights at higher elevations, and hikers should be equipped for foul weather.

Getting to Atlanta

The best route from Boise leaves State Route 21 nineteen miles above Idaho City or fifteen miles south of Lowman (Section E). The next thirty miles of dirt are graded and signed, on Forest Roads 384 and 327, with a final fifteen-mile grind up the Middle Fork Road (268). The slow route is to take the latter road all the way up, as the lower stretch where it branches off State Route 21 near Boise is a tedious crawl past Arrowrock Reservoir. Thus the "nine soaks tour" along the middle stretch is recommended as a side trip en route to or from Atlanta.

Atlanta can also be reached from Featherville (Section G) via twenty five miles of seasonal roads with a steep clumb over James Creek Road (126)—a short cut from Forest Road 156. The latter connects Featherville with the Middle Fork Road fifteen miles west of Atlanta—a longer but easier route that also accesses the Trinty Alps.

64 Atlanta Hot Springs

General description: A roadside delight near the Atlanta trailhead into the Sawtooths, just east of Atlanta. Skinnydippable with discretion. Elevation 5,400 feet.

Map: Boise National Forest.

Finding the hot springs: Follow the directions above to Atlanta. Continue a bit over a mile northeast on the road to Power Plant Recreation Area (just past the turnoff to Chattanooga), then watch for a large pond on your right. A spur just beyond it has room for a car or two to park, and a short path leads to the pool. The springs aren't marked on the forest map.

The hot springs: A comfortable rock-and-masonry soaking pool sits in a grassy clearing in the woods a scant quarter mile from the Atlanta trailhead. It's usable by late spring since it's well above the river. Two pipes (one at 116 degrees the other at 96 degrees) supply spring water, and the soak averages around 105 degrees. The user-built pool measures a good six by twelve feet and has a hand-hewn bench at one end. An outlet pipe allows easy draining. The runoff

The present pool at Atlanta Hot Springs was tastefully designed and solidly built complete with plumbing.

flows into the pond below, which doubles in hot weather as a fine swimming hole. You may have a few hungry chiggers for company, but the soak is worth the risk.

"Over and out:" After a soak a few years back, I remembered a call I'd promised a friend. I sped into town to find that the only contact Atlanta had with the outside world was a radiotelephone on the counter of the cafe.

I was briefed by the short-order cook on the art of conducting a one-way conversation. Precision timing was required. You pushed a button to transmit and released to receive. Release too soon and your sentence was cut off; release too late and you lost the reply. Remember to end every remark with a loud "OVER," or the other party wouldn't know it was time to speak. As I stood there fumbling with the button and shouting birthday greetings into the microphone, I must have provided the townsfolk of Atlanta with the best live entertainment they'd had in some time!

Shortly thereafter, probably around 1989, Atlanta joined the rest of modern civilization and had standard service brought in via a microwave link. The old radiotelephone and its live entertainment are now just history.

65 Chattanooga Hot Springs

General description: A five-star soaker on the Middle Fork Boise River near the Atlanta trailhead into the Sawtooths, just east of Atlanta. Swimwear optional. Elevation 5,360 feet.
Map: Boise National Forest.

Finding the hot springs: Follow the directions above to Atlanta and continue a mile northeast on the road to Power Plant Recreation Area. Just west of the pond by Atlanta Hot Springs, look for a left turn marked by a tree that bisects the road. Follow a short spur north to a grassy flat by the cliff. (The flat is on private land—no camping allowed.) Park here and choose between two steep paths dropping down to the pool. Chattanooga isn't shown on the forest map.

The hot springs: Bubbly springs cascade over a cliff into a large, knee-deep pool lined with rocks. The clear pool has a sandy bottom, and the temperature seems to stay a steady perfect. This topnotch retreat, near the trailhead for the following hikes, is tucked between the base of the 100-foot cliff and the nearby river. The jagged Sawtooths across the canyon form a dramatic backdrop. This is a great place to pause and unwind between the rigors of a long, dusty trail and those of an even longer, bumpy road!

Chattanooga offers wayfarers a scenic soak and showerbath.

66 Greylock Hot Spring

General description: Yet another hot dip on the Middle Fork Boise River at the Atlanta trailhead into the Sawtooths, jst east of Atlanta. Keep swimwear within reach. Elevation 5,460 feet.
Map: Boise National Forest.

Finding the hot spring: Follow the directions above to Atlanta and continue 1.3 miles northeast to Power Plant Recreation Area (just past Atlanta and Chattanooga Hot Springs). You'll see a meadow at the campground entrance. On the right is the Atlanta trailhead and on the left is a primitive camp on the bank. Park here and follow a track down to the riverside pool(s). This spring isn't marked on any map—not even the state geothermal.

The hot spring: Some recent sleuthing unearthed one more hot soak near Atlanta, and it couldn't be closer to either the trailhead or a fine campsite. The spring flows across a gravel bar into one or more rocky soaking pools. The biggest has a sandy bottom that four to six bodies can shoehorn into. The temperature runs around 104 degrees and can be adjusted by adding river water.

Greylock would be submerged during spring runoff, but since the following

Hot water channels into a late-season pool at Greylock.

hikes are best done in mid to late summer, the timing would coincide. The site is visible only to people camping on the bank above, and the view across the river to jagged Greylock Mountain (its unofficial namesake) is nothing short of spectacular.

HIKE 66a *Spangle Lakes*

General description: A rugged thirty-one-mile, round-trip backpack featuring alpine meadows and lakes in the heart of the Sawtooth Wilderness, near Atlanta, Chattanooga, and Greylock Hot Springs.
Elevation gain and loss: +3,480 feet, -320 feet.
Trailhead elevation: 5,440 feet.
High point: Upper Spangle Lake, 8,600 feet.
Hiking quads: Atlanta East and Mount Everly USGS.
Road map: Boise National Forest.

Finding the trailhead: Follow the directions above to Atlanta and continue 1.3 miles northeast to Power Plant Recreation Area. The trail sign is located on the right side of a large meadow at the campground entrance. Give the car a well earned rest and put your boots to work.

Increasing glimpses of granite peaks and ridges above the river canyon ease the strain of the long climb to Spangle Lakes.

The hike: A bonsai effect of delicate meadows, rock gardens, and dwarfed, twisted trees is the setting for Little Spangle Lake. Upper Spangle is a deep blue circle rimmed by thick woods and cream colored granite walls. The basin sits on the threshold of the magnificent high country, and lonesome campsites tempt the visitor to linger and explore farther (Hikes 66b,c). The price of admission is a lengthy access on a trail that doesn't give much to write home about for the first twelve miles—a gradual ascent through a uniform forest of Douglas fir relieved by occasional meadows.

The first few miles east on the Middle Fork Boise River Trail (460) are an easy stroll. The route then crosses Leggit Creek (difficult to ford during high water in early summer) and hairpins up a hill. Leggit Lake Trail forks south from the top of a rocky knoll at 6,050 feet. *Note:* A mystery hot spring on Leggit Creek, unmarked on any map but the state geothermal, hides away about a mile upstream undiscovered. However, one unlisted even on the geothermal has been found on the trail side of the river just up ahead (see Hike 67a).

You'll pass Mattingly Creek Trail in five miles and cross the creek itself in another 0.5 mile. This stream, another difficult ford during high water, is a good late-season water source and has fine campsites on both sides of the log crossing.

The four-mile stretch north to Rock Creek is a moderate climb up the east side of the canyon. A few campsites hide in the woods west of the trail at the end of a meadow 0.25 mile before the first river crossing. The route crosses two wide channels here in a rocky outwash that could be dangerous too early in the summer. Just beyond the second ford, at 6,400 feet, the trail splits. The left branch climbs Rock Creek to Timpa Lake, and the main trail turns east.

The trail crosses the river four times in the 3.5 miles to Flytrip Creek. Scout for footlogs hidden up or downstream. Next, wade a meadow with chin-high wildflowers and a view of Mattingly Peak over your shoulder. Later, the path reaches a few campsites in a flat where the river (just a small stream by now) splits into several channels and the trail disappears. Wade the stream and aim for a grove of tall trees ahead, where you'll find more campsites. The Flytrip Creek Trail junction (at 7,500 feet) branches off to your right.

A scenic side trip can be made up the steep 1.5-mile trail to Camp Lake at 8,500 feet. Follow a faint path southeast from its inlet to reach Heart Lake in another 0.25 mile. Low ridges separate the many tiny lakes just south and east. Beyond them rises the jagged crest of the Sawtooths topped by 10,651-foot Snowyside Peak. To explore these lakes, you'll need the Snowyside Peak quad.

The final three-mile stretch offers broad views as the trail switchbacks up the headwall. Continue over the crest past a meadow to Little Spangle Lake. Peninsulas and inlets around the shallow basin offer a variety of photogenic scenes; rocky islands breaking the surface adopt a new shape from each viewpoint. An idyllic campsite lies across a small meadow at the northeast corner.

Cross a low ridge 200 yards north to reach Upper Spangle Lake at 8,600 feet. The large, circular lake is hemmed in by a steep basin crowded with subalpine fir, lodgepole and whitebark pine. The only decent campsites lie up a small valley on the northeast side. The Middle Fork Trail ends at Spangle Junction near the south shore. Two new trails begin here—both easy day trips from Spangle Lakes.

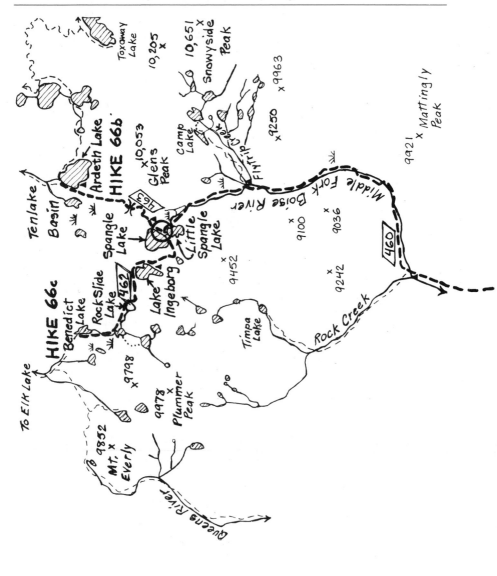

HOT SPRINGS 64 *Atlanta Hot Springs*
HOT SPRINGS 65 *Chattanooga Hot Springs*
HOT SPRINGS 66 *Greylock Hot Spring*
HOT SPRINGS 67 *Lynx Creek Hot Spring*

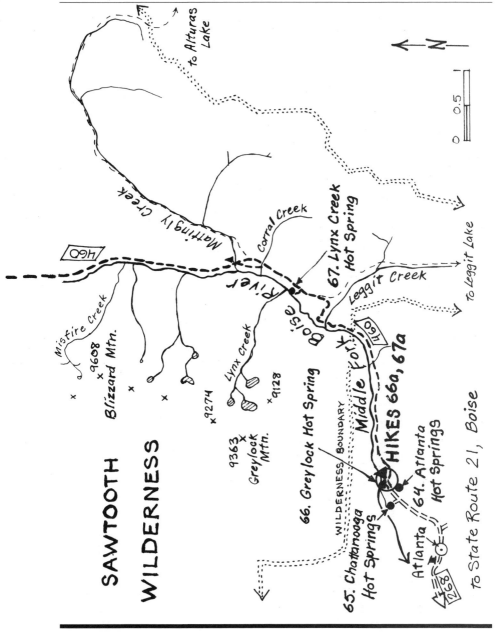

HIKE 66b *Spangle Lakes to Tenlake Basin & Ardeth Lake*

General description: A moderate five-mile, round-trip day hike or overnighter from Spangle Lakes to more high views and lakes in the Sawtooth Wilderness.
Elevation gain and loss: +352 feet, -712 feet.
Trailhead elevation: 8,600 feet at Upper Spangle Lake.
High point: Spangle Summit, 8,952 feet.
Maps: Same as Hike 66a.

Finding the trailhead: Follow Hike 66a to Spangle Lakes.

The hike: Look south from Spangle Summit to jagged peaks rising above the river canyon far below. To the west, above Spangle Lake Basin, is the snow-capped escarpment by Lake Ingeborg. Look straight up at 10,053-foot Glens Peak to the east. To the north lies the rocky Tenlake Basin—you can count at least six of the many small lakes from here.

To get there, turn right (northeast) at Spangle Junction and climb the ridge above the east side of the lake on a well maintained trail (463). Enjoy the panoramic views from the 8,952-foot summit (the high point on the hike) just a mile up the trail.

Drop down the steep talus slope on the north side of the ridge. You may still find snow patches here in midsummer. The route passes just west of a marshy pond and continues north through a forest of subalpine fir and lodgepoles leading down to Ardeth Lake at 2.5 miles, 8,240 feet.

The path emerges from the woods to overlook beach campsites on the southwest shore. Follow the trail down the west side of the lake to more camp-sites and viewpoints near the outlet on the northwest side. There's a marvelous outlook from here of the permanent snowfields and jagged silhouette of Glens Peak mirrored in the clear water.

HIKE 66c *Spangle Lakes to Ingeborg, Rock Slide, & Benedict Lakes*

General description: A moderate six-mile, round-trip day hike or overnighter from Spangle Lakes to the highest lake reached by trail in the Sawtooth Wilderness.
Elevation gain and loss: +320 feet, -640 feet.
Trailhead elevation: 8,600 feet at Upper Spangle Lake.
High point: 8,920 feet.
Maps: Same as Hike 66a.

Finding the trailhead: Follow Hike 66a to Spangle Lakes.

The hike: No trek to Spangle Lakes is complete without a side trip to these beautiful lakes. The lightly traveled route offers unlimited opportunities to explore and enjoy the magnificent alpine scenery on all sides. Don't miss it!

The trail (462) begins at Spangle Junction and zigzags up the steep basin

Rock Slide Lake earned its new name from the slide falling directly into the small triangular lake from a nearby peak.

on the southwest side. The grade tapers off near a small gem of a lake rimmed with granite walls. Bear northwest a mile across the 8,920-foot plateau to reach sky-high Lake Ingeborg at 8,890 feet (the highest major lake accessible by trail in the Sawtooths) on a bench between the Boise River and Benedict Creek drainages. Rosy granite juts above the western side; the shoreline is dotted with limber pine and subalpine fir between tiny campsites.

Circle the east side, then drop 200 feet to Rock Slide (a smaller lake in a similar setting) in another 0.75 mile. The trail descends through the maze of boulders that give the lake its present name. The label shown on the forest map, Robert Jackson Lake, came from a man who decided to name it after himself! When the USGS learned that Mr. Jackson was not only still alive but had no historical connection with the lake, they changed it to the present name.

The path follows the east side of Rock Slide Lake and descends a wooded hillside to a large pond. The meadow on the east shore is cut by serpentine channels that resemble dragons in an oriental rug pattern. Continue north across a marsh sprinkled with tiny wildflowers, then drop down a wooded ridge to reach Benedict Lake at three miles, 8,260 feet. Green meadows and a thick border of subalpine fir line the west wall, and two sharp peaks mark the south end of the valley.

67 Lynx Creek Hot Spring

HIKE 67a *To Lynx Creek Hot Spring*

General description: A moderate nine-mile round-trip day hike to the uppermost hot spring on the Middle Fork Boise River, and the only one to be found in the Sawtooth Wilderness. Swimwear superfluous baggage.

Elevation gain and loss: +780 feet, -620 feet.
Trailhead elevation: 5,440 feet.
High point: 6,050 feet.
Hiking quad: Atlanta East USGS.
Road map: Boise National Forest.

Finding the trailhead: Follow the road access for Hike 66a.

The hike: Those not planning to backpack into the Spangle Lakes (Hikes 66a-c) may yet be interested in a day's jaunt to a pristine soaker hidden at the river's edge at the base of a steep bank below the trail. This wild gem, probably the best kept secret around Atlanta, isn't marked on any map at all.

Stroll the Middle Fork Boise River Trail (460) east through a uniform forest of Douglas-fir and scattered meadows. On the far side of Leggit Creek (a difficult ford during spring runoff), the route hairpins up a hill to a high point of 6,050 feet at the Leggit Lake Junction. This is the four-mile mark. The route continues well above the river, and in another 0.25 mile a user-built path plunges down the bank to the spring.

The hot springs: Totally screened from the path above, Lynx Creek Hot Spring bubbles into a cozy soaking pool at the river's edge a short distance downstream from the mouth of Lynx Creek on the opposite bank. Rebuilt by the few souls who frequent it each year after the river level drops, the pool offers a toasty soak in a tranquil alpine setting. The temperature is adjustable by shifting a rock or two in the dam.

68 Weatherby Hot Springs

General Description: Potluck hot dips up a creek on the wrong side of the Middle Fork Boise River, west of Atlanta in the Boise Mountains. Naked bodies welcome. Elevation 4,500 feet.
Map: Boise National Forest.

Finding the hot springs: Refer to "Getting to Atlanta" above and take the Middle Fork Road (268) about thirteen miles downstream. Watch for a sign labeling Hot Creek between Mileposts 55 and 54. Turn left to an airstrip and park on the bank near the windsock end. By mid-August you should be able to wade safely across to the mouth of the creek. Weatherby isn't marked on the forest map, but the creek is. The USGS quad is Phifer Creek.

The hot spring: Weatherby, one of the least known springsalong the Middle Fork, has the advantage of not being visible from the road. The strike against it is the problem of crossing the river to investigate. One spring issues from the ground at 113 degrees near an old corral at the mouth of Hot Creek, and another spring can be reached via an overgrown path about 0.25 mile up the creek. With perseverance and a dash of luck, you may find a soaker worth developing.

The shower shack at Phifer shows you can't judge a book by its cover. You gotta check out the inside. . .

69 Phifer Warm Spring

General description: A roadside shower shack supplied by an artesian well along the Middle Fork Boise River, west of Atlanta in the Boise Mountains. Wear whatever you normally bathe in. Elevation 4,400 feet.
Map: Boise National Forest.

Finding the warm spring: Refer to "Getting to Atlanta" and take the Middle Fork Road (268) about fifteen miles downstream to the intersection of Forest Roads 327 north and 156 south. Cross the river bridge and turn left on a spur that crosses Phifer Creek and soon ends at a primitive camp. The spring isn't marked on the forest map, but you can't miss the container.

Note to hikers: The Trinity Alps, a tiny wonderland of lakes on a five-mile trail between Big Trinity Lake Campground and the lookout capping 10,000-foot Trinity Mountain, can be reached via Forest Road 156 or 255.

The warm spring: Spring water gushing from an artesian well is piped into a funky but functional bathhouse to provide the passerby with a torrent of warm (86-degree) bath water. The five by seven-foot shack is lined with plastic and floored with bright green astroturf. A partition separates a changing room (stumps for clothes) from the shower cubicle. Other facilities include a home-built outhouse labeled "Bullbuck's office." The site, once part of the old Weatherby Mill, is currently a mining claim on public land.

70 Granite Creek Hot Spring

General description: A scenic soaker on the Middle Fork Boise River, southwest of Atlanta in the Boise Mountains. Swimsuits essential when standing up. Elevation 4,200 feet.
Map: Boise National Forest.

Finding the hot spring: Refer to "Getting to Atlanta" and take the Middle Fork Road (268) about fifteen miles downstream to the junction of Forest Roads 327 north and 156 south. Continue 3.4 miles past Dutch Creek Guard Station to a pullout 0.5 mile east of a sign for Granite Creek and hop down the rocks to the pool. The spring isn't marked on the forest map.

The hot spring: Sun-warmed boulders line a large soaking pool at the river's edge below the road. The outflow from the nearby spring keeps the sandy-bottomed pool clean, and the temperature can be lowered by removing a rock or two in the dam. Except for Loftus, this may be the best of the downstream dips. Its only drawback is the proximity of the dusty road.

Granite Creek can be counted on for a user-friendly pool after spring runoff.

71 Dutch Frank Hot Springs

General description: Steamy springs and tiny pools on the Middle Fork Boise River, southwest of Atlanta in the Boise Mountains. Swimwear advised. Elevation 4,100 feet.

Map: Boise National Forest.

Finding the hot springs: Refer to "Getting to Atlanta" and take the Middle Fork Road (268) about twenty-one miles downstream (two miles past the Granite Creek sign) to the junction of Forest Road 255 signed to Trinity Lakes, at the Roaring River bridge. (*Note to hikers:* See 69.) Park across the river and follow a short path upstream. Dutch Frank, called "Roaring River" by locals, isn't marked on the forest map.

The hot springs: A cluster of springs issues from the ground at temperatures up to 150 degrees, and steamy channels flow across a broad and highly visible flat on the south side of the river. A few small pools dug out of the rocks right at waterline allow a variable blend of temperatures. As the river level drops through the season, new dips must be dug lower down.

72 Brown's Creek Hot Spring

General description: A hot "showerfall" on the wrong side of the Middle Fork Boise River, southwest of Atlanta. Swimwear and a life preserver recommended. Elevation 3,900 feet.

Map: Boise National Forest.

Finding the hot spring: Refer to "Getting to Atlanta" and take the Middle Fork Road (268) about 24.5 miles downstream (3.5 miles past the bridge at Forest Road 255). Watch for a sign labeling Brown's Creek Trail, just east of Brown's Creek. There's a pullout where you can look directly across at the plunge. The spring isn't marked on the forest map.

The hot spring: Hot water gushing from fissures in the rocks at 122 degrees cascades down a cliff in several graceful falls. One lands on a tiny beach exposed at low water. This lovely stand-up shower would be tricky to reach even when the river's at its lowest (usually in late August). It's swift and deep at this bend, sheer walls except for the take-out point, and rapids just downstream. Possibly an inner tube or raft? Or, maybe just a pleasant fantasy.

The magnificent showerbath at Brown's Creek is a windowshoppers special.

73 Ninemeyer Hot Springs

General description: A cluster of springs flowing down an open hillside on the wrong side of the Middle Fork Boise River, southwest of Atlanta. Swimwear advised. Elevation 3,800 feet.
Map: Boise National Forest

Finding the hot springs: Refer to "Getting to Atlanta" and take the Middle Fork Road (268) nearly thirty miles downstream (five miles past Brown's Creek) to Ninemeyer Forest Camp at Milepost 38. The springs, directly across from Ninemeyer Creek, aren't marked on the forest map.

The hot springs: Early morning steam blankets the slopes above Ninemeyer as scalding 169-degree water channels rivulets downhill. It's possible to ford the river here from around mid-August through early October (an island in the center eases the crossing), and folks often dig out a dip or two right at waterline, where the hot and cold stand a chance of mixing.

Geothermal note: Between Mileposts 35 and 36, 2.5 miles downstream from Ninemeyer, you can spot a spectacular hot waterfall across the river near Pete Creek. It's not marked on any map, but sure looks like a potential shower when the river's low enough to cross!

A ponderosa tipping downhill provides a towel rack at Loftus.

74 Loftus Hot Spring

General description: A roadside grotto pool on a wooded bank above the Middle Fork Boise River, southwest of Atlanta. Swimwear recommended when standing up. Elevation 3,600 feet.
Map: Boise National Forest.

Finding the hot spring: Refer to "Getting to Atlanta" and take the Middle Fork Road (268) nearly thirty-four miles downstream (four miles past Ninemeyer) to a pullout at Milepost 34. Park here and climb the short path up to the pool. Loftus isn't marked on the forest map.

The hot spring: Users have dug out a pool beneath an overhanging rocky ledge, and the hot spring trickles directly over the lip into the water below. The shallow pool, which runs around 105 degrees, is about ten feet in diameter with a clean sandy bottom. Once seated in the pool, users have a sense of total privacy. Loftus, a popular hideaway, can be enjoyed virtually year-round.

75 Smith Cabin Hot Springs

General description: Hot springs on both banks of the Middle Fork Boise River, southwest of Atlanta. Swimwear advised. Elevation 3,600 feet.
Map: Boise National Forest.

Finding the hot springs: Refer to "Getting to Atlanta" and take the Middle Fork Road (268) about thirty-four miles downstream (0.2 mile past Loftus) to a bridge where the road crosses to the south bank. Continue 0.7 mile and park wherever you can find room. Several tracks drop down to converge at the springs. Smith Cabin isn't marked on the forest map.

The hot springs: Spring water emerges from the riverbank at 138 degrees, and users sometimes dig out a pool in the rocks right at waterline where the temperatures can blend. And by mid-August, you should be able to safely ford the river upstream to a line of bushes that conceal more hot springs and a potential dip or two on the opposite bank.

Geothermal note: Locals report a number of springs and seeps in the stretch downstream to Sheep Creek Bridge. Not marked on any map, they can only be pinpointed by their early-morning steam.

From the roadside dips at Smith Cabin Hot Springs, you can spot more springs across the river just upstream.

76 Sheep Creek Bridge Hot Spring

General description: A "has been" spring on the Middle Fork Boise River, southwest of Atlanta. Bare buns not recommended. Elevation 3,400 feet. **Map:** Boise National Forest.

Finding the hot spring: Refer to "Getting to Atlanta" and take the Middle Fork Road (268) around thirty-eight dusty miles downstream (2.7 miles past Troutdale Forest Camp) to a bridge at Milepost 30 where the road recrosses the river. Park at the east end by a trail sign and follow a short path that forks to the right from the trail. The spring, on a rocky bench above the river, isn't marked on the forest map.

The hot spring: Last on the Middle Fork list, this 142-degree spring is piped into a scalding hot, algae-laden soaker around ten feet in diameter. The outflow trickles through a small adjacent pool, then down a boulder slope to the river. Dipping diehards might try digging a cooler pool lower down. Reports indicate the output has been diminishing and the main pool was more usable in the past. Worth keeping tabs on. Who knows—it may perk up again.

G. OUT OF FEATHERVILLE

Note: The only services you'll find in Featherville are a bar, cafe, and public phone.

Hot springs and hikes

The remote outpost of Featherville, faintly marked on the state map midway between Boise and Ketchum, is the gateway to a series of hot springs along the Featherville-Ketchum Road (227) into the Smoky Mountains. Heading east through Sawtooth National Forest, the scenic route leads to easy-access soaks at Willow Creek (77) and popular Baumgartner (78). Next is the elusive Lightfoot (79a), then a hike-in soak at Skillern (80a) and a roadside dip at Preis (81). Last but not least comes a geothermal delight at Worswick (82).

Season

The limit on these soaks is the seasonal dirt road (open from about mid-May through October) and the spring runoff at Skillern's creekside pools. The hiking season ranges from May through October in the lower elevations to late June through late September in the higher country farther east. Summer weather is generally hot with scattered thunderstorms, with cold nights at higher elevations.

Getting to Featherville

The most direct access from the outside world is via sixty miles of pavement leaving Interstate 84 at Mountain Home: U.S. Highway 20 leads to the South Fork Boise River Road (61) which takes you north past Anderson Ranch Reservoir and Pine. Featherville can also be reached from Atlanta (Section F).

Travelers from the Twin Falls area would take State Route 46 north to Fairfield (home of the district ranger station) then continue north on Forest Road 94 to hit 227 near Worswick, midway between Featherville and Ketchum. The eighty-five-mile route is paved to the turnoff to Soldier Mountain, but the last ten miles are slow. From Ketchum, the route west on Forest Road 227 is all on dirt with a tedious crawl over Dollarhide Summit. From either starting point, the tour would be done in reverse—from east to west.

G. OUT OF FEATHERVILLE

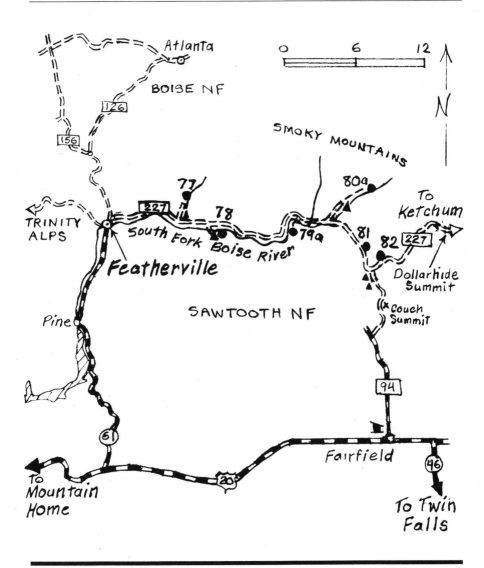

77 Willow Creek Hot Spring

General description: An all-season soak by a creekside path near the South Fork Boise River east of Featherville. Swimwear optional. Elevation 5,100 feet. **Map:** Sawtooth National Forest.

Finding the hot spring: Refer to "Getting to Featherville" above and take the Ketchum Road (227) seven miles east to Willow Creek Road. Turn left past the campground and drive 1.7 miles to the end. A wooded path follows the creek a scant 0.5 mile upstream to the pools. The spring is marked on the forest map.

The hot spring: Bubbles rise to the surface of a source pool at 131 degrees through a jungle of algae, and several soakers have been formed in the thermal stream. The uppermost is ten feet square and knee deep, dammed with logs and a tarp, and it registers a toasty 105 degrees. One or more cooler dips can be found in the bushes where the stream joins the creek. The day I was there, the sandy path displayed one bike track, a few footprints, and mostly deer prints. A gathering of huge golden butterflies shared the sunny clearing around the springs.

The perennial pool at Willow Creek is a little-known dipper's delight.

For a bit of civilized soaking, check out Baumgartner's popular swimming pool.

78 Baumgartner Hot Springs

General description: A campground hot swimming pool on the South Fork Boise River, east of Featherville. Public nudity prohibited. Elevation 5,100 feet.
Map: Sawtooth National Forest.

Finding the hot springs: Refer to "Getting to Featherville" and take the Ketchum Road (227) about ten miles east to Baumgartner Campground (a fully developed site, rare in these parts). You'll find the pool at the road end. Baumgartner is prominently marked on the forest map.

The hot springs: A fifteen-by-twenty-foot concrete pool houses the outflow from Baumgartner Hot Springs. The pool, furnished with decking and benches, is maintained by the Forest Service and kept at 104 degrees. There's a fee for camping, but passersby can use the pool free of charge. It's open from 6 a.m. to 10 p.m. daily (no alcohol or glass containers), from May 20 through September.

The site was deeded to the Forest Service by John Baumgartner for public camping and bathing "in its natural state so far as that is practicable." While it's about as far from its natural state as any you'll find in this guidebook, it's equally far from the commercial resorts at the other end of the spectrum. All things are relative, and the Forest Service has done a tasteful job of development.

79 Lightfoot Hot Springs

HIKE 79a *To Lightfoot Hot Springs*

General description: An easy three-mile round-trip walk to thermal streams and a dip or two on the wrong side of the South Fork Boise River, east of Featherville. Swimwear optional.
Elevation gain and loss: Minimal.
Hot springs: 5,400 feet.
Map: Sawtooth National Forest.

Finding the trailhead: Refer to "Getting to Featherville" and take the Ketchum Road (227) about 20.5 miles east (1.5 miles past the Lightfoot Hot Springs sign) to a footbridge across the river to Boardman Creek Trail. The springs are named on the forest map.

The hike: What's worthy of note about Lightfoot is that there's more to it than the algae-laden swamp in the ditch beside the road. The rest lies hidden across the river. It can be reached by fording near the sign (not recommended during high water) or by driving upstream to the footbridge and following a user-built path back on the opposite bank. Start hunting for clues after you pass an abandoned cabin in the woods and enter a clearing.

The hot springs: Three adjacent springs issue from the ground at 133 degrees and form shallow streams. One boasts a 110-degree pool dammed with rocks and a log; it's clean except for a layer of algae on top and bottom. Another, closer to the river, contains a tiny pool dug out of a rocky wash. Either is usable in a pinch, and chances are you'll have them all to yourself.

80 Skillern Hot Springs

HIKE 80a *To Skillern Hot Springs*

General description: An easy five-mile round-trip day hike to secluded pools on Big Smoky Creek, east of Featherville in the Smoky Mountains. Swimwear superfluous.
Elevation gain and loss: +300 feet, -100 feet.
Trailhead elevation: 5,600 feet.
High point: 5,900 feet.
Hiking quad: Paradise Peak USGS.
Road map: Sawtooth National Forest.

Finding the trailhead: Refer to "Getting to Featherville" and take the Ketchum Road (227) about twenty-four miles east to a turnoff signed Big

The highlight at Skillern Hot Springs is a rock pool with a showerbath, partway up the cliff.

Smoky. From the other direction, it's the same distance from Fairfield, and 5.5 miles from Forest Road 94. The road forks right, passes Big Smoky Guard Station, and ends in 1.3 miles at Canyon Campground. The trailhead is at the end of the loop. Skillern is named on the maps.

The hike: Big Smoky Creek Trail (72) hugs the stream a bit too closely, requiring four crossings, so an alternate route has been built up the bank. The high trail not only keeps your feet dry but offers views up and down the canyon. Grass and sagebrush speckle the southeast facing hills, while the cooler slopes across the canyon are wooded with ponderosa. At two miles the trails converge by the creek, and you'll reach the springs in another 0.5 mile. *Note:* You'll pass several trails branching left including two signed to Skillern Creek. Don't be tempted—stay in the main canyon.

The hot springs: Water gushing from the rocks at 140 degrees cascades down a cliff, then flows across a grassy flat to the creek. Here you'll find a few late-season pools where the temperatures can be blended into a first-class soak. Upstream, around the side of the cliff, there's a hidden pool partway up the side. This little gem, a depression in the rocky wall well above the high water mark, features a steamy shower spraying the surface and a rock/log dam to contain it.

Geothermal note: A second hot spring six miles upstream (marked on the forest map and named Big Smoky on the state geothermal) is reported by locals to be unusable for humans but very popular with the elk and deer population. Just thought you'd like to know.

HIKE 79a *To Lightfoot Hot Springs*
HIKE 80a *To Skillern Hot Springs*
HOT SPRINGS 81 *Preis Hot Spring*
HOT SPRINGS 82 *Worswick Hot Springs*

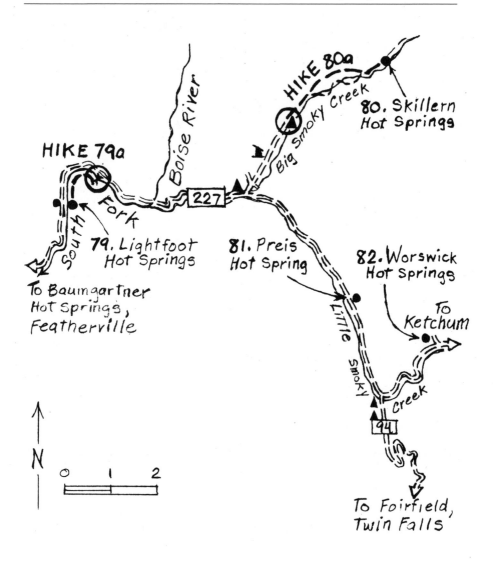

81 Preis Hot Spring

General description: A roadside hot box above Little Smoky Creek, east of Featherville in the Smoky Mountains. Swimwear recommended. Elevation 5,500 feet.

Map: Sawtooth National Forest.

Finding the hot spring: Refer to "Getting to Featherville" and take the Ketchum Road (227) about 27.5 miles east (3.5 miles past the Skillern turnoff at Big Smoky Creek). From the other direction, it's 2.1 miles from Forest Road 94. There's no landmark but a rock pile near the road. Preis is named on the forest map.

The hot spring: Rocks form a border screen around a three-foot square box recessed into the ground. Spring water bubbles up into the cozy container at 106 degrees, and the temperature can be lowered by plugging the inflow. The box can be drained and refilled after each soak, and a submerged bench makes a handy seat. The dubious function of the border (besides providing the only landmark) is to conceal the box itself. It's not high enough to screen any soaker over age five from full view by passing motorists.

82 Worswick Hot Springs

General description: A hot springer's fantasy spread out on both sides of the road, east of Featherville in the Smoky Mountains. Swimwear advised. Elevation 5,600 feet.

Map: Sawtooth National Forest.

Finding the hot springs: Refer to "Getting to Featherville" and follow the Ketchum Road (227) 2.1 miles east of the junction with Forest Road 94, a distance of nearly thirty-two miles from Featherville. There's ample space south of the road to park or pitch a tent. The springs are signed by the road and named on the forest map.

The hot springs: A complex of about fifty springs issues from a grassy hillside at temperatures up to 180 degrees and branches into a thermal stream flowing at a staggering rate of 250 gallons/min. It runs through a series of pools, is piped under the road, and then snakes across a flat into Little Smoky Creek. The temperature rises through the summer as the output of an incoming cold stream diminishes.

There's a toasty soaker dammed with a log partway up the hill, a rocky pool by the culvert, and a broad shallow one near the creek. Smaller dips are scattered in between. When I was there in early June, the upper pool clocked in at 110 degrees, the "culvert pool" at 100, and the creekside one at 95 degrees. Take your choice!

The area around Worswick is home to a number of unique plants including a variety of tiny sunflower. Wildlife frequent the springs when human life has left. The number of visitors has increased over the years, and it's important to remember the basics—tread lightly and leave no trace.

The tiny soaking box at Preis can't be seen until you're right on top of it.

The pools at Worswick Hot Springs appeal to a variety of happy soakers.

HIKING NOTES

H. OUT OF KETCHUM & STANLEY

Hot springs and hikes

West of Ketchum comes a roadside soak at Frenchman's Bend (83). State Route 75 runs northwest of town through the Sawtooth NRA; the eye-catching drive parallels the Salmon River and the jagged Sawtooths. A number of roadside hot pools (84-89) combine well with trips into the Smoky Mountains and eastern Sawtooths near Stanley. Next, a remote trail north of Sunbeam leads to wilderness hot springs on Upper Loon Creek (90a). To the east comes a dip at Slate Creek (91) and a nearby hike into the White Clouds. And farther east off State Route 75, a back road accesses the White Clouds and ends with soaks at remote West Pass and Bowery (92,93).

Season

In the Sawtooth NRA, Elkhorn's "boat box" is usable year around, and the tubs at West Pass and Bowery would be except for the seasonal road. The riverside pools are mostly underwater during spring runoff. Access to Upper Loon depends on road closures; prime time is July through October. The high Sawtooths are often obscured by snow until late July and snowed in again by mid-September. Summer weather brings warm days and cold nights at higher elevations, and hikers should travel prepared for rain or even snow.

83 Frenchman's Bend Hot Springs

General description: A popular roadside soak on Warm Springs Creek, west of Ketchum in the Smoky Mountains. Public nudity a no-no. Elevation 6,400 feet.
Map: Sawtooth National Forest.

Finding the hot springs: From State Route 75 in Ketchum, take the Warm Springs Road (227) about 10.5 miles west to a sign welcoming visitors to the springs. Park in the designated area and step down to the pools. The springs, labeled Warfield on the map, are more widely known as Frenchman's Bend and are so named on the sign.

The hot springs: Two attractive soaking pools, four feet across and two feet deep, nestle side by side in the creekside boulders next to the road. The temperature ranges up to 115 degrees but can be lowered by shifting rocks in the dam. While not as spacious as the previous four-by-eight footer, they're an improvement over the old "two-holer" soaking shack that once stood 0.25 mile down the road.

The current site has rules posted and strictly enforced: No public nudity, no alcohol or glass containers, no parking except in designated areas, and no soaks between 10 p.m. and 4 a.m. The "no-no" list may be objectionable to

H. OUT OF KETCHUM & STANLEY

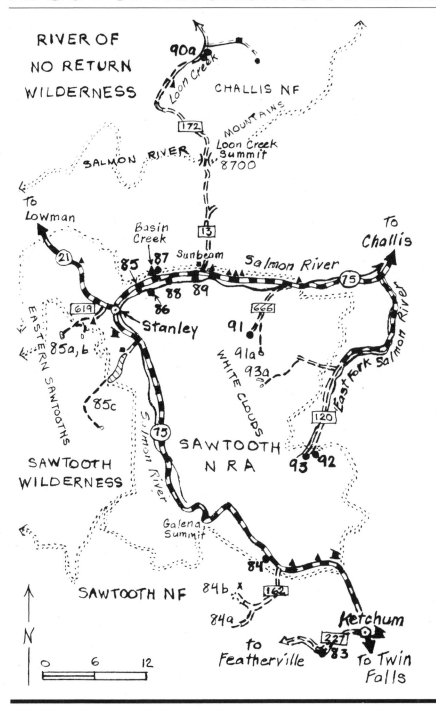

RIVER OF
NO RETURN
WILDERNESS

90a

Loon Creek

CHALLIS NF

MOUNTAINS

172

SALMON RIVER

Loon Creek
Summit
8700

To
Lowman

Basin
Creek

21

85   87

Sunbeam

Salmon River

75

88 89

619

86

Stanley

666

91

91a,b

To
Challis

East Fork Salmon River

85a,b

WHITE CLOUDS

93a

85c

Salmon River

75

120

SAWTOOTH
NRA

EASTERN SAWTOOTHS

93 92

SAWTOOTH
WILDERNESS

Galena
Summit

SAWTOOTH NF

84

84b

162

84a

Ketchum

to
Featherville

227

83

To Twin
Falls

N

0   6   12

251

A dyed-in-the-wool skinnydipper takes his chances in the roadside pools at Frenchman's Bend.

some, but it's alleviated the overuse/abuse problems encountered in the past. The access road is plowed up to homes a few miles back, and folks sometimes ski in for a quiet winter soak.

84 Russian John Warm Spring

General description: A roadside warm soak northwest of Ketchum in the Sawtooth NRA. Skinnydippable. Elevation 6,900 feet.
Map: Sawtooth National Forest.

Finding the hot spring: From Ketchum, drive about eighteen miles northwest on State Route 75. The turnoff is located 2.5 miles past Baker Creek Road. Turn west onto a dirt road near Milepost 146, then south to the parking area by the pool. The spring isn't marked on the forest map.

The hot spring: A huge pile of logs shelters an old sheepherder's soaking pool from sight of the busy highway 200 yards away. The clay bottom stirs up easily, and the temperature hovers around 85 degrees—on the lower edge of warm. The popularity of the small pool is probably due to its semi-secluded setting and to the fact that it's a long drive to the next dip.

HIKE 84a *Baker Lake*

General description: A brisk two-mile, round-trip stroll to a popular lake in the Smoky Mountains, near Russian John Warm Spring.
Elevation gain and loss: 880 feet.
Trailhead elevation: 7,920 feet.
High point: Baker Lake, 8,800 feet.
Hiking quad: Baker Peak USGS.
Road map: Sawtooth National Forest.

Finding the trailhead: Follow the directions above to Baker Creek Road (162). Turn left and drive eight dusty miles to the road-end parking area and trail sign.

The hike: This pretty lake, a pleasant family outing, is well worth the short walk. Tall stands of fir rim the grassy shore, and pink granite cliffs cast their reflections in the clear water. Baker Lake Trail (138) starts off by crossing a branch of Baker Creek and then follows a track up a grassy hillside. Continue west on a sneaker-worn path that follows a wooded ridge leading up to the lake.

HIKE 84a *Baker Lake*

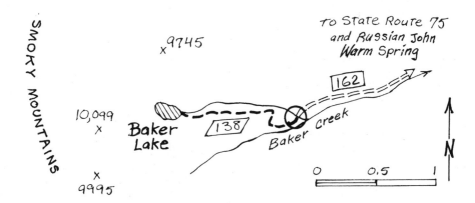

HIKE 84b *Norton Lakes Loop*

General description: A strenuous 5.5-mile, round-trip day hike (including a 3.5-mile, partially cross-country loop) to secluded lakes in the Smoky Mountains, near Russian John Warm Spring.
Elevation gain and loss: 1,840 feet (520 feet to start of loop; loop, 1,180 feet; to Upper Norton Lake, 140 feet).
Trailhead elevation: 7,640 feet.
High point: 9,300 feet.
Maps: Same as Hike 84a.

Finding the trailhead: Follow the road access above, taking Baker Creek Road six miles southwest to Norton Creek. Turn right on Norton Lake Road (170) and drive a mile to the end. Park wherever you can find room and dig out your boots.

The hike: Most visitors take the steep trail to the Norton Lakes, pause for lunch, and head back the way they came in. The adventurous hiker can make a loop that circles from Lower Norton Lake through a maze of granite ridges and basins past Big Lost and Smoky Lakes before dropping down a canyon to rejoin the trail. In addition to excellent scenery, the off-trail route offers the fun of exploration and discovery.

Wade the deep gulley of Norton Creek (treacherous during high water). Turn right at the register box and climb the wooded west bank on Norton Lake Trail (135). Cross a side creek and continue up a valley with a view of a serrated ridge. The two-mile trail to the lakes has a gain of 1,300 feet.

Lower Norton Lake is fringed with wildflowers spaced between stands of tall trees; rocky slopes back the far shore. Upper Norton is reached by a short path that climbs the flower-choked inlet.

Leave the trail behind at Lower Norton Lake and walk around to the west end. Pick a route heading due south up a scree-filled gulley. Cross over the lowest point on the ridge (and the highest point on the hike) at 9,300 feet.

Driftwood logs hug the outlet of Lower Norton Lake—the first stop on the Norton Lakes Loop.

HIKE 84b *Norton Lakes Loop*

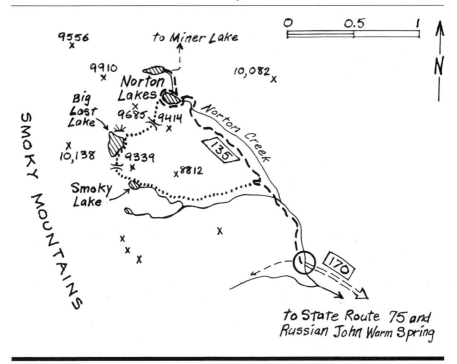

Bear right (southwest) as you descend the far side and head across a rocky valley to the next lake.

The moonscape setting for Big Lost Lake is a wide shoreline strewn with giant boulders; a jagged ridge tops the scree slope rising directly above the west side. Huge chunks of gnarled driftwood punctuate meadows and wide beaches along the eastern shore. This is a prime place to explore and take a break for lunch.

Cross a low saddle at the south end of the lake and wind down a rocky hill on a faint path curving east to Smoky Lake. This emerald green gem lies in a rocky bowl backed by wooded ridges. Skirt the northeast shore and follow an overgrown path down the north side of the outlet through clusters of shooting stars and monkeyflowers.

Contour eastward down the widening canyon, staying high to avoid a tangle of downed trees below. Continue about 1.5 miles below Smoky Lake to intersect Norton Lake Trail in a forested area. Not to worry—you can't miss it. Follow the trail back down the hill for the last mile.

85 Elkhorn Hot Spring

General description: A riverside hot box below a highway, near Stanley and the eastern Sawtooth trailheads, in the Sawtooth NRA. Swimwear essential. Elevation 6,100 feet.

Map: Sawtooth National Forest.

Finding the hot spring: Drive two miles east of Lower Stanley on State Route 75. Watch for a small pullout by the river in the middle of a curve 0.7 mile east of Milepost 192 (local folks call the spot First Bend Hot Spring or the "boat box"). Park here and climb down the rocks. Elkhorn isn't marked on the forest map.

The hot spring: This is the first of several hot dips along the Salmon River Scenic Route east of Stanley. A few shallow pools and a one-body soaking box tucked between boulders mark the highly visible spot. Scalding hot, 136-degree water is piped under the highway to the tub, and the only way to cool it is to scramble back and forth over the rocks to the river with a bucket. If somebody has made off with the bucket, you're out of luck!

Locals call this tub at Elkhorn the "boat box" because of it popularity with kayakers and commercial raft groups. It's normally usable all year.

HIKE 85a *Alpine, Sawtooth, and McGown Lakes*

General description: A moderate twelve-mile, round-trip day hike or overnighter featuring alpine views and the largest lake in the Sawtooth Wilderness, near Elkhorn Hot Spring.

Elevation gain and loss: +2,090 feet, -280 feet.

Trailhead elevation: 6,710 feet.

High point: 8,800 feet.

Hiking quad: Stanley Lake USGS.

Road map: Sawtooth National Forest.

Finding the trailhead: Drive 2.5 miles west of Stanley on State Route 21. Turn left onto gravel Iron Creek Road (619) and drive three miles to a campground loop at the road's end. The trailhead for these lakes as well as Goat Lake is located near the far end of the loop.

The hike: The star attraction of this highly popular trip is the giant sapphire oval of Sawtooth Lake. Craggy Mount Regan dominates the skyline directly across the granite bowl, and trails around both sides offer a variety of unobstructed views. This may well be the most shutterbugged scene in the Sawtooths; it's a hard one to beat! *Note:* Campfires aren't allowed within 200 yards of either Alpine or Sawtooth Lake.

The Iron Creek Trail (640) meanders southwest for the first 1.25 miles to the wilderness line. Next, it intersects Alpine Way branching east, signed "to Marshall Lake." (Alpine Way also accesses the following hike to Goat Lake, 85b). The route curves gently to a second junction in a boggy flat, then angles up an open slope above Iron Creek Valley. Splash across Iron Creek and climb to an overlook of Alpine Lake in four miles. A spur drops to the north shore and Alpine Peak stands out to the south above the treetops.

The main trail snakes above Alpine Lake. The ridgetop has views of peaks to the north and south and overlooks the Iron Creek Valley stretching east toward Stanley. A bit more scenic climbing brings you past a small tarn in an alpine valley to the outlet and northern end of the largest lake in the Sawtooths at five miles, 8,430 feet.

Starkly beautiful Sawtooth Lake stretches a full mile from head to toe and a half mile across. A deep basin of granite slabs outlines the oval shape, and a few twisted trees cling for survival to the steep walls. The jagged contours of Mount Regan shoot 1,760 feet skyward from the surface at the far end.

There is a junction by the outlet. Before going on to McGown Lakes, take the left fork to a granite knoll with a full view across the lake. The scenic path hugs the shore for an easygoing mile to a flower-lined pond directly beneath Mount Regan before dropping through a glacier-cut gap to reach Baron Creek Trail in six lightly traveled miles (see Hike 59b).

The main trail branches west to climb 360 feet in a 0.5-mile traverse across the north wall. This eye-catching stretch offers an eagle's perspective across the full length of the lake to Mount Regan and the gap carved in the far wall. The path crests at 8,800 feet, the high point on the hike, then quickly drops into a rocky valley to reach the largest McGown Lake just south of the trail at six miles.

The McGown Lakes lie in shallow rock basins below low peaks. They haven't much to offer other than a couple of campsites, a few stunted trees, and the magnificent route connecting them with Sawtooth Lake a mile away.

Looking down the length of mile-long Sawtooth Lake, craggy Mount Regan dominates the southern horizon.

HIKE 85b *Goat Lake*

General description: A difficult seven-mile, round-trip day climb or over-nighter (for mountain goats only) to a rock-walled lake in the Sawtooth Wilderness, near Elkhorn Hot Spring.
Elevation gain and loss: +1,750 feet, -240 feet.
Trailhead elevation: 6,710 feet.
High point: Goat Lake, 8,220 feet.
Maps: Same as Hike 85a.

Finding the trailhead: Follow the road access for Hike 85a.

The hike: A second trek from the Iron Creek Trailhead offers a challenging route to a lake hemmed in by sheer granite cliffs. Hanging snowfields on the far wall cast chunks of ice into the water. A misty waterfall threads down from two higher lakes, and another borders the climb in. The trip isn't recommended for inexperienced hikers, as much of the route is a steep scramble on loose rock. Good hiking boots are a must. *Note:* Campfires are prohibited within 200 yards of Goat Lake.

Follow Iron Creek Trail (640) 1.25 miles southwest through a lodgepole pine forest, past the wilderness boundary, to a trail junction in a grassy valley. The right fork continues up Iron Creek Valley to Alpine, Sawtooth, and McGown Lakes (Hike 85a); the left fork is signed "to Marshall Lake" and traces the wilderness line southeast.

Turn east onto Alpine Way (528) and cross Iron Creek footbridge. Pass through a boggy forest, then wade a small stream laced with wildflowers where the trail contours around a wooded ridge. It swings slowly southward and then veers sharply northeast a second time at 2.75 miles.

Leave the main trail and turn right on a primitive path climbing below a cliff. A spur branches downhill in 0.25 mile to the base of Goat Creek Falls. The track to the lake becomes increasingly eroded and slippery. Look south at the first switchback to another ribbon of falls across the basin; farther south, Williams and Thompson Peaks slice into the horizon. The path shoots up the north wall to the top of the falls, gaining 800 feet in the 0.75-mile climb from Alpine Way.

Cross the creek above the falls, then hike the last hundred yards to reach the north shore of Goat Lake at 3.5 miles. Cliffs on three sides rise 1,500 feet above the surface, and jagged towers lean out as if ready to leap. Experts can boulder-hop around the east shore to compare views, but the traverse is steep and tricky.

"The Leaning Latrine": Iron Creek Campground, at the time I was there, had an unusual feature—an outhouse tipped forward on a slant. I was unaware of this as I approached one night without a flashlight. The door seemed hard to open, and then it slammed shut behind me! In total darkness, I found myself staggering to stand upright and reach the seat. I couldn't understand what was wrong—I'd only had one beer after the hike. The following morning it all became clear when I saw that it was the outhouse, and not me, that was tipsy.

A jumbled mass of ridges and peaks, seen from the log jam at the outlet, walls in the south shore of Goat Lake.

HIKE 85a *Alpine, Sawtooth, and McGown Lakes*
HIKE 85b *Goat Lake*

HIKE 85c *Cramer Lakes*

General description: A moderate 14.5-mile, round-trip backpack up a glacial canyon leading to high lakes, wildflowers, and breathtaking views in the Sawtooth Wilderness, near Elkhorn Hot Spring.
Elevation gain and loss: 1,840 feet.
Trailhead elevation: 6,560 feet.
High point: Upper Cramer Lake, 8,400 feet.
Hiking quads: Mount Cramer and Warbonnet Peak USGS.
Road map: Same as Hike 85a.

Finding the trailhead: Drive 4.5 miles south of Stanley on State Route 75 and turn right on Redfish Lake Road. Drive two miles to a sign on the right marking the backpacker's parking lot. This is the only spot you can leave your car for overnight trips.

The hike: A boot-beaten path up a deep canyon bordered by the best known and most climbed peaks in the Sawtooths branches south to the Cramer Lakes in a popular hike from Redfish Lake. Inviting campsites at Middle Cramer face a waterfall across the blue-green water. Upper Cramer, the largest of the three, sits directly beneath the towering face of a 10,500-foot peak. Mount Cramer peeks from behind the canyon leading south to Cramer Divide.

With the help of the Redfish Lake ferry, you can save 5.5 miles of walking to the far end. The scenic twenty-minute ride offers face-on views of Mount Heyburn's sheer cliffs and the sharp pinnacles of The Grand Mogul guarding the head of the lake. The ferry drops hikers at Redfish Lake Inlet Transfer Camp. Trail mileage and elevation gain are given from this point.

Redfish Lake Creek Trail (101) starts above the developed inlet campground in heavy timber and climbs alongside the rushing creek into the wide, U-shaped canyon. Pop out of the woods at the base of Mount Heyburn and zigzag past a junction with the lakeside trail. Continue with a moderate climb past a stretch where house-sized boulders almost block the path. Climbers enjoy this area for its solid rock and easy access.

The path continues alongside the plunging creek and passes occasional waterfalls, then climbs through a forest of lodgepole pines, spruce, and fir with frequent glimpses of the spires and domes rimming the canyon walls. You'll pass the orange-hued Saddleback at two miles, nicknamed by climbers the Elephant's Perch. Continue past Goat and Eagle Perches to reach Flatrock Junction at 3.5 miles, 7,400 feet.

At Flatrock Junction, named for the granite slabs filling the canyon floor, the trail splits. The right fork branches off to cross Baron Divide, drop to Baron Lakes and finally exit at Grandjean in a total of 18.5 miles (see Hike 59b). The left fork climbs past the Cramer Lakes over 9,480-foot Cramer Divide, and offers access to many classic lakes and peaks farther south.

Turn south onto Cramer Lakes Trail (154). You can ford Redfish Lake Creek on a log jam downstream or wade across on slabs 200 yards above. Stroll 0.5 mile upstream through forest, then follow switchbacks up the wall to a hanging valley where the route swings southeast. Enjoy views across to craggy Reward and Elk Peaks. A last gentle stretch brings you to Lower Cramer Lake at 6.8 miles. Settle down here for a bit of solitude, or walk another 0.5 mile to the upper lakes for less privacy but wall-to-wall views.

The graceful twenty-foot waterfall at Middle Cramer Lake makes an idyllic setting for the large campsite facing it at the outlet, while tiny tentsites along the narrow shelf between the upper two lakes combine a vertical view down the broad falls with a panorama of jagged peaks rimming Upper Cramer Lake. It's a delightfully difficult choice!

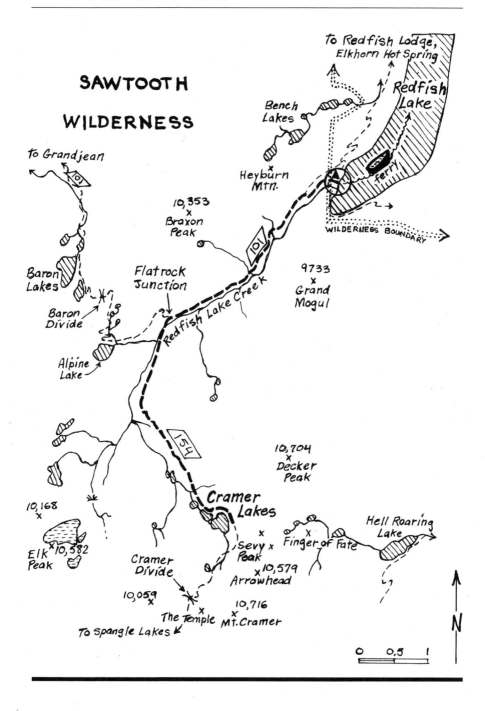

SAWTOOTH

WILDERNESS

To Redfish Lodge,
Elkhorn Hot Spring

Redfish
Lake

Bench
Lakes

To Grandjean

Heyburn
Mtn.

10,353
x
Braxon
Peak

Ferry

WILDERNESS BOUNDARY

Baron
Lakes

Flatrock
Junction

9733
x
Grand
Mogul

Baron
Divide

Redfish Lake Creek

Alpine
Lake

10,704
x
Decker
Peak

10,168
x

Cramer
Lakes

Hell Roaring
Lake

Elk
Peak

x 10,582

Sevy x
Peak

x Finger of Fate

Cramer
Divide

x 10,579
Arrowhead

10,059
x

10,716
x
Mt. Cramer

The Temple

To Spangle Lakes

N

0   0.5   1

86 Mormon Bend Hot Spring

General description: A hot pool on the wrong side of the Salmon River, near Stanley and the eastern Sawtooth trailheads, in the Sawtooth NRA. Swimwear advised when standing up. Elevation 6,100 feet.
Map: Sawtooth National Forest.

Finding the hot spring: Take State Route 75 two miles east of Lower Stanley to the first bend in the river past Elkhorn Hot Spring (see 85 above) and just west of Milepost 193. Dig out your wading shoes and aim for the far bank—but only when the river is low. The spring isn't shown on the forest map and is misplaced three miles east on the state geothermal.

The hot spring: A channel of steamy water flows across a meadow into a small but pleasant rock-lined soaker. The pool, about 350 yards downstream from the "boat box" at Elkhorn, is barely visible on the far bank. It requires a major river ford, which by late summer shouldn't be too tricky, but offers the finder a quiet soak unobserved by passing cars. Why, passers-by would never know there was a hot pool there unless they happened to be looking at the precise spot when it was occupied.

87 Campground Hot Spring

General description: Soaking pools hiding out in a campground, near Stanley and the eastern Sawtooth trailheads, in the Sawtooth NRA. Daytime skinnydipping not recommended. Elevation 6,100 feet.
Map: Sawtooth National Forest.

Finding the hot springs: Drive seven miles east of Stanley on State Route 75 to Basin Creek Campground. Pull into campsite four and wander casually into the bushes. You'll have to wade the small creek to reach the pools. The riverside dips across the highway (see below) are larger but more heavily used. The spring isn't marked on the forest map.

The hot spring: What most folks stopping here never discover is that there happens to be a small hot spring on the creek flowing past the campsites; the bushy border screens a couple of pleasant soaking pools from view. The temperature can be controlled by adjusting the creekside rocks. A semi-private spot in a public campground!

HOT SPRING 85 *Elkhorn Hot Spring*
HOT SPRING 86 *Mormon Bend Hot Spring*
HOT SPRING 87 *Campground Hot Spring*
HOT SPRING 88 *Basin Creek Hot Spring*
HOT SPRING 89 *Sunbeam Hot Springs*

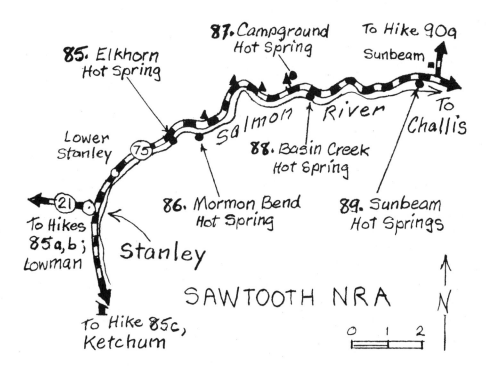

88 Basin Creek Hot Spring

General description: Hot dips sandwiched between the highway and the Salmon River, near Stanley and the eastern Sawtooth trailheads, in the Sawtooth NRA. Swimwear advised. Elevation 6,100 feet.
Map: Sawtooth National Forest.

Finding the hot springs: Drive seven miles east of Stanley on State Route 75. Just beyond Basin Creek Campground (see above), turn right onto a short spur that dead-ends at the soaking pools and an unofficial camping area by the river. The spring isn't shown on the forest map.

The hot spring: This semi-secluded spot may be the best of several roadside dips east of Stanley. It's at the base of a bank below the busy highway; motorists wouldn't be likely to notice a few bathers unless they knew just where to look.

Two family-sized soakers (often filled to capacity) border the river. Rocks enclosing them can be moved to either divert the 137-degree spring water or admit cold river water. The pools swamp during high water and the rocks wash away; they take on a new look every summer depending on the talents of the volunteers who rebuild them.

The pools at Basin Creek Hot Spring lie at the river's edge and must be rebuilt every year when the water level drops.

89 Sunbeam Hot Springs

General description: Highly visible pools squeezed between the highway and the Salmon River, east of Stanley in the Sawtooth NRA. No nudes, just "prudes and prunes." Elevation 6,100 feet.

Map: Sawtooth National Forest.

Finding the hot springs: Drive about eleven miles east of Stanley on State Route 75 (four miles past Basin Creek Hot Spring or a mile west of Sunbeam Resort). Look for an old stone bathhouse and interpretive signs at a large turnout. A short path leads down the bank to the pools. (The nearest campgrounds are Basin Creek four miles west (see 87 above) and Dutchman Flat two miles east.) The springs are named on the forest map.

The hot springs: One last cluster of highway hot soaks lines the Salmon River Scenic Route from Stanley to Challis. Boiling water is piped beneath the highway from the springs and flows across a gravel beach into several popular pools at the river's edge. Bathers can adjust the rocks to create a variety of soaking temperatures. Succeeding pools, each cooler than the one above, emerge as the river recedes through the summer.

The historical bathhouse has recently been repaired and restored, and a stone outhouse in the same style has been built nearby. This work was done in conjunction with the Idaho Centennial Historical Site near Sunbeam Dam, at the mouth of Yankee Fork, and was just completed in 1992.

With a few buckets of river water tossed in, this former soaking box at Sunbeam was quite enjoyable. The stone building above it was built in the 1930s as a public bathhouse.

90 Upper Loon Hot Springs

HIKE 90a *To Upper Loon Hot Springs*

General description: An easy 11.5-mile, round-trip day hike or overnighter to a chain of pearls lost on a creek above the Middle Fork Salmon River, northeast of Stanley in the River of No Return Wilderness. A skinnydipper's delight.
Elevation gain and loss: +240 feet, -640 feet.
High point: Trailhead, 5,400 feet.
Low point: Owen cabin, 5,040 feet.
Hiking quads: River of No Return Wilderness, South half (Forest Service) or Castro, Falconberry Peak, and Rock Creek USGS.
Road map: Wilderness quad or Challis National Forest.

Finding the trailhead: Drive about twelve miles east of Stanley on State Route 75 (a mile past Sunbeam Hot Springs) to Sunbeam Resort. Turn left on the Yankee Fork Road (13) and drive eight easy miles north to Bonanza, home of the historic Yankee Fork Dredge that sits marooned in a small pond walled in by the rocks it dredged out of the creek.

Bear left beyond the barge onto rocky Loon Creek Road (172) which follows Jordan Creek north past other historic sites to Loon Creek summit. The seasonal road (July 1 to November 1) snakes over the 8,700-foot crest that forms the wilderness boundary and down the far side to eventually reach the road-

This five-star, crescent-shaped pool at Upper Loon was built right under a hot waterfall.

end trailhead in a total of thirty-three dusty miles. Tin Cup Campground, a mile from the end, provides a welcome rest. The springs are marked on the forest maps.

The hike: Five wilderness hot springs lie at close intervals on Upper Loon Creek in the Salmon River Mountains north of Sunbeam. All are located on the east (trail) side of the broad creek, and all branch into steamy channels that either trickle or tumble down the rocky banks. They vary in appearance from interesting to spectacular and in usability from "for display purposes only" to outstanding.

Loon Creek Trail (101), a pleasant stroll, is far less tiring than the access road. The canyon walls are coated with grass and sagebrush on the south-facing slopes while the hills facing north are lightly wooded with Douglas-fir. The upper canyon consists of talus slopes and rock outcrops patched with lime-yellow and orange lichen. Beyond an 800-foot rock face, the path fords small streams fringed by grassy flats. The route closely follows the lively creek, and in August and September you can sometimes see salmon struggling up the rapids to reach their spawning grounds.

The trail bridges Loon Creek at three miles, passes a few campsites, and soon reaches a stretch of midsummer berry picking interspersed with more easy stream hopping. At five miles are the remains of a log cabin (still in one piece) hidden in a tangle of greenery down by the creek. The first hot spring branches into a broad flow over the rocky flat, and a few shallow pools edge the creek. There's a shaded campsite in the grass beside the cabin.

HIKE 90a *To Upper Loon Hot Springs*

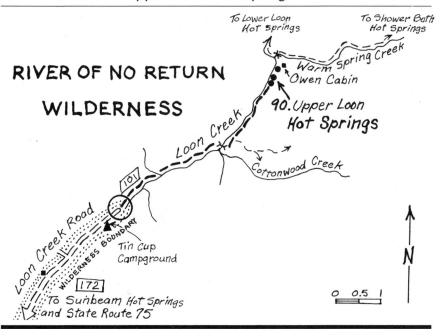

The hot springs: Just around the next bend, hot waterfalls from the two largest springs plunge over twenty-foot cliffs into Loon Creek. A totally outstanding pool in the shape of a crescent has been built against the cliff directly below one of the falls. Green moss and ferns hug the bank beneath the misty spray. The temperature may be a smidge too hot, but the rocks lining the bubbly can be rearranged to admit a cold mix from the creek. The outflow swirls with a delicious marbling of hot and cold currents into a protected alcove alongside.

The last two hot springs emerge in a meadow a scant 0.5 mile farther on. They flow gently through the grass into pools of rust-colored algae, then continue down the bank to fill shallow, rock-lined pools by the creek. The crumbling ruins of the historic Owen cabin, engulfed in vegetation, lie just beyond the wide meadow.

With time to spare: From this point, there's a choice of extensions. One could take Warm Spring Creek Trail 8.5 miles upstream as an alternate way to Shower Bath (see Hike 94a). The primitive route involves fording the creek six times, but it passes another wild gem—a shower shack plus hot tub affair (privately owned but rarely visited) at Foster Ranch. Or, one could continue down Loon Creek Trail all the way to Lower Loon and Cox Hot Springs (see Hike 95/96a), which might be an easier access than the one described.

91 Slate Creek Hot Spring

General description: A hot bath in a wooded canyon near a dirt road, southeast of Stanley in the Sawtooth NRA. Keep swimwear handy. Elevation 7,040 feet.
Map: Sawtooth National Forest.

Finding the hot springs: Drive about twenty-three miles east of Stanley on State Route 75. Turn right on Slate Creek Road (666) just beyond a bridge over the Salmon River. Drive seven bumpy miles south to a roadblock, climb the gate, and walk a few hundred yards up the road. The spring is named on the forest map.

The hot spring: Until recently, a funky but functional bathhouse straddled a hot spring (also known as "Hoodoo") on the wooded bank above a creek. An incoming pipe fed 122-degree water into a recessed, soaker-friendly box big enough to hold two cozy couples, and a second pipe admitted cold water. A removable slat in the wall let the water drain out. The system worked great!

The crude structure was pieced together from whatever materials came to hand. The walls were a mixture of logs, planks, and plywood. The roof was open to the elements at the end above the soaking box, and a hole for a window lets the bather enjoy the view downhill.

Update on Slate: Bad news! The old bathhouse and plumbing are gone, kaput. As of the summer of '92, all that remains at the site are the toasty soaking box sans cold water pipe, a creekside dip or two, and a nearby hot "culvert shower."

HOT SPRING 91 *Slate Creek Hot Spring*
HIKE 91a *Crater Lake*

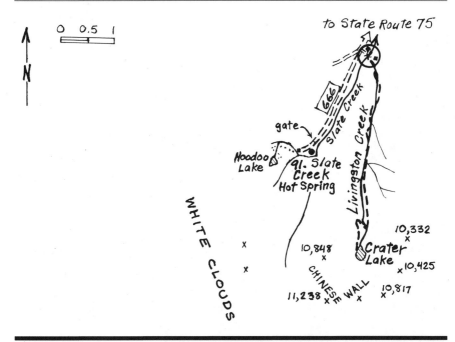

You can't judge a book by its cover. The shack at Slate Creek had a way of eliciting smiles of contentment from those who ventured within its patchwork walls.

HIKE 91a *Crater Lake*

General description: A moderate eight-mile, round-trip day hike or over-nighter to a quiet lake in the White Cloud Mountains, near Slate Creek Hot Spring.

Elevation gain and loss: 2,480 feet.
Trailhead elevation: 6,440 feet.
High point: Crater Lake, 8,920 feet.
Hiking quad: Livingston Creek USGS.
Road map: Sawtooth National Forest.

Finding the trailhead: Follow the directions above to Slate Creek Road and drive upcanyon 5.6 miles. Turn left at the second ranch to the road-end parking area at Slate Creek. The trail is shown on the forest map but not on the USGS quad.

The hike: A pleasant walk up a lively creek reaches grey-blue Crater Lake tucked between twisted ridges in a lightly used part of the Sawtooth NRA. The route has many stream fords but is easy to follow. Hoodoo Lake, the only other hike near Slate Creek Hot Spring, is a tough scramble up a hill riddled with eroded mining roads. Of the two, Crater Lake is much easier to find, has a better track to hike, and offers closer views of the surrounding White Clouds.

Cross the creek on a footbridge and walk an abandoned mining road. At most of the stream crossings, you'll find rocks or logs to balance across on. The route for the first mile or so is a fairly gentle climb through deep woods, then it begins to steepen. At three miles, there's an open traverse with increasingly broad views as the track heads up the rocky canyon wall. Make one giant switchback at the head of the canyon to reach the outlet of Crater Lake at four miles.

Wander around the lake on either side and enjoy views of the contorted Chinese Wall—a striated ridge that buckles in the center as if someone had tried to lift it off the ground from both ends! Across from the Chinese Wall is the rounded end of Railroad Ridge. A sawtoothed crest fills the gap in between. The unusual basin gives a touch of class to an otherwise modest lake.

"Pain remedy": Halfway through a peanut butter and carrot sandwich, as I sat on a warm rock gazing up at the Chinese Wall, the sky suddenly turned darker than Slate Creek below. I'd just gulped down the last bite when the drops started to fall, and the drizzle turned to a spitting downpour before I was halfway down the trail. The harder it poured, the faster I ran!

I'd no sooner leaped into the car when the sky turned a sickly shade of yellow and let loose a wild volley of hailstones. The ground, covered with dancing snow peas, turned white in an instant. I slithered the last mile up the road with a smile on my face because the perfect antidote to nasty weather was close at hand. Ten minutes later, I slid into a cocoon of steamy water and leaned back against a handy plank. Sleet and hail pelted the crude shelter at Slate Creek Hot Spring while I waited out the storm in total comfort.

92 West Pass Hot Spring

General description: A remote pair of aging bathtubs on a grassy slope near a dirt road, southeast of Stanley in the Sawtooth NRA. Wear what you normally bathe in. Elevation 6,800 feet.
Map: Sawtooth National Forest.

Finding the hot spring: From Stanley, take State Route 75 about 36.5 miles east (five miles past Clayton) and turn south on East Fork Salmon River Road (120). Pavement turns to gravel in seventeen miles, and Big Boulder Creek Road (Hike 93a) continues while the main road veers left. The seasonal road (May 1 through December 1) eventually passes a winter gate and a primitive camp, and two miles later bridges West Pass Creek by an old cabin. Bear left on a track that climbs above the creek to a grassy flat. Park here and take a short path past an abandoned mine down to the tubs. The spring, a total of twenty-nine miles from the highway, is marked on the forest map.

The hot spring: Pipes running downhill from a steamy source pool hidden inside the old mine shaft supply 110-degree water to each of two bathtubs perched side by side above West Pass Creek. The old tubs both have gaping holes a football could pass through, but they're lined with sturdy plastic that can be rinsed off before use. The soaking temperature can be lowered by diverting the pipes, and bathers enjoy a broad view that includes an old cabin in a meadow just upstream.

93 Bowery Hot Spring

General description: A secluded soaking tub and rocky pools on the East Fork Salmon River at the end of a dirt road, southeast of Stanley in the Sawtooth NRA. Highly skinnydippable. Elevation 6,800 feet.
Map: Sawtooth National Forest.

Finding the hot spring: Follow the road access above to the turnoff to West Pass and continue a mile to a closed gate. Walk the road toward Bowery Guard Station, cross a bridge and go left on a short path to the tub. The guard station, thirty miles from State Route 75, is marked on the forest map.

The hot spring: A baby-blue bathtub of recent vintage nestles in the rocks above the stream. The 125-degree water piped from the spring can be cooled by diverting the flow and adding a few buckets of river water, and a plywood deck offers a dry spot for clothes. Below you'll find one or two small pools at waterline. The temperature can be lowered by adjusting the rocky border.

The water bucket at Bowery plays a key role in getting the tub temperature just right.

HIKE 93a *Island and Goat Lakes*

General description: A strenuous thirteen-mile round-trip day hike or over-nighter to alpine lakes bordered by the White Clouds, en route to or from West Pass and Bowery Hot Springs.

Elevation gain and loss: +2,220 feet, -240 feet.

Trailhead elevation: 7,160 feet.

High point: 9,240 feet at Island Lake.

Hiking quads: Boulder Chain Lakes and Livingston Creek USGS.

Road map: Sawtooth National Forest.

Finding the trailhead: Follow the road access in 92 above to Big Boulder Creek Road (667) and drive just under five miles to a trail sign near the dilapidated Livingston Mill. Turn left to the trailhead parking area.

The hike: This popular trail, which also accesses Walker Lake and the Big Boulder Lakes, is the shortest route into the White Cloud Mountains. The Boulder Chain Lakes to the south see fewer visitors but also require twice the hiking distance to reach. Bordered by granite slabs and lofty peaks, these lakes offer stiff competition to the well known Sawtooth Range farther west.

Big Boulder Creek Trail (680) crosses sagebrush flats backed by redrock towers, and in two miles a side path branches south to Frog Lake and Boulder

HIKE 93a *Island and Goat Lakes*

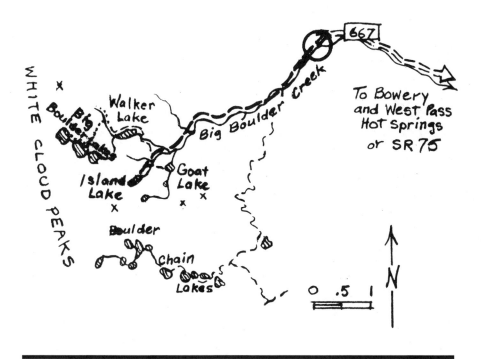

Chain Lakes. The main trail works up through a forest of lodgepole and aspen, dips across Quicksand Meadows crossing side creeks on logs, then climbs past the rushing outlet of Goat Lake to the Walker Lake junction in just over five miles.

Climbing to Island Lake, the path weaves back and forth across the stream. In a marsh 0.4 mile up, a 0.5-mile path forks left across a rocky saddle to Goat Lake. You'll reach a campsite at Island Lake less than a mile from the Walker Lake junction. Talus slopes and trees border Goat Lake beneath a wall of color-fully banded rock crossing Granite Peak to a skyline of pinnacles. Narrow Island Lake, dotted with two islands, is rimmed by granite benches, a cliff on one side, and a small meadow at the upper end.

With time to spare, this trip combines well with Walker Lake just a mile above the junction. The 0.5-mile long lake, misnamed Walter on the USGS quad, is backed by cliffs and a double-tipped peak. A cross-country route from here climbs two miles to the Big Boulder Lakes—Cove, Sapphire, and Cirque—nestled in the White Clouds at a high point of 10,000 feet.

I. OUT OF CHALLIS

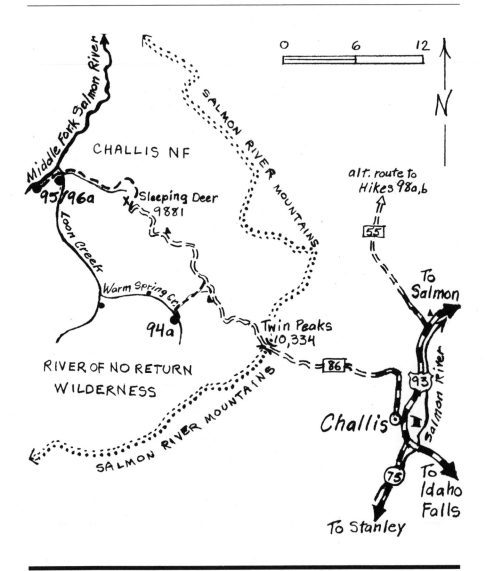

I. OUT OF CHALLIS

Hot springs and hikes

A hair-raising but spectacular drive northwest of Challis climbs a convoluted crest deep into the River of No Return Wilderness. At thirty miles, a path plunges to geothermal delights at Shower Bath (94a). And at the road's end, a long descent to the Middle Fork Salmon River reaches hot soaks at Lower Loon Creek and Cox (95/96a).

Season

Prime time for the wilderness hot spring treks is midsummer through early fall. Off-season use is hampered by seasonal road closures, high-elevation trailheads, and spring runoff. Hikers should prepare for nippy or foul weather at the start to hot and dry climate at the finale.

94 Shower Bath Hot Springs

HIKE 94a *To Shower Bath Hot Springs*

General description: A grueling twelve-mile, round-trip day hike or over-nighter to a geothermal fairyland on a remote creek above the Middle Fork, northwest of Challis in the River of No Return Wilderness. Swimwear superfluous baggage.

Elevation gain and loss: +100 feet, -2,340 feet.

High point: Trailhead, 8,040 feet.

Low point: Shower Bath, 5,800 feet.

Hiking quad: Sheldon Peak USGS or River of No Return Wilderness, South Half (Forest Service).

Road map: Wilderness quad or Challis National Forest.

The vision and the challenge: Imagine stumbling knee deep in a torrent of icy water through a deep chasm that sees maybe an hour of sun a day, rounding the last bend numb and exhausted, and finding paradise spread out before you. Steamy water flows over the sides of a wide alcove and splashes into rocky bowls below. Clouds of spray billow out over a soft green carpet beyond the pools. Peering through the mist, you can almost conjure up a row of angels drying their wings in the sun after a heavenly soak.

But, like the legendary Shangri-la, Shower Bath lies at the end of an exhausting and difficult trek. Some twenty-nine teeth-jarring miles on a knife-edged road are followed by a trail diving downhill into a stream that must be waded through a narrow gorge. The last 300-yard stretch can be waist deep through late July; when it is, Warm Spring Creek can't be waded with any degree of safety. Be sure to check with the Forest Service in Challis before attempting the trip.

Finding the trailhead: The odyssey begins by taking U.S. Highway 93 or State Route 75 to Challis. Turn right at McPherson's store and drive nine paved miles into Challis National Forest, where pavement ends and Sleeping Deer Road (86) begins. Bear right at 10.5 miles and right again at a confusing junction at fifteen miles. Climb a rocky surface to crest at 10,334 feet on Twin Peaks (the wilderness boundary). The seasonal road (August 1 to October 1) irons out somewhat beyond the top but becomes very narrow; sheer dropoffs are offset by wall-to-wall views.

Shortly past a turnoff to Mahoney Springs Camp at about twenty-eight miles, you'll see the first of two signs a mile apart that both read "to Warm Spring Creek Trail"; the second (located opposite the Fly Creek trailhead) is the shorter route. Shower Bath is named on all three maps. See the following hike for another adventure at the end of the road and Hike 90a for an alternate route to Shower Bath by way of Upper Loon Hot Springs.

The hike: Drop over the edge on a path that plunges 760 feet in the first mile to reach a spring, two old log huts, and a junction where the two trails join together to follow Mahoney Creek downhill. The grueling route dives another mile through heavy timber to a side stream, after which the grade becomes more moderate.

The sinuous track weaves across Mahoney Creek wherever the canyon walls get too snug on one side. When you're not fording the main creek, you'll be jumping the many side streams that feed it. Continue down through a colorful

The persevering hiker will find one or more rocky soaking pools at Shower Bath Hot Springs hidden behind a curtain of steam and fine spray.

blend of pine, fir, and aspen to finally bottom out on a sagebrush flat at Warm Spring Creek with a total loss of 2,340 feet in five miles.

Take a breather and stroll upstream on Warm Spring Creek Trail past the old Warm Spring Ranger Cabin (built in 1910) and on to the mouth of the narrows. Prepare for a cold plunge as rock walls 200 feet high funnel the path into the swift moving creek. Work your way upstream taking care to avoid the deeper holes. The path emerges briefly along the west bank, then drops back into the stream. Tiny hot springs trickle down the sheer walls, but these aren't the ones you came this far to see. Round the final bend and haul out on dry land on the west bank at six miles.

The hot springs: Shower Bath is the ultimate experience in wilderness hot springs—guaranteed to meet your wildest dreams! A broad wall of water

---

HIKE 94a *To Shower Bath Hot Springs*

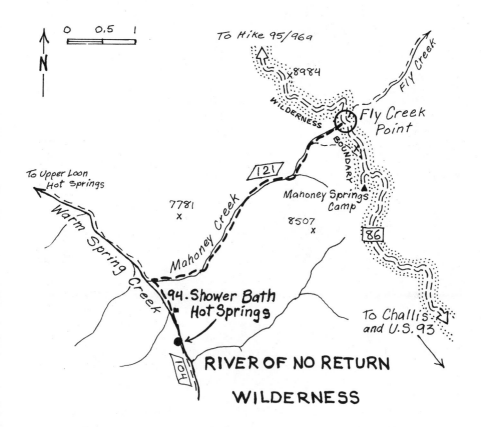

---

trickles and tumbles in a forty-foot drop over the rim, and rainbows shimmer overhead as sunlight pours through the mist. Gushing from the ground above at 120 degrees, the flow cools to a perfect soak in the tiny soaking pools directly below.

Colorful lichen speckles the rock-ribbed walls, and moisture-loving grasses carpet the floor with inviting campsites. A warm stream meanders through the meadow to another soaking pool spread out by the creek. Enjoy your stay, but please treat the fragile ecosystem around the springs with the respect it deserves.

95/96 Lower Loon & Cox Hot Springs

HIKE 95/96a *To Both Hot Springs*

General description: A rugged thirty-five-mile, round-trip backpack featuring hot dips in the Middle Fork Salmon River Canyon, northwest of Challis in the depths of the River of No Return Wilderness. "Prudes out, nudes in" seems the Middle Fork motto.
Elevation gain and loss: +120 feet, -5,420 feet.
High point: Trailhead, 9,340 feet.
Low point: Lower Loon Creek, 4,040 feet.
Hiking quads: Sleeping Deer Mountain and Ramey Hill USGS, or River of No Return Wilderness, south half (Forest Service).
Road map: Wilderness quad or Challis National Forest.

Finding the trailhead: Follow the spine-tingling access road described in Hike 94a above. Continue along the narrow crest to reach the road-end trail sign in about forty-three total miles. Perch your car in the tiny pullout and dig out your dusty boots. Lower Loon is marked without a name on the USGS quad; Cox is named on all three maps.

The hike: A long and lonesome journey offers the more adventurous hiker a chance to sample a broad cross section of the River of No Return Wilderness as well as a steamy double dip at the rainbow's end. The path begins in subalpine forest on a frosty mountaintop. Two life zones, fourteen miles, and well over 5,000 feet below, it comes to rest in the semi-arid canyon carved by the Middle Fork Salmon River. Sagebrush lines the way to Cox Hot Springs, and a twilight forest of ponderosa pine frames the stroll up Loon Creek to one of the finest hot pools in the wilderness.

High lakes below the trailhead draw an occasional fisherman, and the distant hot springs attract seasonal boatloads of river rats, but the rugged backcountry here sees almost no visitors at all. Pristine scenery and solitude more than make up for the roundabout route.

Note: There's an alternate way to these hot springs that's even more round-about but with a far easier grade and a better trail, via Loon Creek (see Hike 90a). There's also a similar soaking box to that at Lower Loon that can be reached with half the hiking miles but with a grueling plunge of 4,300 feet (see Hike 98a below).

Martin Mountain Trail (103) spends the first mile contouring around a knoll studded with whitebark pine to a three-way junction on a high saddle. The left fork drops to Cabin Creek while the middle path climbs a mile to the lookout cabin on the 9,881-foot summit of Sleeping Deer Mountain. The right fork takes you down a precipitous slope, where it traverses beneath the lookout to another saddle 200 feet below the first. This stretch is usually snow covered until mid-July. The path is hard to trace across the second saddle.

The route drops between granite slabs to a long meadow at the head of Cache Creek. Five glacially-carved lakes fan out at half-mile intervals. You'll pass the first lake in the marshy meadow and see a log cabin nearby that's used by outfitters during the hunting season. Good campsites are at the head of the lake and beside the cabin, elevation 8,685 feet.

The soaking pool at Lower Loon, visited chiefly by river rafting groups, has all the key ingredients to keep a boater or backpacker happy for hours.

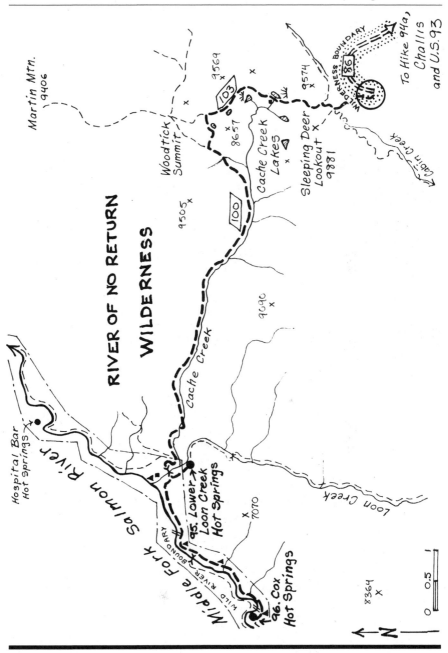

The trail contours an open ridge that overlooks Cache Creek Canyon and the second lake bordered by meadows. As it swings around the headwall, there are views of other lakes and the rugged Salmon River Mountains below. You'll reach a signed junction at about four miles. The right fork branches off to Woodtick Summit and continues on to Martin Mountain.

Turn left and zigzag down a grassy slope on the Woodtick Cutoff Trail past a small lake to reach a branch of Cache Creek 400 feet below. Ford the creek to meet the rugged trail you'll be following down to the river. This ten-mile stretch offers few level campsites and difficult access to water, so it might be best to spend the first night somewhere around the lakes.

Cache Creek Trail (100) dives down the headwall of the craggy canyon. The route passes primeval forests and lush meadows, and at times you'll hear the roar of Cache Creek far below. As you continue the grueling plunge, deep forests are gradually left behind. Grass and sagebrush begin to speckle the dry south-facing slopes, and the cooler hills facing north become wooded with stocky pines.

Finally, near the bottom, come two sets of stream crossings where you can count on wet feet. Shortly beyond the last ford, the trail comes to rest at a junction. Bear left on the Middle Fork Trail to Loon Creek Pack Bridge, at 4,030 feet—fourteen miles and 5,300 feet below the trailhead on Sleeping Deer Mountain. Turn left across the bridge to find Lower Loon 0.25 mile upstream.

The hot springs: You'll discover a rectangular pool lined with split logs—at least twenty feet long, ten feet across, and three feet deep. Fed by several springs with temperatures up to 120 degrees, the flow cools to a blissful soak en route through a long pipe to the crystal-clear pool. One side is shaded by a canopy of evergreen boughs while a few planks on the creek side form a sun deck. The setting is a blend of seclusion and open views.

For the seven-mile round trip from here to Cox, head 0.5 mile downstream to the river and swing west up the Middle Fork Trail. The gentle route passes sagebrush slopes dotted with age-old ponderosas. You'll spot Cox Campground down on a sand bar dominated by one tall pine three miles upstream. The springs are on the second bench above it, at 4,160 feet. The lower bench holds a tadpole-laden pond and the grave of Whitey Cox—a miner who died in a rockslide while prospecting the area.

The few shallow soaking pools here lie in a meadow strewn with wildflowers. There isn't much flow-through by late summer from the 130-degree springs, and the silty bottoms stir up easily. The pools don't have much to offer the gourmet hot springer other than countless acres of solitude, a pleasant view across the canyon, and the highly scenic three-mile stroll along a wild and grand old river.

HIKING NOTES

J. OUT OF SALMON

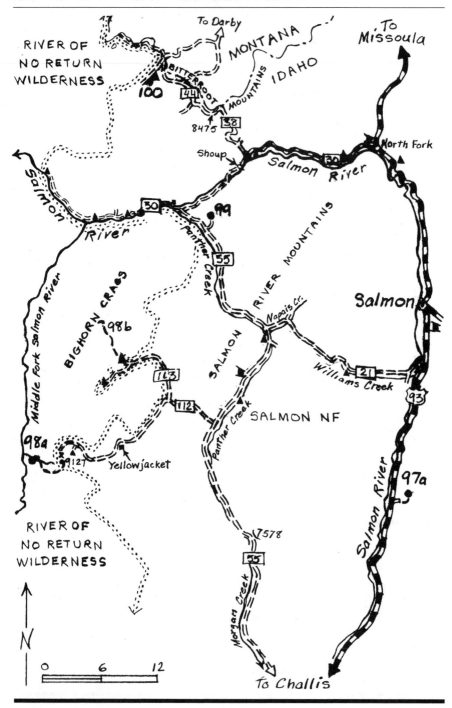

J. OUT OF SALMON

Hot springs and hikes

U.S. Highway 93 speeds north from Challis (Section I), tracing the Salmon River downstream to North Fork before crossing the Bitterroot Range to Missoula. South of Salmon, a hike leads to Goldbug's thermal cascades (97a). West of town, a remote trail in the River of No Return Wilderness plummets to Mormon Ranch Hot Springs (98a) while another climbs to the Bighorn Crags. A jump northward hits a soak at Panther (99). Finally, back roads northwest of town climb to a remote bathhouse in the Bitterroots at Horse Creek (100). This dispersed batch of bubblies resides in Salmon National Forest.

Season

Goldbug's at its best from late runoff in early summer through the fall months, while the wilderness treks are limited to midsummer to early fall due to high-elevation trailheads and seasonal roads. Panther can be reached and enjoyed most of the year, but high elevation narrows access to Horse Creek to the few months between snowfalls. Summer weather varies from hot and dry at Goldbug, Mormon, and Panther to cool and frequently rainy at higher elevations.

97 Goldbug Hot Springs

HIKE 97a *To Goldbug Hot Springs*

General description A moderate four-mile round-trip day climb to steamy soaks and waterfalls in a desert canyon, south of Salmon. Keep a swimsuit handy.

Elevation gain and loss: +920 feet, -120 feet.
Trailhead elevation: 4,400 feet.
High point: Goldbug Hot Springs, 5,200 feet.
Hiking quad: Goldbug Ridge USGS (optional).
Road map: Salmon National Forest (optional).

Finding the trailhead: Drive about twenty-three miles south of Salmon on U.S. Highway 93. Near Milepost 282, turn east on a short gravel road ending at the trailhead parking area. Goldbug isn't marked on either map.

The hike: A brisk climb up a craggy desert canyon ends at a green oasis where lush undergrowth borders a tumbling geothermal stream. Goldbug (known locally as Elk Bend or simply Warm Springs) may be near the bottom of the list in the table of contents but certainly ranks close to the top as an all-time favorite.

A trailhead bridge spans Warm Spring Creek, and switchbacks drag the path 200 feet uphill. The first 0.5 mile crosses private land, but as the route traverses an open slope you'll pass a gate onto BLM land. The trail drops across a second bridge where greedy cottonwoods and willows choke the creek in a green line winding up the valley between dry sagebrush slopes dotted with pinyon and juniper. Ahead, Goldbug Ridge reveals a jagged slit. The path crosses a third bridge near the canyon's mouth then zigzags up the wall. The last 0.5 mile mile (from the national forest boundary to the springs) is very steep and slippery and can be icy in winter.

Camping at the springs is discouraged by the Forest Service and next to impossible because of the tight canyon, but you'll pass a grassy campsite or two near the creek between the second and third bridge. The pools tend to disappear during spring runoff in late April and May, and the creek temperature becomes significantly cooler, so it's usually not worth the trip at that time.

Goldbug Hot Springs offers delightful hideouts to those who enjoy a bit of privacy.

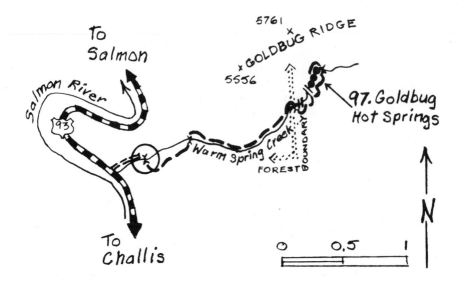

The hot springs: Start peering through the foliage for pools interspersed in the cascade. One of the first is the "rollercoaster" pool which features a bizarre waterslide that tumbles down from upper pools, then bounces up and billows out over the surface. Beyond are many others, most of them closer to the far bank. To reach these without rock hopping, climb to the fourth bridge and drop down the other side.

Hot and cold springs mix underground and emerge as geothermal cascades that flow over dropoffs down the rocky floor. A chain of bubbly pools of varying temperatures punctuates the spaces between falls. They come in a wide variety of sizes and shapes, and the current keeps them scoured clean. Moisture-loving greenery hugs the banks and overhangs the stream to create a private world around each sparkling pool.

98 Mormon Ranch Hot Springs

HIKE 98a *To Mormon Ranch Hot Springs*

General description: A strenuous fourteen-mile round-trip overnighter to a remote soaking box near the Middle Fork Salmon River, southwest of Salmon in the River of No Return Wilderness. Swimwear optional.
Elevation gain and loss: +120 feet, -4,760 feet!
High point: Trailhead, 8,940 feet.
Low point: Hot springs, 4,300 feet.
Hiking quad: Aparejo Point USGS or River of No Return Wilderness, South half (Forest Service).
Road map: Wilderness quads (both north and south halves) or Salmon National Forest.

Finding the trailhead: From Salmon, drive five miles south on U.S. Highway 93. Bridge the river onto Williams Creek Road (21) signed to Williams Lake and climb twenty-four miles west to Panther Creek Road (55), where a right turn leads to Panther (see 99 below). Hang a left and go 12.5 miles (6.5 miles past Cobalt Ranger Station) to Porphyry Creek Road (112). Turn right and follow signs to Middle Fork Peak. In a few more miles, you'll pass the turnoff to the Bighorn Crags (Hike 98b). Next, you'll pass the rustic remains of Yellowjacket—a ghost town featuring a five-story hotel.

The seasonal road (July 15 to October 15) deteriorates badly in the final fourteen miles, but those with high clearance and a modicum of common sense should survive. Continue a few miles past the tiny campground to Middle Fork Peak Lookout (9,127 feet) at the end, a total of sixty-eight long and dusty miles from the highway. The springs are faintly marked on the maps.

The lowdown: Did you read the review of Lower Loon Creek (Hike 95/96a) but decide, like a true "couch potato," that it wasn't worth a fifteen-mile hike? (You may be right. I'm not sure I'd do it again—at least, not from the same direction.) Well, here's a chance to sample a carbon copy at less than half the price. The soaking box at Mormon, except for being half the size, is indeed identical. The hike, however, plunges nearly 5,000 feet in just seven miles! You could almost dive into the pool from the trailhead, but then there's the trip back out. What, no chairlift? Now, I didn't claim free admission, just fifty percent off (seven trail miles vs. fifteen). In any case, if you're a dyed-in-the-wool hot springer, Mormon is worth the experience at any price.

The hike: Middle Fork Peak caps a sinuous ridge high in the Yellowjacket Mountains. The lonesome trail begins just south of the manned lookout and follows the ridge, dropping steadily in a giant half circle around the Warm Spring Creek drainage. As it circles the head of the broad canyon, you'll enjoy panoramic views framed by tall trees.

Shedding life zones, high-elevation forests are gradually replaced by drier slopes dotted with sagebrush and ponderosa. When you reach a point looking back to the lookout, the path begins plummeting in earnest, weaving in and

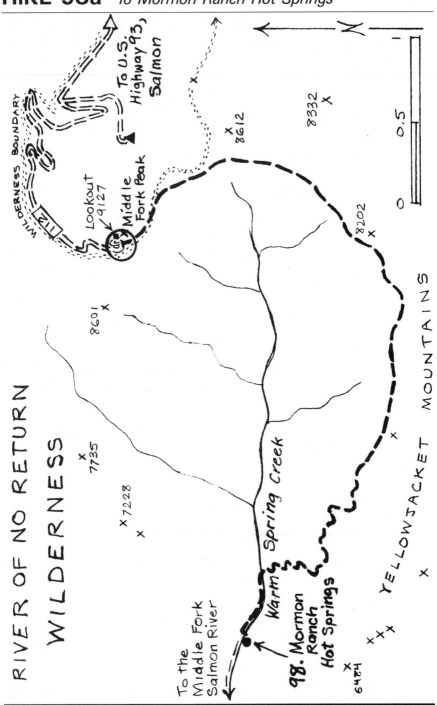

RIVER OF NO RETURN
WILDERNESS

To the Middle Fork Salmon River

98. Mormon Ranch Hot Springs

Warm Spring Creek

YELLOWJACKET MOUNTAINS

x 6424
x x x
x

x 8202

x 8332

x 8612

x 8601

x 7735
x 7228
x

Lookout 9127
Middle Fork Peak

WILDERNESS BOUNDARY

211

To U.S. Highway 93, Salmon

N

0   0.5

The best time to visit Mormon Ranch is NOT when the air temperature matches that in the box.

out of gullies and across open slopes in a long descent to the canyon floor. The path crosses Warm Spring Creek and hugs the north bank en route to the river. Start watching in about half a mile for a side path through the grass on your left. Follow it across the creek and just beyond the woods to the springs.

The hot springs: A length of pipe transports spring water into a tongue-and-groove soaking box that measures four-by-eight feet. The sturdy box can hold up to eight cozy bodies in over two feet of crystal clear water. The temperature runs a bit high, and there isn't any way to lower it short of diverting the pipe and waiting for the water to cool. When I was there in midsummer, the tub clocked in at 106 degrees (as did the air temperature), but in cooler weather I'm sure it would feel great.

There's a plywood deck adjoining the soaking box, handy for changing clothes. The setting is a sunny meadow screened by bushes from the creekside path, and you can pitch a tent nearby. The box gets far less use by passing river rats than the one at Lower Loon since it's located 1.5 miles up the trail from the river.

HIKE 98b *Bighorn Crags*

General description: A strenuous fourteen-mile round-trip overnighter to the first stop in a chain of lakes at the Bighorn Crags, west of Salmon in the River of No Return Wilderness, en route between Mormon and Panther Hot Springs.

Elevation gain and loss: +1,400 feet, -1,520 feet.

Trailhead elevation: 8,460 feet.

HIKE 98b   *Bighorn Crags*

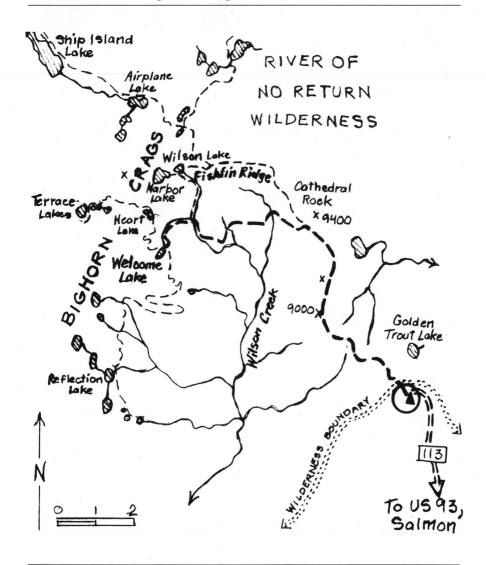

High point: 9,000 feet.
Low point: Welcome Lake, 8,330 feet.
Hiking quads: Hoodoo Meadows and Mount McGuire USGS or River of No Return Wilderness, north half (Forest Service).
Road map: Wilderness quad or Salmon National Forest.

Finding the trailhead: Follow the directions above to Porphyry Creek Road (112) and drive 8.7 miles to a four-way intersection. Turn right on Forest Road

113 and go north over Quartzite Mountain. Pass the turnoff to Yellowjacket Lake and cross a pass at 8,700 feet (usually passable July 15 to October 15) to Crags Campground, 10.7 miles from Forest Road 112 or a total of fifty-six dusty miles from the highway. The register box is at the north end of the loop.

The hike: The Bighorn Crags is a backpacker's paradise of tiny alpine lakes and jagged granite towers, and the Crags Campground trailhead offers by far the shortest access. The hike to Welcome Lake, a fine introduction in itself, also offers a tempting array of side trips, loops, and extensions to those with time to spare.

Ship Island Lake Trail (21) climbs a wooded ridge above Golden Trout Lake to a summit at 8,720 feet, then dips and climbs another ridge north to a high point of 9,000 feet at two miles. Here you'll pass nine or ten rocky towers, then drop past Cathedral Rock to a junction in four miles with the scenic route over Fishfin Ridge to Harbor and Wilson Lakes.

Turn left onto the Waterfall, or Welcome Lake, Trail (45) and plummet to and across Wilson Creek Canyon. In 6.2 miles, at the third stream crossing, a one-mile trail branches north to Wilson Lake. Across the creek, the route switchbacks up to Welcome Lake in seven miles.

From Welcome Lake, the sharp spires and triangular peaks of Fishfin Ridge stand out to the northeast across Wilson Creek Canyon. A dark wall of cliffs towers above granite slabs and scattered trees at the upper end of the narrow lake, and meadows of tiny wildflowers carpet the convoluted shoreline.

Options: The Waterfall Trail continues to Heart Lake and over the divide to the four tiny Terrace Lakes backed by a needle-tipped cliff. This 3.6-mile section has a gain of 670 feet and a loss of 680 feet. South of Welcome Lake, a trail to Puddin Mountain Lakes (not marked on the USGS quad) crosses the divide and drops to Reflection Lake whose surface mirrors a granite wall. The five-mile route gains 850 feet and loses 1,080 feet. Beyond are Buck, Doe, Fawn, Echo, Twin Cove, and Turquoise lakes.

Harbor and Wilson lakes are found north of Welcome Lake at the base of Fishfin Ridge. From the junction at four miles (see above) it's a three-mile trip with a gain of 820 feet and a loss of 360 feet. One could do a loop to include all three lakes in a total of 16.5 scenic miles. Farther north are even more lakes to visit.

99 Panther Hot Springs

General description: A Texas-style soaker on a grassy hillside near a dirt road above Panther Creek and the Salmon River, northwest of Salmon. Skinnydippable with discretion. Elevation 4,400 feet.
Map: Salmon National Forest.

Finding the hot springs: From U.S. Highway 93, there are two routes to Panther. The shortest (thirty-four miles, nearly half on pavement) starts at North Fork, twenty-one miles north of Salmon. Here the Salmon River Road (30) heads west, past the turnoff to Horse Creek (see below) and Shoup. At twenty-six miles comes the Outpost—home of the "Booker Burger," named for chief

At Panther, it pays to test the water before you take the plunge.

cook and bottle washer John Booker. At this venerable landmark, Panther Creek Road (55) turns south. In four miles, Forest Road 60 hairpins four miles up to a pullout where a 0.25-mile path drops to the springs.

The alternate route, for travelers coming from Salmon or points south, is a thirty-nine-mile trip all on dirt. It leaves the highway five miles south of town where Williams Creek Road (21), signed to Williams Lake, bridges the river and climbs twenty-four miles west, ending at Panther Creek Road (55). Turn north and go just under fifteen miles to the final turnoff (see above). Panther is marked on the forest map. *Note:* Forest Road 55 also connects with routes to Mormon Ranch Hot Springs and the Bighorn Crags (Hikes 98a,b).

The hot springs: On a hillside edged by ponderosas, users have carved out a huge waist-deep soaking pool and dug trenches to regulate the temperature. Scalding water at up to 180 degrees is channeled toward the pool but can be diverted by adjusting rocks. A small cold water source (sometimes gone by late summer) also funnels in, and the balance is critical. The system works fine unless some user there before you gets to tinkering and messes up the plumbing.

Panther's at its best in cooler weather and shines on through the winter months. The final road gets icy about halfway up, but locals often walk the last two miles for a steamy winter soak. For those into steam heat, there's even a sauna hut built from rocks.

Historical note: Panther Creek itself was originally called Big Creek. The name changed in the 1920s when some son of a gun reportedly went popping every panther in sight until the creek was littered with them. It's been Panther Creek ever since, but you'll still see Big Creek Hot Springs labeled on the older maps.

100 Horse Creek Hot Springs

General description: A roadside bathhouse near a remote campground in the Bitterroot Mountains, northwest of Salmon. A haven for skinnydippers or "chunkydunkers" as the case may be. Elevation 6,200 feet.
Map: Salmon National Forest.

Finding the hot springs: From Salmon, zip twenty-one miles north on U.S. Highway 93 to North Fork and take Salmon River Road (30) west. At 16.5 miles, where pavement peters out, turn right on Spring Creek Road (38) and climb switchbacks to the Bitterroot Divide on the Idaho-Montana border. The sinuous road follows the crest and state line over a high point of 8,600 feet and becomes Forest Road 44, eventually passing a turnoff to Darby, MT at Horse Creek Pass. A few more miles brings you to Horse Creek Road (65) on the left and the shortest route to Darby on the right. The final lap plummets 3.6 bumpy miles to reach the bathhouse twenty-seven dusty miles from Salmon River Road. Horse Creek, 43.5 miles from the highway and a total of sixty-five miles from Salmon, is named on the forest map.

Note to hikers: Those who enjoy fishing might consider a side trip to Reynolds Lake. The trailhead, signed to Reynolds Creek and Divide trails, is found at the end of Forest Road 44 eight miles past the turnoff to Horse Creek. The 1.5-mile path is a moderate climb, and the marshy lake sits in a basin of granite benches.

The hot springs: Bubbles stream up through the slab rock and sand bottom of a soaker big enough to float a small family side by side. Over the 100-degree pool sits a crude eight-by-ten-foot bathhouse, roofless except for a covered area on the side for hanging clothes. A window looks out across a tree-lined meadow. A footbridge from the picnic area to the shack spans the outflow, which flows through an outdoor dip into Horse Creek. The nearby campground makes a peaceful spot to hang your hat.

"The name game:" *While contentedly afloat, I began to notice the many names inscribed on the walls around the pool—who was here with who. Out of chaos, a pattern began to emerge: "Abe n Deb," "Bear n Deb," "Jo & Jack & Deb," "Deb + Jim," "Pete n Deb," "Zeek n Deb." In the far corner was a noteworthy exception— "Rob '90, w/o Deb." And in case any reader is interested, at the bottom of one wall you'll even find "Deb alone" plus a telephone number.*

A rustic footbridge leads travelers into a private world at Horse Creek Hot Springs.

ABOUT THE AUTHOR

Evie Litton broke loose from a career of fifteen years as a technical illustrator for the University of California in Berkeley to hit the road in 1983. Trading the civilized life for a camperized van she now calls "home," she's been busy exploring the backcountry to find out what secrets lie in wait around the next bend. She avoids developed recreation areas and advertized tourist attractions, preferring the adventure of personal discovery. Her nomadic odyssey stretches from the saguaro deserts, canyon country, and (hot) watering holes of the southwest to the mountain country and wild hot springs in the northwestern states and Canada.

Since Evie's book first came out in 1990, her collection has grown by leaps and bounds. She's been asked to write a companion book on hot springs of the southwest but is undecided. Her obsession with accurate descriptions and directions conflicts head on with concerns over publicizing the many little-known wonders to be found. Evie entreats devotees of wild places and quiet soaking pools to drop her a note via Falcon Press to air their views.

Out here—there's no one to ask directions

...except your **FALCON**GUIDE.

FALCONGUIDES is a series of recreation guidebooks designed to help you safely enjoy the great outdoors. Each title features up-to-date maps, photos, and detailed information on access, hazards, side trips, special attractions, and more. The 6 x 9" softcover format makes every book an ideal companion as you discover the scenic wonders around you.

FALCONGUIDES...lead the way!